D1105984

BLP

DATE DUE

SEP 1 4 2005			

For a Great and Grand Purpose

The History of African-American Religions Series

UNIVERSITY PRESS OF FLORIDA / STATE UNIVERSITY SYSTEM

Florida A&M University, Tallahassee
Florida Atlantic University, Boca Raton
Florida Gulf Coast University, Ft. Myers
Florida International University, Miami
Florida State University, Tallahassee
University of Central Florida, Orlando
University of Florida, Gainesville
University of North Florida, Jacksonville
University of South Florida, Tampa
University of West Florida, Pensacola

Cornish Chapel AMEZ Church seen on the Key West skyline, 1890
photograph. Collection of the authors; courtesy Tom Hambright,
Monroe County May Hill Russell Library.

FOR A GREAT AND GRAND PURPOSE

The Beginnings of the AMEZ Church
in Florida, 1864–1905

CANTER BROWN JR. AND LARRY EUGENE RIVERS

Foreword by Stephen W. Angell and
Anthony B. Pinn, Series Editors

UNIVERSITY PRESS OF FLORIDA

Gainesville · Tallahassee · Tampa · Boca Raton
Pensacola · Orlando · Miami · Jacksonville · Ft. Myers

Copyright 2004 by Canter Brown Jr. and Larry Eugene Rivers
Printed in the United States of America on acid-free paper
All rights reserved

09 08 07 06 05 04   6 5 4 3 2 1

A record of cataloging-in-publication data
is available from the Library of Congress.
ISBN 0-8130-2778-0

The University Press of Florida is the scholarly publishing agency
for the State University System of Florida, comprising Florida A&M University,
Florida Atlantic University, Florida Gulf Coast University, Florida International
University, Florida State University, University of Central Florida, University
of Florida, University of North Florida, University of South Florida,
and University of West Florida.

University Press of Florida
15 Northwest 15th Street
Gainesville, FL 32611-2079
http://www.upf.com

With respect,
to our friend the late Robert W. Saunders Sr.,
hero of the Florida civil rights movement and proud descendant
of pioneers of the AMEZ Church in Florida

CONTENTS

ILLUSTRATIONS

Following page 58

Following page 138

We are pleased to offer *For a Great and Grand Purpose: The Beginnings of the AMEZ Church in Florida, 1864–1905*, by Canter Brown Jr. and Larry Eugene Rivers, an important work that opens to our gaze more unexplored riches from the history of Florida's African American churches. This time, Brown and Rivers have as their theme the work of a small, yet exceedingly important and influential, denomination in Florida, the African Methodist Episcopal Zion (AMEZ) Church for the years 1864 to 1905. This is a fitting companion volume to their previous contribution to our series, one devoted to the history of the African Methodist Episcopal Church, entitled *Laborers in the Vineyard of the Lord: The Beginnings of the AME Church in Florida, 1865–1895*.

The AME and AMEZ denominations have more in common than the obvious similarity of their names. Both arose in the early nineteenth century, nearly at the same time, as a protest against various forms of racial discrimination in the Methodist Episcopal Church. The AME Church was centered in Philadelphia, and its creation was due largely to the labors of Richard Allen, who would become its first bishop. The AMEZ Church, as Brown and Rivers explain, was founded in New York. There was no figure of such Olympian significance as Allen in its formation, although we may note that James Varick became the first superintendent (the name of the office would later be changed to bishop) in the AMEZ Church. The priority of these two denominations is fiercely debated by their partisans, but historians generally assign a very slight lead to the AME Church. Thus, for example, Allen led the AME Church through decisive steps in its formation in 1816, whereas, as Brown and Rivers note, the AMEZ Church went through a similar decisive stage from 1820 to 1822.

While there were unsuccessful attempts to unify the two denominations in the 1860s, missionaries from both bodies arrived as fierce competitors in Florida and the rest of the former Confederacy in the aftermath of the Civil War. In their previous volume on the AME Church, which would assume numerical dominance in Florida, that competition rated only passing mention. Here, however, in drawing a portrait of the smaller denomination, their competition moves closer to center stage.

As the authors note, the AMEZ Church has taken pride in its reputation as a "Freedom Church." In support of this reputation, it is commonly stated that such luminaries in human rights movements as Frederick Douglass, Sojourner Truth, and Harriet Tubman were all associated with the AMEZ Church for shorter or longer periods of time. Thus, an implicit contrast is drawn with the AME Church as slightly more conservative on human rights questions. How does such a contrast hold up in the Florida context, given the fine work of Brown and Rivers?

As the reader might suspect, the contrast provided by our authors does not appear to be quite so simple. In some areas, the AMEZ Church was clearly in the lead on human rights questions. One such instance was the issue of women's ordination. The only AME woman ordained to the ministry during the nineteenth century, Sarah Ann Hughes of North Carolina, in 1885, had her ordination revoked two years later as a result of a backlash among the male ministers and bishops in the denomination. As Brown and Rivers point out, the AMEZ Church moved a little more deliberately, but far more enduringly, on this question. It has been well known that the first AMEZ woman ordained as an elder was a Pennsylvanian, Mary J. Small, in 1898, but Brown and Rivers are the first to unearth the fact that there was an ordination as elder of a Florida AMEZ woman, Mary V. Anderson, within a few years of Small's ordination. Unlike the earlier AME ordination of Hughes, these AMEZ ordinations were permitted to stand.

On the other hand, Brown and Rivers portray the AME Church as far more politically involved during Reconstruction than the AMEZ Church. Some of the political involvement of the AME Church perhaps may be ascribed to the greater responsibilities attendant on a larger membership, but the fact remains that conservatism or radicalism was not to be found exclusively in one denominational corner—in Florida, at least. We await the results of other denominational histories at the state level as lavishly documented and clearly written as these two volumes.

This volume provides a compelling portrait of the dreadful and growing violations of human rights of African Americans during the forty-odd years that it covers, showing that the AMEZ clergy and laity had to figure out what they could do to respond to the onslaught. Choices between radicalism and conservatism, and on any point of the spectrum in between, had both their principled and strategic dimensions. Some of the most important work was exceedingly unglamorous. Simply building up a black denomination—churches were the most important institutions under the firm control of African Americans during much of this period—should be seen as important human rights work, especially during this perilous era.

At any rate, even in the face of such grave difficulties, an inescapable question concerning the AME and AME Zion churches is why they never achieved an "organic union." The authors note that there were several attempts at this, all of which seemed to dissolve in some form of acrimony between the denominations' partisans. Personality factors do crop up repeatedly in this work, as ministers who suffer estrangement in one denomination, or stumble upon a better opportunity, simply switch their affiliations.

The conflict did not simply revolve around personalities, however. The careful reader of this volume and the preceding one by these two authors will note important differences between these two denominations, both at the state and national level. For example, we find out that in Florida the AMEZ Church was located most securely in three widely separated urban areas (Key West, Pensacola, and Tampa), whereas the AME Church had its stronghold in the rural, agricultural heartland of Florida just south of the Georgia state line. So in this volume we have the story of a largely urban denomination attempting to make gains in the surrounding countryside. Of course, we have only begun here to sketch the complexities and subtleties handled expertly by these two authors.

With studies closely focused on the state and local level of the AMEZ Church and other African American denominations, Brown and Rivers have helpfully expanded the paradigm of a history of Florida that unites and responds meaningfully to both religious and secular concerns and issues. The dazzling wealth of information and insight contained in this book deserves a very wide readership indeed.

STEPHEN W. ANGELL AND ANTHONY B. PINN
SERIES EDITORS

ACKNOWLEDGMENTS

We are indebted to many individuals and institutions for their support and encouragement in completing this study. At Florida A&M University, we thank Fred Gainous, president; Larry Robinson, provost; Aubrey M. Perry, professor of psychology; Kyle Eidahl, professor of history; David H. Jackson, associate professor of history; Titus Brown, professor of history; Shanta Haywood, dean of the Graduate School; Frances J. Stafford, history professor emeritus; Charles U. Smith, professor of sociology; Keith Simmonds, professor of public administration and assistant dean, College of Arts and Sciences; James N. Eaton, professor of history and curator, and Muriel Dawson, curator, Black Archives Research Center and Museum; Barbara Proctor, Ann Hinson, Jacquelyn Y. Shuler, Vivian H. Royster, and Carolyn T. Bivens, Coleman Library; Joe Briggs and Jim Davis, president's office; and Charles Lyles, master of applied social sciences program.

Thanks go also to Bob Hall, associate professor of history, Northeastern University; Cynthia C. Wise, Dorothy L. Williams, and Judy Holesmier, Florida Collection, State Library of Florida, Tallahassee; Joan Morris, Jody Norman, and Leslie Sheffield, Florida Photographic Collection, Florida Archives; Tom Muir, Pensacola; Nathan Woolsey, Milton; Betty Jean H. Rivers and Barbara Gray Brown, Tallahassee; Leland M. Hawes, *Tampa Tribune*; the Reverend Curtis A. Swafford, Mt. Sinai AMEZ Church, and Robert W. Saunders Sr., Tampa; Phyllis H. Galloway, director, Heritage Hall Archives and Research Center, Livingstone College, Salisbury, N.C.; Cynthia D. Keever, director, and Faye Taylor, librarian, Hood Theological Seminary Library, Livingstone College, Salisbury, N.C.; Tom Hambright, Monroe County May Hill Russell Library, Key West; Vernon Peeples, Punta Gorda; Gregory J. Harris and Talibah Marin-Coleman, Tallahassee; Anthony Dixon, Fort Valley, Georgia; and James Cusick, librarian, P. K. Yonge Library of Florida History, University of Florida.

We add, as well, special words of thanks for their magnanimous support to series editors Stephen Ward Angell and Anthony Pinn; Peter A. Krafft, director of cartography for the Florida Resources and Environment Analysis Center, Florida State University; and the director and staff of the University Press of Florida, as well as the readers selected by them who shared numerous excellent and insightful suggestions.

Incorrect spellings and usage in direct quotations have been left as they appear in the original, and the use of [*sic*] has been avoided. Responsibility for the interpretation of events and for errors of fact rests with us alone.

INTRODUCTION

This study focuses on the remarkable, yet little known, history of Florida's African Methodist Episcopal Zion (AMEZ) Church in its formative years, which is to say the four-decade period ending about 1905. As an officially sanctioned church with an authorized minister, the AMEZ denomination actually preceded its better-known rival, the African Methodist Episcopal Church (AME), by one year in establishing an official religious presence in the state. When Wilbur Garrison Strong of Hartford, Connecticut, arrived at the Union stronghold of Key West in 1864, he became the first black ordained minister in all of peninsular Florida. As will be seen, the legacies of his mission and those of his fellow pioneering African American preachers continue to exert influence in the state into the twenty-first century.[1]

While some general readers may not be familiar with the AMEZ Church and its history, many knowledgeable persons rightly consider it to be one of the principal religious institutions within the black community today. It boasts an institutional history that stretches back well over two centuries. The Zion Church traces its roots to the establishment during the 1760s of New York City's first Methodist society. Within one decade if not earlier, slave Peter Williams and perhaps his wife, Mary Durham, had adhered to the Methodist cause. They eventually associated closely with the John Street Church, a body that bought Williams's freedom and allowed him to repay the congregation when he was able. Eventually, the John Street Church licensed African Americans to preach. As of 1800, Abraham Thompson, June Scott, and Thomas Miller actively pursued the calling within the city.[2]

Meanwhile, the number of African Methodists in New York City had grown so significantly that, by 1796, a committee including Peter Williams, Francis Jacobs, William Brown, Abraham Thompson, and June Scott secured permission to meet separately from the church's white members. Services soon commenced in William Miller's cabinet shop on Cross Street between Mulberry and Orange, from which event some AMEZ historians and adherents have concluded that the denomination's date of origin should be placed at 1796. Within three years, serious consideration was given to the erection of a house of worship and a more formal organization of what had become known as the African Chapel. By 1801 backers had satisfied formalities sufficiently to call into being the African Methodist Episcopal Church of the City of New York. The same year, thanks to the efforts of Williams and others, a subscription campaign resulted in the beginnings of construction of Zion Church at the corner of Leonard and Church streets, an initiative that reached its final conclusion in 1820. "This was the first church edifice built expressly for the people of color in New York," one chronicler noted. "Mr. Williams laid with his own hands the cornerstone of this building," he added, "and was one of the original trustees."[3]

As these events occurred in New York City, African Methodist churches had begun to flourish in other major cities, and talk soon turned to the concept of an umbrella organization. In particular, Bethel African Methodist Episcopal Church in Philadelphia had grown under Richard Allen's leadership. In 1816 Allen convened delegates representing all churches except those in New York City. This general conference opted to create an African Methodist Episcopal Church. Given the spark provided by Philadelphia's Bethel Church, the denomination often was referred to as the Bethel AME Church. New York City's African Methodist Episcopal Church, to avoid confusion, became known as the Zion Church.[4]

For the time being, the Zion Church remained within the fold of the New York Conference of the Methodist Episcopal Church, but the situation changed in 1820–21. In that period several area congregations withdrew from the white-controlled parent organization, established their own general conference, and published an initial discipline. The first yearly conference of these associated churches was held in New York City on July 21, 1821. The discipline already had prescribed the new denomination's name as the African Methodist Episcopal Church in America. That would remain its official title until 1848 when the general conference renamed the body as the African Methodist Episcopal Zion Church. With this ultimate title still a generation in the future and given that the march of church affairs had not occurred without some controversy and division, by the mid-1820s the Zion Church nonetheless had become established in New York, Connecticut, and Pennsylvania. In 1822 James Varick achieved election as its first superintendent.[5]

Varick's elevation as the first AMEZ superintendent reflected two important facets of the church's institutional development that bear mention and understanding. The birth of the new denomination had come amid serious tensions emanating from Zion Church's relationship with the white-controlled Methodist Episcopal Church and its New York–area episcopal hierarchy. The mother church particularly desired to maintain control over ordination and appointment of ministers and certain other matters of importance. Finding little flexibility on these issues, Zion's congregation, convinced that ecclesiastical law permitted such an action during a time of necessity, opted on September 13, 1820, to elect Abraham Thompson and Varick as its elders. This precedent having been set, the denomination thereupon launched itself upon the future committed to lay influence within the church to a far greater degree than would prove the case within the AME Church. This lay influence especially came to include a right to a role in "law-making" church conferences.[6]

Greater lay influence necessitated some diminution in the power of the denomination's episcopal authority, the second point raised by Varick's selection as superintendent. Varick's title told the story. It began with the church's intention to adhere closely to many, but not necessarily all, of Methodism's historic tenets. "The African Methodist Episcopal Zion Church is a Methodist connection," church historian and bishop William J. Walls observed on the point, "a denomination with churches bound together with each other as congregations of the A.M.E. Zion Church, with a central form of polity governing each congregation while each congregation maintains a separate and distinct identity." He continued, "The A.M.E. Zion Church adopted the pattern of American Methodism, with modification, in the creation of its first Discipline and in development of congregations and conferences."[7]

One such modification involved adoption of the term "superintendent" in lieu of the term "bishop." This usage harkened back to Methodism founder John Wesley's 1784 appointments of Dr. Thomas Coke and Francis Asbury "to be joint superintendents over our brethren in North America." Although in practice the early AMEZ ministers and laymen interchangeably used the titles "superintendent" and "bishop," the former term officially remained correct until 1868 when union with the AME and Methodist Episcopal churches seemed possible. Through those years differences of opinion within the AMEZ Church eventually led to a more powerful bishopric, but until the post–Civil War era the superintendency clearly implied a less august post. A four-year term, rather than a lifetime appointment, reinforced the suggestion. "During the earliest days of Zion," as Sandy

Dwayne Martin explained, "the superintendent or chief officer was an elder who had been set aside for a designated period of time to oversee the connection, with the clear understanding that at the next quadrennium he might be removed from office." Martin added, "Indeed, these pioneer Zionites apparently made a special effort to dissociate themselves from the more episcopal Methodism represented by the Methodist Episcopal Church, out of which they formed, and the African Methodist Episcopal Church, Zion's rival."[8]

Having thus organized itself with a strong laity and an episcopacy of somewhat limited authority, the Zion Church evolved at a measured pace until the Civil War years. This progress naturally found itself subject to various ups and downs, one of which will be considered shortly. By 1840, thirty-eight organizations owned twenty-nine buildings valued at $157,000. Thirty-seven elders, ten deacons, and three preachers, organized into two conferences, shepherded more than three thousand members in nine states. Through this period and until 1860, the church's reach extended almost totally within the North. In that year sixty-four churches serviced more than forty-six hundred members in eleven states. Five annual conferences then possessed sixty-four church buildings worth $248,000. Zion elders totaled eighty-two, with church deacons adding fifteen more officers and eight preachers rounding out the ministry.[9]

One challenge of the pre–Civil War decade merits special attention. Balloting for the superintendency during the 1852 general conference opened wounds that, in the following year, led temporarily to a church split. A majority of members and congregations mostly representing the denomination's westerly and southerly reaches (basically west and south from Philadelphia) formed the Wesleyan Episcopal Zion Church. Church fathers healed the split by 1860, but the prolonged crisis diverted attention and resources as the nation headed toward war, a conflict that, presumably, would create an opportunity for the church to reach out to the freedmen of the South.[10]

AMEZ ministers and laymen yearned to end slavery and reach out to the enslaved. They embraced the abolitionist cause with fervor and served as mainstays of the famed Underground Railroad. "The A.M.E. Zion Church not only was foremost in the carrying on of this struggle for freedom but appears to have been the leader along this line," church historian David Henry Bradley Sr. concluded. "At one time or another," he added, "every great racial advocate of freedom was a member of this organization." Sandy Dwayne Martin concurred. "The Zion Church was well represented as a fierce opponent of slavery and a firm advocate for the empowerment of African Americans by denominational founders James Varick and Christopher Rush," Martin observed, "abolitionists who were either lifelong Zion members or united with the group for at least a portion of their lives (as were Harriet Tubman, Sojourner Truth, Frederick Douglass)." Martin continued, "Entire congregations provided havens for refugees from slavery and permitted their houses of worship to serve as meeting places for antislavery activities, and there were other efforts as well that focused on enhancing the condition of blacks, whether enslaved or 'free.'"[11]

In accomplishing the church's religious and political missions, AMEZ adherents and congregations faced competition from within the African church during the antebellum era, as they also would in the post–Civil War years. Although the Baptists always posed serious challenges in the quest for saved souls and Sunday collections, the AME Church offered Zion— two churches within the same Methodist family—its fiercest rival and competitor. At the national and local levels the two faiths, often cooperating or supporting causes jointly, nonetheless repeatedly locked horns. As it turned out, each denomination prevailed in certain areas and regions while finding itself in second place elsewhere. For example, the AMEZ eventually would predominate in Alabama, North Carolina, and New York, while the AME would take precedence in much of the South and Southwest. Thus, the history of the AMEZ Church cannot properly be told without placing its experience within the context of AME development and evolution, just as the AME story cannot be understood fully without consideration of the AMEZ experience.[12]

In Florida, as will be seen, the AME Church dominated most of the state, while Zion preachers commanded greater strength in certain of its larger towns. The details of that rivalry have remained unreported, a fact that applies as well to the state-by-state experience elsewhere in the South. Although the AME Church can boast several state studies, none come to hand for the AMEZ. With some additional and complementary works, the available history of the Zion Church is contained in Bishop James Walker Hood's *One Hundred Years of the African Methodist Episcopal Zion Church* and *Sketch of the Early History of the African Methodist Episcopal Zion Church*; Bishop William J. Walls's *The African Methodist Episcopal Zion Church: Reality of the Black Church*; David Henry Bradley Sr.'s two-volume *A History of the A.M.E. Zion Church*; Sandy Dwayne Martin's worthy study *For God and Race: The Religious and Political Leadership of*

AMEZ Bishop James Walker Hood; and Bishop James Clinton Hoggard's *The African Methodist Episcopal Zion Church, 1872–1996: A Bicentennial Commemorative History.*

Several general monographs that cover the antebellum and post–Civil War black church add greatly to our understanding of its origins and over-all development. These studies have encouraged interest in the various contributions made by black religious institutions in the southern United States. Of particular interest are Albert J. Raboteau's *Slave Religion: The "Invisible Institution" in the Antebellum South;* John W. Blassingame's *The Slave Community: Plantation Life in the Antebellum South;* Eugene D. Genovese's *Roll, Jordan, Roll: The World the Slaves Made; "Ain't Gonna Lay My 'Ligion Down": African American Religion in the South,* edited by Alonzo Johnson and Paul Jersild; William E. Montgomery's *Under Their Own Vine and Fig Tree: The African-American Church in the South, 1865–1900; Masters and Slaves in the House of the Lord: Race and Religion in the American South, 1740–1870,* edited by John B. Boles; and Eric C. Lincoln and Lawrence H. Mamiya's *The Black Church in the African American Experience.*

Works dealing with specific denominations likewise are very helpful. On the AME Church, these include Stephen Ward Angell's *Bishop Henry McNeal Turner and African American Religion in the South;* and Clarence E. Walker's *A Rock in a Weary Land: The African Methodist Episcopal Church during the Civil War and Reconstruction.* Pertaining to the black Baptist Church, see *A History of Black Baptists* by Larry Fitts; *Redeeming the South: Religious Cultures and Racial Identities among Southern Baptists, 1865–1925* by Paul Harvey; Evelyn Brooks Higginbotham's *Righteous Discontent: The Women's Movement in the Black Baptist Church, 1880–1920; History of the Black Baptists of Florida, 1850–1985* by George Patterson McKinney Sr. and Richard I. McKinney; and Lewis G. Jordan's *Negro Baptist History: USA—1750–1930.*

As noted above, no scholarly case studies published to date have traced the history of the AMEZ Church in any individual state. A person desiring to inquire into the origins of the Florida AMEZ Church, for instance, would find no books or scholarly articles written about any aspect of its origins, involvements, or development. If any clear understanding of the origins and development of this important institution in the African American community is to be reached, however, such state studies obviously must be undertaken.

The authors offer the present study as a beginning toward that larger goal, while noting an unfortunate reality. Especially for the first two decades of the Florida AMEZ experience, little in the way of primary source material comes to hand. Relevant annual conference minutes have suffered loss or destruction for most of the church's formative years, and no letters, diaries, journals, or reminiscences of state or local church leaders and laymen in Florida have surfaced. Public documents such as deed, tax, and marriage records often provide the principal sources for insight, leaving many gaps in the understanding of church complexities and requiring a great deal of informed speculation.

Florida's experience, it also should be acknowledged, does not represent a typical one for the AMEZ Church in its areas of greatest success. It does illustrate, though, how with few resources and little support, dedicated Zionites managed to create and maintain a lasting presence against formidable odds and constant challenges while affording spiritual comfort to thousands and building legacies that remain in force and in place today. How such was possible at all seems to the authors a topic worthy of research and publication.

Any attempt to present Florida's AMEZ experience, as will be true throughout the South, must commence with a recognition of the fact that the church evolved as an extension of the religious experiences of the state's slaves. Sterling Stuckey, for one, has detailed the desires of many slaves to worship within a Christian context but apart from the structure demanded by white masters. Numerous social scientists also have shown that analysis of the black church is of critical importance to understanding the lives of bond servants, the slave family, and the quarter community. It is established from these and other studies that, by the late eighteenth and early nineteenth centuries, the black church had proven instrumental in the formation of the black community in America. Historians generally agree that any attempt to interpret the lives of enslaved blacks in this country must begin with a comprehension of their relationship to religion.[13]

By the 1830s, large numbers of blacks enslaved in the United States professed Christianity, even though many of these individuals held no formal church membership. Whether or not each person willingly embraced the faith, religion became a central part of their lives. Many slaves would attend the religious services of their masters. According to former Florida slaves Mary Minus Biddle, William Williams, and Douglas Dorsey, they would be seated either in the front, back, or balcony of their masters' churches to listen to a preacher, usually white, tell them to obey their masters. Other former Florida slaves such as Margrett Nickerson and Bolden Hall remembered that white preachers never told them much about God, only that they should "obey their master and mistress at all time[s]."[14]

But most slaves clearly understood what religion and spirituality meant to them. In the slaves' world, it was understood that conversion from their worldly ways to those of God's kingdom placed them on equal footing with whites regardless of what their masters said or what white ministers preached to them. They found through the Scriptures confirmation of their humanity. Florida's Mary M. Biddle summed up what most enslaved blacks probably thought about whites when she declared, "Yeah, wese juest as good as deys is only deys white and we's black."[15]

Having embraced Christianity by whatever manner and in whatever form, a substantial—though not easily specified—percentage of enslaved blacks throughout the antebellum South identified with one Christian denomination or another. This was true in Florida as elsewhere. Methodist doctrines and beliefs appealed to the sensibilities of many of Florida's slaves. The faith had grown out of the Holy Club at England's Oxford University around 1729 with emphasis on "righteous living." As it expanded from England to New England and the American South, the church made a conscious effort to recruit and include slaves and free blacks as a part of its membership. The Methodists' joyful praise and preaching compared favorably with slaves' traditional ideas of worship. Bond servants also admired the position taken by northern Methodists that its members and, especially, its bishops should not own other human beings. Overall, enslaved blacks could merge African beliefs and traditions into the ethos of Methodism more easily than was the case with some other faiths.[16]

Bond servants were exposed to Methodism in Florida as early as the mid-1820s. Joshua Nichols Glenn had planted the church in St. Augustine by 1823. Methodism had reached Middle Florida (that region stretching from the Apalachicola River on the west and the Suwannee River on the east) during the same period. In fact, the Methodists were the first denomination to establish a sanctioned mission and organized congregation in the Middle Florida region, having done so at Tallahassee by 1823. As elsewhere, the state's bond servants considered the denomination to offer a plain and simple gospel that appealed to their souls, allowing them to easily mix Methodism with other African religious beliefs.[17]

Nonetheless, many Florida slaves recognized that much of what white ministers preached to them was suspect whether they were in the Methodist church or affiliated with another religious faith. One slave suggested as much when she said that "what the minister had just said was all lies." Given that slaves wanted to blend African beliefs with their brand of religion and hear messages other than those preached by white ministers, they created their own independent churches that allowed them the opportunity to worship as they pleased. Many times these churches operated without slaveholders' knowledge or consent. Albert J. Raboteau noted that the religious experiences of slaves were not "fully contained in the visible structures of the institutional church." Indeed, he concluded that "independent black sanctuaries for slave members did exist in the South before emancipation." Florida slave preacher Henry Call, a Methodist, confirmed Raboteau's assertion of the "invisible church." The enslaved minister operated an unsanctioned Methodist church in the Middle Florida region for bond servants without the knowledge or approval of either the master or the overseer.[18]

Additional slave ministers preached in Florida's Methodist Church as Henry Call had done in Middle Florida. In 1848 at the state capital Tallahassee, for instance, "Isaac, a colored man, belonging to [former governor] R. K. Call, made application for renewal of his license to exhort, which was granted." Yet the state held no ordained black Methodist minister until the arrival of Wilbur G. Strong at Key West in 1864. During the 1850s Florida Baptists likely could boast of only one, the Reverend James Page of Tallahassee. With the Key West area under the control of Union forces during much of the Civil War period, however, slaves and free blacks there could more liberally express their desire for their own churches. As will be considered, they demonstrated as much when they gravitated to the AMEZ Church established by Strong. All told, powerful yearnings for self-determination in directing their own religious activities, more than anything else, led to the creation of independent black faiths such as the Florida AMEZ Church.[19]

Given the dynamic role that religion has played in the black community, we offer this history of one such religious movement in Florida—that of the AMEZ Church from 1864 to 1905. The reason we begin with 1864 will become clear in chapter 1, but our decision to end the narrative in 1905 may require explanation here. C. Vann Woodward and other scholars have shown that the era of legally enforced racial discrimination and effective legal efforts to inhibit voting by African Americans—what often is called the "Jim Crow" era—arrived not in the Reconstruction or early post-Reconstruction period but, rather, in the late nineteenth and early twentieth centuries. Florida commenced this process in earnest in 1889, but the year

1905 stands out for the passage of state laws mandating racial segregation on public transportation. The same year Governor Napoleon Bonaparte Broward urged the expulsion of all African Americans from the state (from the United States, for that matter) and the enactment of measures sufficient "to prevent Negroes from migrating back."[20]

Other developments also brought special attention to the halfway point of the twentieth century's first decade and provided reasons to conclude this study in 1905. Among them, railroad construction by then had opened up much of the state to development and given birth to or nourished most of the towns and cities that now make up urban Florida. Given ups and downs, the AMEZ Church by 1905 had expanded its reach accordingly. This reflected the pioneering church at, arguably, its most mature point before a period of decline commenced. Unfortunately, a gap that begins in 1905 in available runs of the church's national newspaper, the *Star of Zion*, renders documentation for years thereafter extremely difficult. By then, most white newspapers that remain extant had dropped coverage of black church conferences and other events. Our intention, however, always had been to tell of the church's beginnings in Florida. It seemed to us, upon reflection, that this history of the pioneer church appropriately should conclude at the time when Zion had arrived at its zenith in the state. To do so seems a fitting way to pay tribute to the remarkable accomplishments of a heroic, if also very human, era.[21]

As readers will learn, the AMEZ Florida congregations faced many obstacles as Zion attempted to gain a foothold in the state. Among the many issues to note in the following discussion are questions related to idiosyncrasies of episcopal leadership that assisted or frustrated church development; the rivalries between local ministers and episcopal authorities; the influence of politics in church affairs; the role that women played in the church; the influence of social and natural factors on church development and membership; and the effects of education on ministerial growth within the church. By addressing these and additional questions, we hope that this study will tell the story of the AMEZ Church's perseverance and dedication to the spiritual uplift of black Floridians from times when they faced the challenges of newfound freedom through eras of lynching, discrimination, racial segregation, and disfranchisement. We believe a study such as this also offers insight into the larger issues of the nature of institution building within the black community and the greater society.

1

CORNISH CHAPEL, 1864–1865

—•◦•—

the nucleus of all our work
in the far off South

The beginnings of the African Methodist Episcopal Zion Church in Florida sprang from events that occurred as the nation's most tragic conflict, the Civil War, defied final resolution. At the time, with slavery in the United States approaching its demise, clerical officials were contemplating the very future of their denomination just as the millions held in bondage urgently required the attention of church fathers. In the circumstances, one far-sighted individual determined to send the AMEZ Church on a course toward the South. That mission led a church emissary to Florida by late 1864, even as Civil War guns continued to spew deadly fire and as the questions of disunion and emancipation remained in the balance.

Joseph Jackson Clinton, the churchman determined to introduce the AMEZ Church into the South, claimed a personal heritage far removed from southern ties. Born October 3, 1823, he had grown up in Philadelphia. There, he had enjoyed the opportunity as a youth to gain a solid education. "He studied in the common branches of English education in the famous Mr. Bird's school at Philadelphia," his future colleague James Walker Hood explained, "thence went to the Allegheny Institute." At the age of fifteen Clinton had accepted a religious calling. Within three years he had earned his license as a local preacher, and, by 1843, the young minister had emerged as a traveling preacher for the AMEZ Church at a time when the denomination claimed fewer than three thousand members. Ordination as a deacon followed in 1845. Elder's orders ensued one year afterward. On denominational business at Pittsburgh, the rising churchman met and married Letitia Sisco (or Hamilton). The couple would share ten children, and Letitia would prove, in the words of Bishop William J. Walls, "a model wife and great helper to her husband."[1]

Known as a devoted family man, Clinton found time nonetheless to become one of the AMEZ Church's most dynamic leaders. During a church split that occurred in the 1850s, he adhered to the majority faction, the Wesleyan Methodist Episcopal Zion Church. In 1856 he achieved within that denomination election as a superintendent (or bishop), the youngest in the history of the AMEZ Church. The reunified church's general conference ratified the election in 1860, at which time Clinton became one of only three superintendents. "Noble in his personal appearance, Bishop Clinton possessed an equally noble heart," a fellow churchman recalled. "Genial in his manner, easy, graceful and commanding in his bearing, generous and jovial, kind, respectful of all, and especially to the aged; condescending toward the poorer and more unfortunate in life," the man continued, "it was by no means strange that he drew around him hosts of admiring friends—both in and out of church." As a preacher, Clinton also stood high in esteem. "In the pulpit he was a prince in power, dignity, and effectiveness," James Walker Hood observed. "There was in his oratory the happiest result of nature and art combined; his eloquence would sometimes seem to be charged with divine electricity."[2]

Clinton fully utilized his sensitivities, talents, and episcopal authority to the benefit of his church and its causes. "He had a high and holy ambition to make himself qualified to do good among his fellow-men," James Walker Hood related further. "He was faithfully devoted to the cause he espoused, and no service was too hard, no sacrifice too great, for that cause." Abolition of slavery constituted one of those causes. "He was intensely enthusiastic in the struggle for freedom," Bishop Walls noted. Among other aspects of Clinton's service in furthering abolition, he presided over the Freedmen's American and British Commission, an organization whose purpose was "to eliminate suffering of our people."[3]

By 1864 Superintendent Clinton focused on several important issues in addition to the abolition of slavery. Central among them was the future of the AMEZ Church. Membership rolls by then topped five thousand, with the congregations organized into six conferences with ninety-two preachers. Still, the AMEZ Church remained small and poorly financed, partially because it competed directly with the African Methodist Episcopal Church, an institution whose adherents numbered in excess of twenty thousand. Many churchmen believed the solution lay in organic union of the two bodies. The churches' general conferences held in the spring of 1864 had agreed, in fact, to a merger within a few years. A unity conference convened at Philadelphia during June 1864 unfortunately had revealed the troubled side of the arrangement. Historian Stephen Ward Angell explained. "Formidable disagreements surfaced on the means of ordaining bishops and many other issues," he reported. "The conference produced a set of proposals that would be formally adopted or rejected by both denominations in 1868, but the ill-feeling that existed at the conference helped to doom this unity drive."[4]

This undermining of hopes for AME-AMEZ union reinforced for Clinton the urgency of certain other long-held concerns. Foremost among them, he fervently believed that the church carried an immense responsibility for reaching out to slavery's victims, a cause that could not await resolution of the organic union debate. The AMEZ membership, on the other hand, remained essentially northern. The body had adopted in 1820 a bold antislavery declaration. "We will not receive any person into our societies who is a slave holder," it had declared. "Anyone who is now a member and holds slaves, and refuses to emancipate them after notice is given to such member by the pastor in charge, shall be excluded." While word of the church's stance seems to have reached the ears of slaves in many parts of the South, antagonism to the position by southern whites had forestalled any true development of congregations in the region. Clinton on one occasion reportedly suffered imprisonment at Alexandria, Virginia, simply for his temerity in supposing that he could sponsor a church there.[5]

That is not to say that some members of the AMEZ Church had not desired for some time a missionary program in the South. Clinton's episcopal district in 1864, the New England Conference, had interested itself, at least to some degree, in southern missionary work as early as 1858. With the Emancipation Proclamation taking effect on January 1, 1863, the sense of urgency had heightened. Clinton and his conference turned late in the year to James Walker Hood, the young pastor of its Bridgeport, Connecticut, congregation, directing him to proceed to Union-occupied portions of the South to open missionary activities. With key assistance from Postmaster General Montgomery Blair's family maid Melvina Fletcher, Hood made his way to North Carolina. At New Bern, he struggled to win for his church an existing all-black congregation then being wooed by the AME and Methodist Episcopal Church. Thanks partly to Hood's leadership and partly to the fact that one of Zion's superintendents—Christopher Rush— had hailed from New Bern, the AMEZ initiative triumphed. In early 1864, New Bern's Andrews Chapel became the denomination's first organized southern congregation. Superintendent Clinton surveyed the success with a personal visit in May.[6]

Also in May 1864, the AMEZ General Conference gathered at Philadelphia for what turned out to be a monumental session. Not only did it agree, as mentioned, to organic union with the AME Church, it also endorsed Clinton's southern missionary endeavors. Specifically, the body created several new conferences, two of them in the South. The first centered on North Carolina but covered, as well, parts of Virginia and all of Tennessee. As a result, North Carolina became, in Hood's words, "the great central force in Zion Connection." The second, to be called the Louisiana Conference, encompassed the South below North Carolina and Tennessee, including Florida. Superintendent Clinton accepted responsibility for overseeing their organization.[7]

Thus, as summer heat began to blanket the nation in 1864, the AMEZ Church and Superintendent Clinton faced southward, anticipating a large-scale missionary program but uncertain exactly what form it would take. Just at that moment, events drew Clinton's attention to Key West. There, he learned, an existing all-black congregation required a minister, a situation remarkably similar to that found by Hood at New Bern. Seemingly at a glance, Clinton decided to ensure that the congregation moved under the AMEZ umbrella. In the process, he launched the church's arrival in Florida.[8]

Given that the AMEZ Church's introduction to Florida came at Key West, it should be noted at the outset that the environment in which the denomination soon found itself by no means reflected circumstances typical in most of Florida, much less the cotton South. Literally and figuratively an island, Key West existed virtually as a world unto itself. Essentially destroyed by a hurricane in 1846, it had rebuilt to a comfortable level of prosperity in the 1850s courtesy mainly of U.S. government spending. In the process, it had emerged as a port of considerable importance, a fact that had led to extensive diversification of its pool of residents. "It was a cosmopolitan population," one resident observed, "Bahama wreckers and immigrants, small fishermen from Noank and Mystic, and the Gulf States, business men, commercial adventurers and mechanics from the Northern States, and world wanderers from every portion of the globe." The resident went on to note the presence of "Englishmen, Italians, Spaniards, Cubans, Canary Islanders, South Americans, Canadians, Scotch, French, shipwrecked sailors, deserters, and discharged men from the army, navy and marine corps." The assemblage totaled 2,832 when census takers came around in 1860, making Key West Florida's second-largest town. Pensacola led by a mere 44 residents. Florida as a whole that year contained only 140,424 persons.[9]

Those persons who now would be termed African Americans comprised slightly less than 20 percent of Key West's 1860 population, but the low percentage should not mislead as to either the influence of or living environment enjoyed by the black community. Given the town's isolation and worldly atmosphere, race relations there tended on a day-to-day basis to offer a great deal of flexibility to slaves and to the town's 160 free blacks. "The negroes, in a very large proportion [seemingly] outnumber the white," one alarmed white correspondent reported exaggeratedly in 1853, "and are possessed of such freedom as renders their living in juxta position a matter almost of impossibility; and the day does not beam far distant in the horizon when the African sceptre will sway supreme."[10]

While the 1853 correspondent misconceived the threat of black domination at Key West, the fact remained that the flexible climate offered substantive opportunities for African Americans, not the least of which involved economic advancement. Government contractors chronically lacked sufficient numbers of laborers, skilled and unskilled, to aid construction and maintenance of the local naval facilities, Fort Taylor, nearby Fort Jefferson, and numerous area lighthouses. Local tradition permitted slaves to take advantage of the situation. With Key West serving the Union cause throughout the Civil War, these conditions grew more desirable for black workers. Shortly after President Abraham Lincoln announced the Preliminary Emancipation Proclamation in the early fall of 1862, a Key West man explained local events to the readers of a Boston newspaper. "Slavery is now, here on our Island, being brought to the test of the late order of the President, and the Quartermaster's Department are employing such negroes as are needed for laborers, nurses for the sick, and for all or any purpose of labor," he began. "Those taken who are claimed by disloyal masters are delighted with the change, and others of the same class who are not thus employed are leaving their masters and seeking labor or employment on their own account," he continued. "A custom long in vogue here," the man concluded, "has prepared the negro for this—they having been allowed to hire their own time and make what they could, paying to master a portion of their earnings."[11]

The experience of Thomas H. Darley offers an example, one that also would hold great future significance for the Florida AMEZ Church, of just the type of economic advancement that could occur in such an environment. Born at Key West and, presumably, into slavery about 1829, Darley was the son of Peter and Theresa Darley. His mother claimed a proud heritage as the daughter of an African king, a fact well known in the broader Key West community and recorded in its principal history. Married by the late 1850s to wife Eliza, Thomas Darley labored as a stonemason. His skills honed by years of experience, he emerged from the Civil War as a home-owner and as head of a Fort Taylor work crew. The $200 in assets he reported for taxes in 1866 had grown fourfold by the decade's end.[12]

The life of Cataline B. Simmons offers similar insight. Born at Beaufort, South Carolina, about 1806, he had become by the 1840s the property of Joseph B. Lancaster, one of Florida's premier political leaders. A Whig, Lancaster served as Jacksonville mayor, as speaker of the Florida House of Representatives, and in numerous other capacities. Elected circuit judge in 1847, Lancaster relocated to Key West, taking Simmons with him. When the judge moved to Tampa in 1853, Simmons likely journeyed there, as well. When Lancaster died three years later, Simmons apparently returned to his old island home, leased himself out, and eventually purchased his freedom. "Being among that heroic few who struggling with the adversities and cruelties of slavery," a friend recalled of him, "yet had that craving of spirit, that greatness of soul and nobleness of ambition, by his own exertions freed himself, paying in gold for what the laws of his country should have secured him." When the Civil War closed, Simmons already held $300 in Key West real estate.[13]

Civil War–era prosperity at Key West permitted local blacks to capitalize on government spending indirectly as well as directly. Take, for example, the case of Sandy Cornish (not to be confused with abolitionist minister and journalist Samuel Cornish). Sandy Cornish's roots lay in Cambridge, Maryland, where he was born the slave of William Eccleston. A grown man when his master died in 1838, the bond servant apparently found himself leased out by Eccleston's son to work on a railroad construction gang near Tallahassee. With a portion of the earnings that his master permitted him to retain, Cornish purchased his freedom only to suffer the loss of his "free papers" in a fire. Seized and held for sale back into slavery, the courageous freedman painfully mutilated and crippled himself to frustrate his captors. By the late 1840s, still free, he had arrived at Key West. If not previously, he met there and married Lillah Cornish and began a family. Unusual for most white women at the time and rare for a black woman, she held property in her own right at Key West by 1851. Sandy also purchased land, in his case a twenty-acre tract near his wife's real estate.[14]

Sandy Cornish prospered at Key West because he used his land well. He farmed it. The one-time slave produced delicious vegetables and other products that became ever more desirable as wartime exigencies brought greater numbers of hungry mouths to the island. "Old Sandy is an institution," one officer related in the spring of 1864. "He is a genuine darky, large headed large souled, big of stature, full of vigor & brawn, and the most perfect gentleman in Key West," he described further. "He . . . has the finest garden on the island," the officer added, "has some thousands of dollars in bank and is generally a noble fellow & prosperous as he should be."[15]

Sandy Cornish not only grew affluent at Civil War–era Key West, he emerged as a local celebrity. Visiting dignitaries habitually made their way to his farm where he regaled them with stories of his life and of the island. President Lincoln's aide John Hay certainly found that to be the case. "Sandy talked mostly of his influential friends," Hay recorded following a March 1864 encounter. "'Captains and Colonels and them things,' and gingerly of the rebellious and fugacious," he continued. The next year no less a luminary than U.S. Supreme Court Chief Justice Salmon P. Chase made the trek to "Sandy's Garden," which the former slave referred to as his "plantation." A reporter recorded the conversation that ensued between Cornish and Chase following Cornish's request for a picture of his guest and the former treasury secretary's attempt to respond with the gift of a "greenback," as dollar bills were called. "The scene that followed was curious," the journalist related. "Old Sandie, bareheaded and with his shirt thrown loosely back from his brawny bosom, stooped down, spread the bill out on one knee, and gazed from it to Mr. Chase and back to the bill again for some moments, in perfect silence," he described. The reporter added: "'Now I knows you,' he broke out at last, 'you's Old Greenback hisself. You mout come heah fifty yeah from now and I'd know you just de same, and tell you all about sittin' in dis yeah piazza heah.'"[16]

The Key West black community that boasted Thomas H. Darley, Cataline B. Simmons, and Sandy Cornish swelled just prior to and during the Civil War, bringing to the island hundreds—if not thousands—of individuals, some of whose efforts would prove instrumental to the AMEZ Church's work in Florida. One small group involved relatively well-to-do slaves and freedmen who sought protection from rising secession sentiment or Confederate excesses. Sampson Forrester offers a case in point. Born as a plantation slave in northeast Florida at the end of the eighteenth century, he found himself captured by Indians during the Second Seminole War of 1835–42, a conflict that likely constituted the largest slave rebellion in U.S. history. Forrester fought for a time on behalf of his captors, but then, sensing that his best interests dictated otherwise, he changed sides. After hiring on as a U.S. Army guide and interpreter, he received his freedom from General Zachary Taylor at Tampa on April 30, 1840. Maintaining lucrative government employment for years thereafter, Forrester bought Hillsborough County farmland and established a plantation. He also purchased Rose Bennet for his wife. Her former owner recalled her as "the most beautiful colored girl I ever saw." A love match from the beginning, the couple remained together, as will be seen, until Sampson's death decades afterward.[17]

Military operations likewise pulled black men and women to the island. Especially during the spring of 1864, repeated raids into the southwest Florida interior resulted in the seizure of "contrabands" and their relocation to Key West. In May 1864, for instance, Union troops occupied Tampa for two days. Among those who departed the town with the occupiers were Romeo Dupont and Aaron Bryant. The slave of merchant Thomas P. Kennedy, Dupont seemingly was literate and had much-demanded skills as a carpenter. Within less than one decade at Key West, he possessed property worth at least $600 and had emerged as a political and community leader. Bryant had known Dupont for years. He had arrived at Tampa from Thomas County, Georgia, with his mother, Dorcas, and brothers Samuel, Berry, and Peter about 1856 as slaves of owner Eleanor Prine. Twenty years of age in 1864, Aaron ached to fight for the cause of freedom. He enlisted that December in the Second Regiment, U.S. Colored Infantry. He ached, as well, to return to his family at Tampa.[18]

Union raids attracted numerous others to the community. Many of the incursions directed from Key West during the spring of 1864 centered on the Peace River valley in the central and southwest peninsula and the Polk County town of Fort Meade. They resulted in the coming to the island of, among others, Joseph Sexton. Fort Meade, situated roughly fifty miles east of Tampa, served as the center of the South Florida cattle industry and, as such, held great importance to the Confederacy and to the Union. Numerous prominent cattlemen and their families, many of whom had not supported secession, resided at the town or within a few miles to the north at a rural community that soon would be known as Homeland. Sexton, who had been born in Georgia about 1830, apparently lived as the slave of the Hendry family, whose members had relocated from Thomas County, Georgia, to Hillsborough and Polk counties in the 1850s. Hendry County, Florida, today commemorates their contributions to their new home. In Polk County by 1861, Sexton had started a family with Hannah Shaw. She gave birth to their second son on April 1, 1864. Whether Union forces seized Sexton during their May 19 occupation of Fort Meade or whether

Unionist Hendry arranged for his protection is not known. In any event, Sexton found himself at Key West in the late spring. Like Aaron Bryant, he ached to return home.[19]

Finally, the U.S. government brought to its Key West bastion several regiments of the U.S. Colored Infantry. Importantly, the Second Regiment, USCI, which formed at Washington, D.C., came on the scene early in 1864. Some of the men of the Ninety-ninth Regiment, a part of the famed "Corps d'Afrique," traced their origins to Louisiana. They off-loaded that fall. As already noted in the case of Aaron Bryant, area men supplemented their ranks. In another example, James A. Roberts, born at Key West in 1845, opted early on to serve as a soldier. He enlisted during February 1863 in the Thirty-fourth Regiment, USCI, and served until discharged at Jacksonville three years later.[20]

As Key West's black population swelled in late 1863 and early 1864, two of its members—Sandy Cornish and Cataline B. Simmons—grew concerned about their own spiritual needs and those of others such as Darley, Roberts, and, eventually, Bryant, Dupont, Sexton, and their loved ones. The two leaders focused particularly on the issue of who would determine the nature and substance of their religious associations, preferring control in black, as opposed to white, hands. At the same time, a similar dynamic seemed to grip a significant portion of the state's African American community. In distant Jackson County, for instance, slave Henry Call quietly was organizing a secret African Methodist Episcopal congregation, while on the peninsular frontier's edge at Bartow, Baptists had laid the foundations for Providence Missionary Baptist Church. At Key West, though, white churchmen and lay leaders took umbrage at the effrontery of Cornish and Simmons. "The colored people of the place are in sad want of teaching and preaching," recorded James H. Schneider, chaplain of the Second Regiment, USCI, in March 1864. "They have been driven from the churches, in which they were members," he added. "They now worship by themselves."[21]

As Schneider suggested, Cornish and Simmons had withdrawn from communion with local white churches, but no black gatherings yet had coalesced. The two men did not even share the same denominational affiliation. For some time Cornish had belonged to the Methodist Church; Simmons had associated with the Baptist. Now, the two men decided to form their own separate congregations. They probably did so with the encouragement of General Daniel P. Woodbury, then commanding Union forces on the island. Chaplain Schneider left his impressions of Woodbury and of the general's concerns. "Our general commanding this district of 'Key West and Tortugas' is Woodbury, a very fine man,—a Christian," Schneider wrote. "Almost the first thing that the general asked the colonel, when he reported to him for duty, was whether he had a good chaplain, and an important question with him seemed to be, where our men would go to church."[22]

Cornish and Simmons acted to further their plans shortly before Schneider's arrival at Key West in late February 1864. Local church historian Marion L. Newman recounted that what would become Cornish Chapel AMEZ Church "was organized by a group of Negroes under a tree listed as a Spanish Lime in the 200 block of the now Hutcherson Lane." The founders quickly moved their meetings indoors into a small building or home, with separate Baptist and Methodist societies convening there. On March 5 Schneider visited the facility for the first time. "I was glad that I preached to the colored people," the chaplain related. "The house was well filled (it is a small church), and they listened well, and seemed affected for good," he continued. "Soldiers were there, and sailors, too," Schneider added. "I shall preach for them regularly,—once every Sabbath," he concluded. "I shall find a large field of labor here, and I shall do all I can."[23]

One thing that Chaplain Schneider believed that he could do was to combine and expand the two congregations. "I want to organize the colored churches, too," he recorded on March 10, "to unite the Baptist and Methodist in one society." Available evidence suggests that he quickly succeeded. "This has been a happy Sabbath," he penned on April 10. "I went up to the church and it was filled very well." His account continued:

> Many of the women brought their children. I had spoken to them about it, and encouraged them to accustom their children to visit the house of God. The size of my audience cannot be much enlarged, because the house is filled, galleries and all. They listened very well, and seemed to understand and feel. I preached upon this: "take my yoke upon you, for my yoke is easy." After service the people were very cordial, and seemed to think that I was their friend.[24]

Now, enthusiasm gripped Schneider and the church. He and its members envisioned a building program that would combine religion with the educational needs of Key West's black community. "In order to encourage the colored people to contribute toward the building of their church, I promised to secure one dollar for them for every five that they should raise," he noted on April 16. "I can get this in the regiment and elsewhere," the chaplain added. "The church is to be used as a school-house, too. I think we must make these people help themselves, but encourage them all we can by assisting them." Schneider then explained the direction of his thinking: "The people are very depraved and vicious on this island. Drinking-saloons are numerous. Sabbath-breaking is almost the general practice. I think I shall be thoroughly initiated in the practical part of a minister's work."[25]

Just at that moment fate took a hand in the chaplain's plans, and it did so in a manner that would echo profoundly in Florida and within its AMEZ churches for the remainder of the century. Yellow fever struck Key West. The dreaded "yellow jack" customarily forced residents of the Gulf coast to live in fear of the onset of summer. The medium of its transmittal, mosquito bites, remained unknown to medical science. No cure was available to its victims, and there was no relief from their intense suffering. And, once the plague had descended, it typically inflicted its lethal punishment until the frosts of late fall or early winter killed its carriers. Sometimes the yellow jack played tricks on potential victims terrorized by its threat and anxious to believe that it could not be so. In such times the disease might come on slowly, lingering for months, before exploding into deadly fury. "I regret to have to state that after all yellow fever has unmistakably broken out in this city," a Key West correspondent advised on June 28, two months after the fever actually appeared. "A few persons have died of the disease," he added. Then, one month later a completely different tone and climate prevailed. "It is painful to place on record," the man declared, "but truth impels me to say that there seems to be no abatement of yellow fever in this little pest stricken city." He appended: "As if a panic had seized the residents and the floating inhabitants, every one who can get out of it is striving to do so. The staple topic of conversation, day after day, is who and how many are dead, who are past the worst, who are out for the first time, who are likely to have a relapse through imprudence, and who may be the next stricken down by the pestilence."[26]

As it happened, one of the last victims of Key West's 1864 yellow fever outbreak was General Woodbury and one of its first was Chaplain Schneider. The minister succumbed on April 26. "It is with much regret I have to announce the death, early this morning, of the Rev. James H. Schneider, chaplain of the Second colored United States regiment," a correspondent informed the *New York Herald*. "I heard Mr. Schneider preach to a few companies of his swarthy congregation, on the green sward before the United States barracks, one evening," the man observed, "and I must certainly say that, without descending to any low language, he adapted his words wonderfully to his audience." Reporting in May concerning the Key West freedmen's school to the *Freedmen's Advocate*, a New York publication, Woodbury also lamented Schneider's passage. "The 2d U.S. Colored Regiment, stationed in this district, has met with a very great loss in the death of its chaplain, the Rev. Mr. Schneider, who had devoted himself like a faithful missionary to the instruction of the men," he reported. "Without any cant in his walk, without any desire to see his name in print, this good man did his work with rare intelligence, fidelity, and energy—and with great success." The general added: "Who can take his place? What good man of similar qualifications, not having the fear of yellow fever before his eyes, will apply for that place?"[27]

Woodbury's *Freedmen's Advocate* letter, published in June 1864 just as the AME-AMEZ Unity Conference pricked the balloon of optimism about organic union and following Superintendent Joseph J. Clinton's first North Carolina sojourn, likely prompted Clinton's interest in carrying the AMEZ Church next to Florida. No evidence survives as to when he might have seen the item, but circumstances hint that in September Clinton learned that the Key West congregation and the school it sponsored yet required leadership. At that juncture, he turned his eyes to New Jersey, where a possible solution to the problem resided.[28]

The person to whom Superintendent Clinton addressed his call was Wilbur Garrison Strong, another black northerner. A native of Hartford, Connecticut, where his parents remained AMEZ members, Strong served by the late 1850s as principal of the Plane Street School in Newark, New Jersey. Observing firsthand the young man's abilities as an orator and educator, Clinton kept him in mind for a time when the right opportunity might come along. That moment arrived in September 1864. "Your humble servant received a letter from Superintendent J. J. Clinton . . . containing the information that he desired me to go to Key West, Fla., and in which he gave me one week to answer," Strong later related. "One of his greatest characteristics was, when he said anything he meant business," Strong continued. "In that communication he requested me to meet him at Newark, N. J., at the house of Mrs. Sarah Simmons, on a certain Saturday," the minister detailed. "I was then the principal of the Fair St. Grammar School, in Newark." He concluded: "We met, and he informed me that a minister was urgently needed at Key West, Fla., and he honored me by desiring my acceptance of the mission. I said to him: Bishop, how do you propose to send me? He replied: I propose to make you a man."[29]

Already a local AMEZ deacon, Strong acceded to Clinton's overture. "Believing it to be my duty to labor for Zion in the field which promised the best results, I assured him that I would go," he recorded. Clinton challenged the seriousness of Strong's quick commitment. "Holding a good position and thinking I might change my mind, he said that he did not want any foolishness," Strong recollected. "I gave him my hand and pledged my services to Zion."[30]

Events then moved at a rapid pace. Clinton arranged for Strong's ordination as a church elder at Zion Wesley Church in Washington, D.C. The congregations of the nation's capital then offered the missionary $75 to defray his expenses to Key West, and with that modest sum he sailed for Florida on October 26, 1864. On the island by mid-November, he claimed Sandy Cornish and Cataline Simmons's church for Zion. "I organized a church there on my arrival, with seventy-five members," Strong observed twenty years after the event, "which was the nucleus of all our work in the far off South."[31]

Strong's easy success at Key West, as opposed to James Walker Hood's struggle to win New Bern's Andrews Chapel for Zion, stemmed from several causes. For one thing Cornish, Simmons, and other local leaders likely had exhausted themselves in lending aid and comfort to families struck by yellow fever. Their ministrations at the risk of their own lives certainly endeared them to the community and cemented the loyalty of dozens of families to their congregation, a dynamic that would revisit the church in years to come at Key West and in other Florida locales. On the other hand and with some victims still recuperating in November, the local people could have kept little energy in reserve. Strong's willingness to come to their plague-ridden island surely impressed them, and no other ordained clergymen seemed likely to venture their way. But, in the end, Strong's enthusiasm, his excitement about his new work, and his take-charge attitude probably carried the day. "In Strong, Bishop Clinton was fortunate in getting the man he wanted for that particular work," Hood explained as church historian. "He had a good education [that is, he had some formal education] and was a splendid preacher," Hood continued. "He was affable, genial, and pleasing in his manners." Hood, a leader who knew how to weigh the qualities of his peers, added, "No one could know him and not love him."[32]

It also could not have hurt Wilbur G. Strong's cause at Key West that he promised to build the local people a new and grand church. Chaplain Schneider's death had forestalled earlier fund-raising efforts, but now

Strong took charge. Especially, he prevailed upon Sandy Cornish to back construction on a lot at Whitehead and Angela streets. The cornerstone was laid before year's end, possibly, as will be discussed shortly, with Superintendent Clinton presiding. Work continued into the new year, as the Civil War entered its final months. By June 1865 a visiting reporter observed, "Sandie . . . has contributed largely to the erection of a handsome church for the negro congregation, of which he is the leading spirit." One congregation member described the sanctuary modestly as a "white, rectangular, two story, frame building, with bell." An architectural historian, commenting one hundred years later, offered a description in somewhat grander language. "The church was built as the cathedrals of Europe were—by the volunteer labor of the parish," he began. "They quarried stone for the ground floor and then craftsmen trained by ship's carpenters fitted together great timbers with mortise and tenon joints and wooden pegs to build the superstructure."[33]

The groundswell of spirit stirred by Wilbur G. Strong at weary Key West in late 1864 likely roiled into a wave of enthusiasm in December with a visit to the community by Superintendent Clinton. The known facts are these. On December 17, with responsibility for establishing the AMEZ Louisiana Conference remaining ahead of him, Clinton joined J. W. Hood and ten others at New Bern to organize the North Carolina Conference. That historic gathering, Hood later insisted, took place "around a stove on a cold winter day." Hood also recalled the superintendent's subsequent actions. "Soon after organizing the North Carolina Conference," the then-bishop recalled, "[Clinton] went by sea to New Orleans, which, like New Berne, had been captured by the Federal forces." Key West, of course, also stood as a Union strong point and offered a port of call for many, if not most, vessels approaching New Orleans from the Atlantic. Leaders of the Florida church later insisted that Clinton stayed at Key West on one occasion. Thus, circumstantial evidence points to an interlude during late December 1864 and early January 1865 when the AMEZ Church offered an episcopal presence in support of its new island congregation. Doubtlessly, Clinton welcomed the warm, tropical climate after his frigid stay in North Carolina. The stopover, if it occurred at that time, stood out as the first visit by a Methodist bishop, white or black, to Key West.[34]

Whether Wilbur G. Strong remained at Key West long enough in 1865 to see his new sanctuary completed also is not known with certainty. Following his own Key West interlude, Superintendent Clinton had continued his journey to New Orleans, where he intended to organize the Louisiana Conference created by the 1864 general conference. That event occurred March 13, 1865, with fifteen preachers present, including Strong. "I remember when he requested me to meet him in New Orleans, where he organized the first colored conference in Louisiana," he explained. "I was its secretary, and compiled the minutes." At the gathering Clinton declared, quite characteristically, "It [is] Zion's mission to take ignorance by the throat and choke it to death." He then directed Strong to remain in place, watching over the maturing of the seeds that he had planted in Louisiana. "He left me in New Orleans to attend to Zion's interest there," Strong added, "while he went to Mobile to raise our banner." The founding pastor of the AMEZ Church in Florida would not return to Key West until October.[35]

In Strong's absence, Sandy Cornish and Cataline Simmons kept the spiritual fires kindled on the island. "While they were not regularly ordained ministers," commented one local man, "[they] held regular services among them until one could be procured." At their ministerial tasks, the two lay preachers succeeded very well. So revered did the name of Sandy Cornish become, that Wilbur Strong's sanctuary soon took on, and has carried ever since, the name Cornish Chapel. One army officer, following a single visit, took their joint accomplishments as representative of the potential for freedmen and freedwomen everywhere. "Compare the negro with the whites in reference to his desire for education, his respect for religion, or his disposition to lead an industrious life," he began. Concluding, the northern man added, "He is in none of these respects their inferior."[36]

Thus, as peace settled on the nation in April and May 1865 following four terrible years of Civil War, the AMEZ Church had established a presence in the Deep South that remains today a living symbol of the church and its ministry. Thanks to the initiatives of Joseph J. Clinton and Wilbur G. Strong, with the local leadership of Sandy Cornish and Cataline B. Simmons, the church's banner first flew in the Deep South at Key West, Florida. From there it was taken up and transported to Louisiana, from whence the AMEZ message and clergy carried the church's cause throughout the region. Now, with the peace, the seeds planted in wartime could begin to flower elsewhere in the ravaged land of Florida.

OUTREACH, 1865–1868

denominational organizers
rather than missionaries

The Civil War's final year saw the African Methodist Episcopal Zion Church reach out to the freedmen of the South, an initiative that soon introduced the church into Florida. Superintendent Joseph J. Clinton, who spearheaded the effort, organized two conferences designed to serve as springboards for missionary probes into all of the region's parts. The North Carolina Conference served much of the Upper South, while the Louisiana Conference facilitated church extension into the Deep South. As peace and emancipation succeeded the four-year conflict, Clinton pursued his dream of outreach despite the sometimes violent and almost always turbulent times that descended upon the states of the former Confederacy. In the process, ministers in Florida built upon the church's Key West beginnings to spread the gospel under the AMEZ banner into the state's panhandle and peninsula. Modest beginnings to be sure, but, despite challenges that offered themselves in wide variety, by 1868 the church had positioned itself for a permanent presence in the state.

Two separate prongs of AMEZ initiative touched the Sunshine State within the months that followed immediately upon the Confederacy's demise; each, though, depended upon the manner of J. J. Clinton's approach to church expansion and the building up of the clergy. Wherever the superintendent determined to plant a church, he looked among the local population for the greater number of his missionaries. Future Bishop James Walker Hood explained the dynamics as they applied to the birth of the North Carolina Conference in late 1864: "Bishop Clinton had no hidebound notions," he wrote, "whatever was necessary for the success of the Church he was ready to do." Hood continued, "At his suggestion several persons were licensed to preach, most of whom made successful preachers." With reference to potential ministers in Alabama, Hood added in a similar vein, "Bishop Clinton found [them] on the spot and ordained [them] for the work." He did so, as will be seen and understandably for the circumstances under which he was working, without overmuch concern for education or training.[1]

The authority of men selected and ordained in such a manner by Superintendent Clinton remained subject under church law to many limitations. On the most basic level, AMEZ strictures created several categories of clergy. At the lowest reach in the church hierarchy could be found exhorters, defined as "religious public speakers, licensed by the Quarterly Conference, a local court of the society." Licensed or local preachers comprised "a higher order of licentiates, [who were] licensed by the same local court in the society, to preach as local clergymen." Itinerant preachers were "sent out by an annual conference, appointed by a bishop to their field of labor, to collect and organize societies, and to serve those already organized as pastors."[2]

The ordained clergy, on the other hand, consisted of two orders, deacons and elders. They were in each case supposed to be approved for the ministry by an annual conference and ordained by elders and a bishop "by the imposition of hands." Despite the apparent lack of conformity in Superintendent Clinton's approach just described, a deacon usually was required to travel two years as an itinerant preacher prior to being ordained. "His duty is to preach at the requisition of the elder in whose charge he is," one authority explained. The eldership represented "the highest of holy orders, as resting upon the divine appointment of orders in the Christian Church." Within the AMEZ family, an elder was expected "to take pastoral charge wherever the bishop may appoint him, to preach on the same as often as practicable, solemnize Matrimony, administer the sacrament of the Lord's Supper and Baptize." As the authority observed, "Only the Elder may consecrate the elements for the Holy Communion."[3]

Likely during a visit to Key West in late December 1864 and January 1865, Superintendent Clinton seems to have repeated his North Carolina and Alabama patterns by selecting local men to represent the church. Sandy Cornish, the cofounder of Cornish Chapel, emerged in charge of his church as either an itinerant preacher or a deacon under Elder Wilbur Garrison Strong's supervision, usually a distant supervision. The stonemason Thomas H. Darley also may have accepted some level of clerical appointment connected with Cornish Chapel. Importantly for the church's future in Florida, one-time Polk County slave Joseph Sexton, brought to Key

West in spring 1864 in the aftermath of Union raids in the southwestern peninsula, accepted a call to the pastorate and received Clinton's blessing. Sexton's initial designation probably was as an itinerant preacher, with deacon's status coming to him within two years or so.[4]

The church's first opening to expansion in Florida may have come with Sexton's embrace of the AMEZ ministry. The young man yearned to return to his wife and two small children near Fort Meade, the cattle industry center located in southern Polk County. Soon after the peace he arranged to go by ship from Key West to Tampa, from whence he could venture eastward into the peninsula's interior toward his family. At Tampa, still only a tiny and isolated village, the war had taken a great toll, but Sexton surely knew in advance that he would be welcomed there. Refugee Aaron Bryant would have informed his fellow freedman at Key West that Bryant's mother, Dorcas, his brothers Samuel, Berry, and Peter, and other local black Methodists had withdrawn from Tampa's white congregation and begun meeting separately by 1863. By September 1864 the small society had formalized its organization in a ceremony held on the Hillsborough County courthouse steps. In March 1865 they ceased meeting at the courthouse, having secured "a small, one room, frame building" on Tyler at Pierce Street for use in worship.[5]

As expected, the Tampa congregation did welcome Sexton to their town and quickly agreed to associate with the AMEZ Church. "Reverend Joseph Sexton, an ex-soldier, came from Key West to become first pastor of the African Methodist Episcopal Zion Church of Tampa," one of its historians wrote, "which the struggling Christian group had elected to become known as." In future years the congregation would take on the name by which it continues to be called today, Mt. Sinai. Meanwhile, having accepted Mt. Sinai into the AMEZ Church, Sexton continued his journey to Polk County. There, on September 21, 1866, he married formally his long-time partner, Hannah Shaw.[6]

The Sexton marriage raises an issue that would have an impact in an important and unfortunate manner upon AMEZ missionary activities in Florida during the immediate post–Civil War years and which stemmed directly from the church's limitations on the authority of some of its ministers. Prior to 1876 the church discipline forbade deacons to perform marriages or baptisms unless accompanied by an elder. In the year or two following the Confederacy's surrender, though, marriages, as well as baptisms, very much commanded the attention of Florida's freedmen and freedwomen. In early January 1866 the Florida legislature specified that all freed couples then living together (and who previously had been prohibited from marrying under the law) had nine months to decide whether to marry or separate. If they desired to stay together, the law required formal marriage.[7]

Consequently, at the crucial moment when the church could have opened itself to the public by offering happy performance of the rites of marriage and thus sealed personal connections with actual and potential AMEZ members, most of its representatives found themselves unable to act. At best Elder Strong visited Florida sporadically, and the only weddings he is known to have performed were two in Key West early in 1867. Although this situation certainly did not doom the church in Florida, the inability to act in those crucial times permitted other denominations to gain advantages by offering memories that were not forgotten easily. "Opinions differ as to whether [Joseph] Sexton had been ordained at the time he took charge of the church," a member of Mt. Sinai related to an interviewer in 1936. "One old resident of the city," the account continued, "states that she was married in another church because he was not." Similarly, at Key West in 1889 an account of Cornish Chapel's early years made clear that Sandy Cornish was "not regularly ordained."[8]

This stumbling block touched on AMEZ activities beyond Tampa and Key West, for the second of its postwar expansionist initiatives already by 1866 had offered an anchor for the church in Florida's panhandle. The beginnings of these efforts centered at and near Pensacola, which had claimed pride of place in 1860 as the state's largest town. They occurred as an outgrowth, though, of the church's establishment in Alabama.

The events that set the stage for the panhandle missionary efforts were these. In March 1865 Superintendent Clinton, with important assistance from Wilbur G. Strong, had organized the Louisiana Conference in New Orleans to govern church activities in the southern states below North Carolina and Tennessee. With the coming of peace, the superintendent left Strong in charge in Louisiana while he traveled on to Alabama. There, Clinton believed, a rich harvest of recruits awaited in a state where African Methodist Episcopal Church outreach had not yet penetrated. In Alabama by June, he began recruiting and ordaining preachers to assist him. North Carolina native Solomon Derry numbered among them and soon emerged as a key figure, assuming within the year the position of Louisiana Conference secretary.[9]

With the assistance of talented men such as Derry, early successes attended Clinton's Alabama efforts. The superintendent centered his work at that time at Mobile and its Little Zion (later Big Zion) and State Street churches. Often the going proved rough. Late in 1865, for example, Little Zion's minister in charge, Ferdinand H. Smith, in the words of Bishop William J. Walls, "was arrested and sent to the penitentiary for refusing to bow to the authority of a rebel preacher."[10]

At Mobile, word reached Clinton of the existence of a small gathering of black Methodists near Pensacola. That he received the news in Alabama, rather than elsewhere, occurred for a number of reasons. Most of the Methodist churches of the isolated panhandle were administered not from Florida but from its sister state to the north and west. "I am told," Solomon Derry later recounted, "that there was a body of Zion worshippers about six or seven miles from Pensacola at a place called Turpentine Orchard in 1865, with about seven members." Before the year's end, Clinton managed to bring the tiny society within the AMEZ fold, likely as a result of a personal visit. The local pastor, an Alabama native named Harrison Williams, then was forty-seven years of age. He remained in charge. Among his small flock were Georgia native Warren Calway Vesta (born in about 1840) and youthful Simon Brown (also born in Georgia about 1848). Rounding out the group were Williams's wife, Matilda, Aaron Wilkinson, Liza Wilkinson, and Mary Davis.[11]

At the time of Clinton's visit, circumstances ill-favored any attempt to found a church within Pensacola, but the same did not apply in certain locales outside the town. "Turpentine Orchard" lay at or near the U.S. Navy Yard (Warrington), southwest of Pensacola. There, Union forces had employed a large number of black laborers, many skilled, in support of the war effort. "At Warrington, the United States government reservation, nine miles from the city . . . ," one observer noted, "the work of the Negroes was [very] pronounced." The description continued, "Following the war and the final emancipation of the slaves, some rewards for their years of work on fortifications at Warrington were given to them." It added: "The government permitted the ex-slaves and their descendants to settle in Warrington and build themselves homes outside the Navy Yard. These homes were tax free [because they sat upon federal government property], and there were no charges for [using] the land."[12]

Within Pensacola, on the other hand, the situation for whites and for blacks appeared gloomy. "During the war we remember to have visited Pensacola," one correspondent recalled, "and according to our recollections it was the most desolate and deserted of Southern cities." A white teacher added detail in a letter penned in April 1866: "The destruction which the war accomplished here was more extensive upon all classes, more terrible, than any place I have seen." He continued, "About seven eights of this town was destroyed." The abandoned Methodist church had burned, the victim of boys playing with fire that they could not control. The result, according to the church's historian, was "a general scattering of the membership and confusion."[13]

During 1866, though, the Pensacola scene brightened to the point that the place became attractive to AMEZ leaders. Already in late 1865, a local man could report, "The restoration of peace has caused the old inhabitants to return to their homes, and commercial intercourse has been resumed between New Orleans and this place." Indicative of the amelioration of conditions, black Baptists revived their St. John Baptist Church, continuing a heritage that began well before the Civil War. "The Colored people have a Church here also & hold meetings," one report detailed in March 1866, adding, "They have a large Sunday school." Before long a regular freedmen's school had opened in the Baptist sanctuary under the sponsorship of the American Missionary Association.[14]

Superintendent Clinton quickly endeavored to take advantage of the Pensacola resurgence. When the second annual session of the Louisiana Conference convened at Mobile in early May 1866, he created a "Tenth District" to encompass the church's Florida outposts, existing and planned. In doing so Clinton assigned a key Alabama aide, Deacon Ephraim S. Winn, to raise the AMEZ banner at the West Florida port town. The superintendent's plans also anticipated future congregations at Apalachicola, Cedar Keys, and Dry Tortugas (a military installation near Key West). Thomas H. Darley and Samuel Frazier, not yet ordained, received responsibility for Tampa, Cedar Keys, and Dry Tortugas, with a ministry at Apalachicola "to be supplied." The plans ratified, as well, Wilbur G. Strong's assignment to Cornish Chapel.[15]

The founding of what would become Pensacola's Talbot Chapel AMEZ Church followed at some time between the conference's adjournment and early November 1866 with a visit to the town from Alabama by preachers Solomon Derry and E. S. Winn. Superintendent Clinton perhaps accompanied them. Seemingly, at the 1866 conference the body had ordained Pensacola's Warren C. Vesta as a deacon. This and a November visitation of the Alabama clergymen is suggested by the fact that Vesta performed a marriage in Escambia County on November 6, presumably under the supervision of either Elder Winn or Superintendent Clinton. In any event, the Pensacola congregation coalesced by late 1866, with Winn taking personal charge not later than February 1867.[16]

The congregation soon found itself housed in a sanctuary. "The first

Zion church built in Pensacola (Fla) was built on leased land near the ice factory," Solomon Derry reminisced. "Elder Winn was pastor." The designation of E. S. Winn, an ordained elder, to the Pensacola church clearly aided the AMEZ attempt to ingratiate itself within the community. Not only did a figure on the scene possess authority to guide all church activities within the region, but he could perform rites such as marriages and baptisms without limitation. Whether Winn did so on a full-time basis is open to question. African American churches generally and the AMEZ Church specifically struggled to glean sufficient financial support for southern outreach. Accordingly, few dollars made their way from the Alabama church or the Louisiana Conference to Pensacola, and economic conditions prevailing there minimized local collections. Deacon Vesta earned his living during the period as a laborer.[17]

Whether circumstances permitted Winn to work on the church's behalf full-time or only part-time, plenty of work awaited him. Not only did he oversee construction and development of the Pensacola church and its congregation while keeping a careful eye on the Navy Yard society, he also managed responsibility for grasping desirable opportunities for expansion. Within one or two years Winn, in fact, reached out to take advantage of two such opportunities. At a rural location nine miles northwest of Pensacola, a small assemblage of black Methodists had continued a fellowship that traced itself to 1841. When Winn welcomed the congregation into connection, it became Spring Hill AMEZ Zion Church. Similarly, at nearby Milton, Santa Rosa County's seat located northeast of Pensacola, one-time Methodist congregants coalesced as an all-black society in a region where the white-run Methodist organization stood moribund. With Winn's encouragement, the Milton residents formed Isaiah Chapel AMEZ Zion Church.[18]

These early AMEZ organizational efforts shared a common characteristic that first saw its manifestation in James Walker Hood's New Bern, North Carolina, experience in 1864. The Florida AMEZ Church up to 1867 attempted to build itself directly upon the ruins of the Methodist Episcopal Church, South. It did so, of course, by offering freedmen and freedwomen a familiar religious context but one operated and controlled by African Americans. As Sandy Dwayne Martin explained in his study of Hood's life and ministry, "In some ways we might more accurately speak of these northern workers as 'denominational organizers' rather than 'missionaries' in the strictest sense of the word." He added, "These northern workers in the southern field were to a great extent incorporating into their connections congregations and individuals already committed to the Christian faith." In 1861 the ME South Church in Florida contained nineteen thousand members, some eight thousand of whom (42 percent) were African Americans. Those numbers began dropping in 1862. More than 10 percent of the total slipped away in 1863 alone, the year that Tampa's black Methodists departed their white-controlled church.[19]

Still, thousands of African Americans remained within the ME South church when emancipation became a reality for most in 1865, a condition that would not last for long. Church fathers attempted to organize special missions for freedmen, but the effort quickly met with disastrous results. In 1866, twenty-five hundred fled. Embittered white clergymen, unable to see their own failings or those of their church, blamed outside agitators. "It was utterly impossible for us to keep our missions," J. C. Ley declared from a perspective held in common with many of his colleagues, "still we tried to render them all the service possible, and could we have served them with the whites, until they could have ministers of their own color, at least partially educated, it would have been better for them." Ley then added, "But the perfect flood of 'carpetbaggers' in their endeavors to obtain power and wealth for themselves by the votes of the enfranchised freedmen, so operated upon them that before the close of this year [1866] most of them had withdrawn from our communion." It mattered little to Ley, of course, that freedmen had no vote in 1866. In any event, by 1869 fewer than five hundred African Americans remained within the fold of Florida's ME South church.[20]

Superintendent Clinton and his AMEZ allies thus enjoyed easy entrée within its Florida fields of operations during the period from 1864 to 1867. The white Methodist churches at Pensacola and Milton had closed, with no minister available to reopen them until 1867. At Key West, Cornish Chapel's backers had won so much respect and loyalty during the Civil War and especially the yellow fever epidemic in 1864 that they easily blunted postwar mission efforts by white clergymen. As of December 1867, not one African American belonged to the white church there. The story at Tampa closely resembled that at Key West. Separation of the races within the Methodist community in that tiny village seemingly occurred without rancor. Although some cooperation continued to occur across racial lines, black Methodists during the period associated almost exclusively with Mt. Sinai AMEZ Church.[21]

One problem that boded poorly for the future, though, concerned the early AMEZ fields of operations. Congregations at Apalachicola, Cedar

Keys, and Dry Tortugas failed to coalesce according to Superintendent Clinton's 1866 plans. That left one church on a remote island, another on an isolated frontier, and perhaps a few others in a panhandle region in which pine trees far outnumbered humans and which lay distant from the rest of the state by one hundred and fifty miles or more. Most of Florida's African American population lived elsewhere. True, in 1860 Key West and Pensacola had vied for honors as Florida's largest town. Their counties' populations in 1867, however, totaled less than ten thousand persons. When Santa Rosa and Hillsborough were added to the mix, the total rose to less than fifteen thousand. This constituted only 9 percent of the state's population. When the focus is shifted to African Americans alone, the figure comes to less than four thousand, or 5 percent.[22]

The large majority of Florida's African American residents in the immediate postwar years lived, not surprisingly, within the bounds of the state's one-time plantation district of Middle Florida. This region of stretched from Jackson County and the Apalachicola River on the west to Madison and Hamilton counties and the Suwannee River on the east. Civil War–wrought destruction virtually had passed it by. After the peace most of the seventy-one thousand African Americans who lived in the state, as well as most of the former slaves who had belonged to Methodist congregations, were attempting to survive there by farming on their own, farming on shares, or working for hire.[23]

Thinly stretched resources in personnel and finances kept the AMEZ Church from approaching this huge pool of potential church members in the immediate postwar years, but the AME Church hesitated not at all to pursue its organization with fervor. That denomination's South Carolina Conference organized on May 16, 1865, and immediately dispatched an ordained minister to venture westward into the panhandle from Jacksonville, reaping Methodist congregations in an AME harvest of the territory. In Jackson, Gadsden, Leon, Jefferson, Madison, Columbia, and Duval counties, he scored triumphs for his church's brand of African Methodism. Subsequent church leaders consolidated and expanded upon these initial conquests. By June 1867 the church's reach had grown substantially enough to command the organization of an AME Florida Conference. Already, it claimed 5,240 members. "We are all looking forward to a glorious future," its presiding elder, Charles H. Pearce, pronounced.[24]

The rapid success of AME expansionist efforts directly touched upon AMEZ efforts. For one thing, they effectively blunted any thoughts Superintendent Clinton may have held regarding AMEZ movement east of

Santa Rosa County and its vicinity. Even within the AMEZ fields of operations, problems could arise when ambitious undertakings, however well intentioned, were launched with insufficient forethought and support. This occurred particularly with an 1867 attempt at outreach from Tampa north into Hernando County and its seat of Brooksville.

Although little information has come to light concerning the Hernando County foray, its rationale and the reasons for its disappointing results seem clear. The idea likely arose when Elder Wilbur G. Strong visited Key West and, possibly, Tampa in January–February 1867. He came to realize during the sojourn that, while relatively few African Americans lived in the remote Tampa Bay frontier region, Hernando (present-day Pasco, Hernando, and Citrus counties) represented in important ways the southernmost reach of the Old South plantation system. Although the county's population amounted to less than three thousand persons, almost one thousand of them were black. An approach to these individuals essentially would double the AMEZ scope of activity in the region. Moreover, the AME Church had yet to extend its reach so far south, leaving a Methodist vacuum in the county.[25]

With such a missionary field ripe for the plucking, Strong faced an important challenge. Whom should he send to Brooksville, given that time was of the essence? He found his personnel resources very limited. Joseph Sexton, ministering at Tampa, remained unavailable. The only clergyman at Strong's disposal turned out to be a disabled Civil War veteran named James H. Roberts who, obviously as events would prove, was a man of great conviction and determination. Lacking acceptable alternatives, Strong dispatched Roberts. The emissary arrived at Brooksville during the summer, but progress came painfully. By early 1868 he found himself compelled to turn to other means for support. "A school has been started at Brooksville, by a Mr. Roberts, a Colored preacher," a Freedmen's Bureau agent reported in February. "He reports that he has about thirty day scholars, who promise to pay him one Dollar and fifty cents each per month, [but] the charges are too high and more than the freedmen can afford to pay," he continued. "Besides Mr. Roberts is not a very Good Teacher, as he can neither write or Cipher, both arms being paralized, he is perfectly honest however in his efforts to improve his race, and is deserving of consideration." One month later the agent described Roberts's school as "very small." A final note came in a report of June 17. "Mr. Roberts broke up his school on the 1st Inst. & has come to Tampa, with the intention of opening a school here," the agent observed.[26]

Beyond the obvious problems involved in dispatching a seriously hand-icapped man on such a mission, several factors contributed to Roberts's frustrations at Brooksville that hinted at future concerns for the AMEZ Church if it intended to move into Florida on a grander scale. First, Roberts launched himself deep into the peninsula's interior without sufficient backing from the church. Always chronically short of funds (again, as were other churches, white and black, at the time), the denomination's inabil-ity in 1867 to support its missionary work to the extent desired glared brightly in the incident, a situation that would come back to shadow AMEZ endeavors in future years. Also, at the critical point when creative leadership from Strong or elsewhere might have bolstered Roberts's sag-ging fortunes, the elder's influential presence ended abruptly with no substitute in sight. This occurred because of another nagging AMEZ chal-lenge, the need for talented and experienced clergymen elsewhere than in remote and underpopulated Florida. In Strong's case, Superintendent Clinton required his old friend to serve as his right-hand man in Alabama, where church growth had resulted by April 3, 1867, in the creation of the Alabama Conference. Clinton "sent for" Strong prior to the gathering, probably because he remained in Florida. Once in Alabama, Clinton desig-nated the elder as pastor of the Mobile church, a position that he retained for the following eleven years.[27]

One other significant dynamic illustrated itself in the Brooksville ini-tiative. AMEZ authorities recognized during these early years the futility of battling the much larger AME Church head-to-head. The Brooksville experience, though, pointed out the need to be alert for overwhelming competition from the Baptists, as well as from the AME disciples. In Her-nando and at Brooksville in 1867, an especially talented and determined group of Baptist ministers with longtime ties to the area had committed to building up their church while also furthering the educational and political needs of their fellows. Centered around the Bethlehem Baptist Church, individuals such as Arthur Sinclair (or St. Clair), his brother Hampton Sinclair, Prince McKnight, Abe Timmons, and Henry Harper grew to exer-cise tremendous influence in county, regional, and state affairs. An out-sider such as Roberts, even one so obviously dedicated and sincere, enjoyed little chance in opposition to such men in such a locale.[28]

That Baptist ministers in Hernando County might exercise important political clout raises other issues, especially that of AMEZ involvement in politics and government and how that involvement compared to and contrasted with the attitudes and actions of AME and Baptist clergymen.

By way of context, the Presidential Reconstruction policies in place from 1865 until 1867 effectively had handed control of most of the southern region back into the hands of the class of men who had taken the same states out of the Union in 1860 and 1861. In Florida, for example, a legislature dominated by former Rebels had enacted a harsh "black code" aimed at regulating the lives of freedmen in an attempt to reinstate slavery to the extent permitted by federal authorities. At the same time, Florida's state government had turned a blind eye to widespread violence aimed at former slaves and, particularly, white Unionist (sometimes called Loyalist) sympathizers.[29]

This situation took a dramatic turn following congressional elections held late in 1866. "Radical" Republicans gained control of both houses of Congress, intent upon replacing President Andrew Johnson's Reconstruction policies with ones aimed at protecting and uplifting freedmen and white Loyalists. Congressional or "Military" Reconstruction ensued the following year with the passage of several Reconstruction acts. For the first time, adult male freedmen were permitted to vote while, pursuant to terms of the new laws that addressed key leaders and supporters of secession and the subsequent war, some former Rebels found themselves excluded from polling places. In Florida, Republicans drafted a new state constitution early in 1868 that, by the summer, resulted in the installation of a Republican state government at Tallahassee. Seventeen of fifty-three members of the Florida house of representatives then were African American, while three black senators sat in the twenty-four–member state senate.[30]

As these events occurred, AMEZ clergymen joined in urging African American participation in politics and the Republican Party's cause. When Republicans gathered at Pensacola in February 1868, for instance, the session "was opened by a prayer from the Rev. Mr. Winn." At Tampa, James H. Roberts and Joseph Sexton pursued similar courses of conduct. As early as August 1867, Sexton had joined church members Aaron Bryant, Samuel Bryant, Mills Holloman, Adam Holloman, and Isaac Howard, among others, to demand immediate appointment of Republican (and black) officials for Tampa and Hillsborough County. Most likely Roberts, then at Brooksville, offered the same leadership. After he arrived at Tampa in June 1868, he certainly did so. At one gathering Sexton and Roberts joined with Brooksville's Baptist leader Arthur Sinclair in a particularly spirited rally. A local newspaper labeled the meeting "a decided success."[31]

What Florida's AMEZ ministers mostly did not do during these initial stages of Congressional Reconstruction was to seek political office for themselves; rather, they encouraged members of their local congregations to do so. Thus, Mills Holloman took a seat on the Hillsborough County commission in 1868, rather than Joseph Sexton or James H. Roberts. This stance may or may not have reflected Superintendent (beginning in 1868, Bishop) Clinton's philosophy. James Walker Hood, for instance, recalled a warning that he received from Clinton after his own elevation to the episcopacy in 1872. "The senior Bishop . . . advised me," Hood recorded, "that it would not be well for me to take a further active part in politics." Hood continued to encourage AMEZ laymen to carry the church's message to the corridors of political power, but, otherwise, he heeded the advice. On the other hand, something as basic as a lack of time to devote to public office may have driven policy for the AMEZ preachers. In any event, the church's message, as suggested by Hood's actions and as possibly derived from Clinton's inclinations, came in a moderate tone that encouraged cooperation with well-intentioned whites.[32]

The paths taken by many AME and Baptist ministers stood in marked contrast to that trod by their AMEZ counterparts. These men concurred with AMEZ policies in supporting the Republican Party, but they differed in that Florida's AME and Baptist ministers in 1867 and 1868 felt little compunction about running for or accepting appointment to political office. Take the example of AME leaders. The Florida constitutional convention of 1868 contained eighteen black members (out of forty-six). Four of them were AME ministers. At least six AME laymen joined them. Eight of seventeen black members who took seats in the legislature that summer were AME ministers or laymen, while the entire black presence in the state senate consisted of three of the denomination's leading preachers. So aggressive and successful was the AME Church's early political militancy that, by 1871, one of its pioneers could boast, "African Methodism is about to rule Florida."[33]

The Baptists failed in these early years of Reconstruction to claim the electoral successes that greeted AME efforts, but the denomination exercised real political muscle in any case. Offering conservative counterpoise within the Republican Party to the AME Church's more radical image, Baptist leaders participated in most levels of government.

A few examples can illustrate the point. The state's leading minister, Leon County's James Page, served as voter registrar in 1867–68 before accepting appointment to the local county commission. Cataline B. Simmons, the cofounder of Key West's Cornish Chapel, had relocated about

1866 to Jacksonville where he had taken the pastorate of a Baptist church. Like Page, Simmons served as a voter registrar before taking a seat on the Duval County commission. Later he held office as a Jacksonville councilman and as the county tax assessor. Arthur Sinclair also served as a voter registrar. His term on the Hernando County commission commenced in 1875.[34]

In the early days of Congressional Reconstruction, the relative lack of direct participation in political office by AMEZ ministers may have lessened the church's attractiveness to some black voters in Florida, although this may have opened the way for church action in other areas by affording time to act. Within the limits of its always difficult financial picture, to cite examples, AMEZ activists worked for good schools and other social services needed by African Americans in their communities. As seen in the case of the Baptist ministers at Brooksville, Baptists joined in this cause as did AME leaders. Still, AMEZ pastors found themselves better able to concentrate on the goals at hand. This dynamic of church endeavor, which would mark the AMEZ ministry in Florida through the century's end, had manifested itself as early as 1864, when Superintendent Clinton dispatched a teacher, Wilbur G. Strong, to minister at Key West. On a visit back to the town in late 1865, Strong had accepted direct responsibility in the matter. "Isaac Brown, principal of the school here having resigned his position," he recorded, "we have taken charge of the school for the present, and we are doing the best we can with it, and bid fair to have abundant success." He continued, "We propose to continue teaching, until we find that the two-fold labor of teaching and preaching is too much for us physically."[35]

Others followed Strong's lead. As seen, James H. Roberts opened schools at Brooksville and Tampa in 1868. Surviving documentation suggests that Joseph Sexton helped to organize one on the Alafia River southeast of Tampa the same year. Soon, Tampa's black school trustee board consisted of the AMEZ minister (John G. Williams, about whom more will be discussed in subsequent chapters), lay member Peter W. Bryant, and one white man. Williams filled in as teacher. In AMEZ communities Milton, Pensacola, and Warrington, the state's superintendent of schools, an ME South minister, discovered strong local support for quality education by 1867. From Warrington in 1868 came this note: "The colored school house being erected by the Freedmen's Bureau near the colored people's church is progressing rapidly, and bids fair to be a good substantial structure, capable of containing a goodly number of pupils. It is two stories high, and will

have a male and female department." At Key West the state school superintendent actually met with the community at Cornish Chapel. "I had a
large church full of a very respectable order of freedmen intelligent and
many prominent for piety," he reported. "They had a teacher," he continued. "His school numbered 70."[36]

Beyond schools and education, some AMEZ adherents already were involved in efforts to offer other needed services to the community. Little
information is available on the subject, but AMEZ churches seemingly
were sponsoring fraternal and mutual benefit societies by 1868. "Fraternal
societies created what anthropologists call fictive kin," David M. Fahey
observed. "Quasi-religious initiation rituals instructed members to regard
one another as brothers (and sisters)," Fahey explained further. "Benevolent societies differed from fraternal ones in that they lacked ritual and
typically had only a local membership, but a mutual benefit society easily
could evolve into a fraternal society." The historian also noted that religion
played a greater part in the development of black fraternal life than it did
for white fraternal bodies. Thus, the known experience at Warrington,
where the AMEZ congregation backed a "Colored Benevolent Association" against the active opposition of the local Baptist church, both stands
out and melds with the trend of future developments. When in the spring
of 1869 the benevolence association ran into financial problems, the Navy
Yard congregation bought its beautiful association hall for use as the
church's sanctuary.[37]

These early accomplishments of the AMEZ Church in Florida may
appear modest, but in a short time with few resources the denomination
had accomplished some solid results against a backdrop of immense and
sometimes threatening challenges. In particular, violence against freedmen and Loyalists, mentioned earlier, plagued the western edge of the
panhandle. The problem mounted in 1866 to the point that military authorities declared martial law in Escambia and Santa Rosa counties and
arrested all of the local public officials (all white). When Mt. Sinai member Thomas Clarke spoke out too openly at Tampa, whites trumped up
charges against him. The judge had Clarke whipped "in a very brutal
manner" after a previous sentence of nailing his ears to a post had failed
to dissuade the activist. Eventually the local judicial system grew so racist and corrupt that the military suspended its application to African Americans.[38]

On top of problems with violence and racism, AMEZ counties con-
tended with immense economic concerns and natural disasters during the

period. Although a Freedmen's Bureau agent at Pensacola could report in October 1867 that "the moral effect of military authority has been very great," he nonetheless felt required to lament "depressed business and the unsettled state of the country." He added, "There has been much want resulting from this stagnation." Only a few miles to the west and south, Warrington residents were hit by waves of layoffs at the Navy Yard. Meanwhile, the withdrawal of most U.S. forces from Key West at war's end complicated economic matters there. Tampa lay in such economic doldrums by late 1868 that a general collapse of its economic viability was feared. As to the local black community, a report commented, "[They] are by no means in a prosperous condition." It concluded, "How many of them make a living is yet unexplained."[39]

To make matters worse, Mother Nature lent a cruel and destructive hand. An October 1865 hurricane tore through the Florida Keys. Its damage, combined with military cutbacks, left one local man exclaiming, "The effect of all these disasters has been ruinous." The weather mostly cooperated during 1866 when racial violence loomed so immediately, but in 1867 its destructive face returned with a vengeance. Constant rains prompted general flooding throughout the peninsula, leaving Tampa essentially cut off from the outside world. This occurred just after a fire destroyed Tampa's "scrub" area, home to many black residents. During the same period, yellow fever attacked Key West, Tampa, and Pensacola. It returned to Key West in 1869.[40]

Through the trials and tribulations, the successes and failures, the infant AMEZ presence in Florida nonetheless persisted. As had occurred previously in 1864, tragedy sometimes offered the church the ability to build community loyalty and respect, solidifying the AMEZ foundation. By 1868, in fact, the church appeared hardy enough to command its own district. The following year would see the organization of a Florida Conference. Perhaps with solid leadership and the setting of preferential priorities in the allocation of resources for its growth, Florida's AMEZ could compete with AME and other black churches. Unfortunately, resources remained scarce, while Florida's priority ranked far from the top.

THE FLORIDA CONFERENCE, 1868–1875

with the blessings of peace
smiling upon our land

In 1868 Florida's weary freedmen and freedwomen, having faced dire and often tragic challenges for three years of what had passed for peace in the immediate post–Civil War era, beheld the glimmering possibility of true freedom at long last. Thanks to a Congress dominated by Radical Republicans, Florida and other one-time Confederate states stepped into a new era of government based upon the power exercised by African American voters allied with white Loyalists and northern newcomers. Meanwhile, the black community against the odds had established foundations for the building of institutions, including churches, that would serve its interests for generations to come. Given relatively good economic conditions for half a decade, many of those institutions would thrive. That others—including the African Methodist Episcopal Zion Church—would survive at all, given the circumstances, also amounted to an achievement. As will be seen, numerous factors, many of which involved frustrations, combined to influence the AMEZ experience. Amid the frustrations, the church's ministers would find themselves playing increasingly crucial roles. Sometimes the roles, unfortunately, revealed themselves to be something far different from what all had hoped would be the case.

The Florida AMEZ Church began the era by manifesting what might be described as a more mature status. On April 27, 1868, Bishop Joseph J. Clinton held the first Zion conference ever convened on Florida's soil. The session, likely convened at Pensacola, seemingly resulted in the creation of a Florida District of the Alabama Conference. Not much else is known about the gathering except that Deacon Joseph Sexton received ordination as an elder.[1]

On the other hand, certain dynamics and intentions may be inferred from the conference meeting. Most particularly, it may have reflected Bishop Clinton's concern for survival of the church in Florida so long as that survival depended upon the generosity and decision-making authority of the Alabama Conference. With the possible exception of Key West's Cornish Chapel, none of the Florida churches could be considered self-supporting. The state as a whole constituted a mission district that required a constant flow of financial assistance. If AMEZ preachers carried the cause deeper into the peninsula and panhandle, the tax on its sponsors would rise proportionately. The rapid expansion of AMEZ membership rolls in Alabama soon would transform that state into a Zion bulwark, but it also created tremendous monetary demands that argued loudly against exporting scarce funds to poor Florida.[2]

Clinton's solution lay in the creation of a separate Florida Conference that would receive its support directly from the national church. Just how he intended to achieve that goal in light of the limited Zion presence in the state remains an intriguing question. The available evidence hints that he grasped hold of the then-waning cause of organic union with the AME Church to find justification sufficient to command action by the AMEZ General Conference. As discussed earlier, the two denominations in 1864 had agreed to a union vote in 1868. Events and personalities subsequently had undermined the fragile consensus; still, the vote's outcome remained anyone's guess in early 1868. So, prudent management practices required responsible planning for merger, whenever it should come. The Florida AME Church—which, by then, encompassed more than seven thousand members in thirty-three churches—had organized as an independent conference in 1867. Clinton thus could argue for a Florida AMEZ Conference based upon the need to align the two churches' conference boundaries.[3]

When combined with the force of Clinton's personality and the persuasiveness of his other arguments, whatever they were, the approach carried the day. At the Twelfth General Conference, which opened at Washington, D.C., on May 6, 1868, delegates created five new AMEZ conferences, among them one for Florida, even though organic union failed to gain approval. In the heady atmosphere at the nation's capital in May 1868—with the promise of Congressional Reconstruction reverberating like a brass band throughout the South—anything seemed doable. To Bishop Clinton and his allies it must even have seemed possible to build an AMEZ Church in Florida strong enough to compete directly with the AME and other black churches.[4]

The bishop's desires took living form at Pensacola on April 22, 1869, with the Florida Conference's organizational session. Clinton presided over the assemblage with Alabama's Edward Johnson acting as its secretary. Reports suggested a rather substantial gathering of thirteen ministers, but they masked reality. The greater number of those attending served congregations in Alabama or elsewhere.[5]

The new conference, however many witnessed its organization, was tiny. Nationally the church claimed 125,000 members in seventeen conferences, but in Florida it could boast only 348 members spread through the five counties of Escambia, Santa Rosa, Hillsborough, Polk, and Monroe. Congregations met at Warrington (Good Hope), Pensacola (the future Talbot Chapel), Milton (Isaiah Chapel), Tampa (Mt. Sinai), and Key West (Cornish Chapel), as well as at one or two rural Escambia County locations. Also, because Elder Joseph Sexton had undertaken following his ordination to organize several new societies in the hinterlands interior from Tampa, the church's banner flew fifteen or so miles to the east of that village at Simmons Hammock (Mt. Zion) near the plantation of one-time army guide Sampson Forrester. Twenty miles farther eastward, Sexton also established missions or congregations in his home county of Polk. They were situated at Alafia (near today's Mulberry on the Polk-Hillsborough County line) and at some point between the county seat of Bartow and the rural community of Homeland (literally Sexton's homeland).[6]

Clinton did his best, given the paucity of resources that he could command, to afford the new conference a fighting chance. His actions focused especially on personnel. In several instances he ensured that energetic and dynamic preachers and organizers, two of them from Alabama, succeeded earlier designees. Perhaps most important, Alexander C. Fisher joined and soon replaced an ailing E. S. Winn at Pensacola, while Gabriel Sexton (no known relation to Joseph Sexton) arrived to aid the work in Santa Rosa and Escambia counties. Clinton also relieved the severely handicapped Tampa pastor James H. Roberts. In Roberts's place, he sent young John G. Williams, a Civil War veteran then living at Key West. The action allowed Joseph Sexton to concentrate on his newly established churches in eastern Hillsborough and Polk. The bishop's plans suffered one unexpected setback. Cornish Chapel's pastor Sandy Cornish died at Key West. It took almost one year to convince a chapel founder, Thomas H. Darley, to leave his lucrative government employment and other business interests to accept the full-time charge. Receiving ordination as an elder at the second state conference session, Darley had taken over the Key West church by summer 1870.[7]

The Florida Conference membership numbers, already small, reflected, as well, a pool for recruitment that itself remained very small. In future years Florida would distinguish itself as the most urban of the southern states, but in the late 1860s and early 1870s the overwhelming majority of Floridians lived in the countryside, worked in agriculture, and either were poor or else lived only modestly. The AMEZ Church, though, found itself rooted mostly in Florida's largest towns and the counties that surrounded them. This would not have limited the church's potential to the degree that it eventually did, except for the fact that the towns themselves were so small. Pensacola in 1870 contained only 3,347 residents with nearby Warrington adding another 1,697. Key West the same year claimed 5,016. The third AMEZ center of Tampa amounted to little more than a village. Its 1870 population totaled less than one-sixth that of Key West. Grouped together, these communities housed an African American community of just 3,190 persons.[8]

Besides this "urban" orientation, another factor limited the church's ministry and subsequent ability to expand. Florida AMEZ members tended to differ dramatically in economic circumstances from most African Americans in the state, and hence their religious needs tended to differ as well. Good-paying government jobs and opportunities that arose indirectly from the local availability of government employment, as well as other factors that will be discussed shortly, permitted growing economic security for many African Americans at Key West, Pensacola, and Warrington. Minister-to-be John G. Williams's experience offers an example. "I am 30 years of age [and] was born in Georgia," he explained. "I enlisted in the U.S. Navy," Williams continued. "I served two years and six months [and] was a servant in Admiral Baily's mess." He added, "After discharge I was employed as a Clerk in the firm of Jones & Co. at Key West."[9]

The life of another Cornish Chapel member, James A. Roberts, provides an additional case in point. Born at Key West in 1845, Roberts grew up on the island, learning to read and write as he matured. The young man served honorably in the U.S. Army from February 1863 until his discharge at Jacksonville in early 1866. Married at Key West on February 7, 1869, to Rosalee M. Scovey, Roberts already was prospering as a skilled worker who had earned a reputation for being, in the words of one government official, "of good moral character, temperate and industrious habit, and faithful to the Union and Constitution." A strong Republican, Roberts soon emerged as a community leader. He was elected to the office of constable during 1872–74 before entering upon a three-year tenure as Monroe County sheriff. Key West voters also selected him as one of their councilmen in 1875. Deriving immense pleasure from his island life, Roberts especially delighted in his participation as a member (and cofounder) of the Key West Cornet Band, an ensemble that enjoyed immense popularity throughout Florida in the 1870s and 1880s.[10]

Even in the Tampa region, where good economic times most certainly did not always prevail during the late 1860s, circumstances nonetheless drew to the AMEZ Church a membership that remained atypical and somewhat more prosperous than was the norm for African Americans in Florida. The case of Sampson Forrester, who owned a thriving plantation in eastern Hillsborough County, already has been mentioned. Nearby in the early 1870s, various members of the Armwood clan, another well-to-do farming family, settled. Having relocated from Volusia County but able to trace their roots to Revolutionary North Carolina, the Armwoods associated themselves closely with the AMEZ cause. In future years Lewis D. Armwood, in addition to his other community service, would preside as chairman of Mt. Zion's board of trustees.[11]

Tampa's Bryant family likewise stood out. From a combination of hard work and united effort plus the likely assistance of some local whites, Dorcas Bryant commanded for herself and her sons a comfortable living. She operated a washing and laundering business, while Aaron, Samuel, and Peter engaged in construction and other activities requiring special skills. By the 1880s Dorcas's home and the improvements connected with it carried the considerable evaluation of $1,500, far in excess of the average worth of the homes of Tampa's white population. Samuel's holdings during the same period ranged up to $7,000. Each of the sons participated actively in Republican Party affairs, with Peter holding office during 1877–80 as a justice of the peace. After graduation from Howard University's law school, he eventually would establish a practice as Key West's leading black attorney.[12]

Two factors provided special impetus to the increasing prosperity enjoyed over time by numerous Tampa-area families and, in turn, influenced the local AMEZ Church. First, in 1866 the Congress had approved the Southern Homestead Act opening up federal lands for southern blacks. The availability of desirable homestead lands near Tampa, as well as in rural Hillsborough and Polk counties, permitted scores of claimants the possibility of financial independence. This especially proved the case because the semitropical climate allowed them to avoid the trap of dependence upon cotton as a cash crop. Most profited instead from truck farming, but they also helped to develop the citrus industry at a time when few area whites evidenced interest in its possibilities. Good times actually began to pervade the countryside inland from Tampa as the 1870s unfolded. The Simmons Hammock and Lake Thonotosassa vicinity, where a group of one-time Polk County slaves settled in the midst of families of their Hillsborough County peers, especially drew attention for the achievements of its residents. "They have their own school and meeting house," a visitor observed later. "They teach in the one and worship in the other," he continued. "They hold camp meetings, and debating clubs, read essays and sing hymns and songs." He concluded: "They send their children to colored academies, and dress in store clothes. But above all they are the best farmers in the county, and are excelling their white neighbors in the quantity and quality of their products."[13]

The second factor involved the rise of the state's cattle kingdom. African Americans had participated in the southwest Florida cattle industry since black drovers had tended Seminole herds in the early 1800s. Stymied during the Civil War, the cattle trade exploded in the late 1860s as ties with Havana, Cuba, ensured a steady demand for Florida beef. Experienced cow-hunters such as Stephen Harvell, whose family attended Mt. Zion AMEZ, found their services in demand. "I used to be in the woods two or three weeks at a time," he reminisced of time spent on the range.[14]

When considered in light of opportunities generally available for African Americans in Florida, the cattle trade promised substantial rewards. Money earned tending or driving beeves could then support modest investments by black hands in beef production, expanded homesteads, and greater involvement in citrus production. At Polk County's Homeland, the former slave Rachel Davis and her family exemplified the fact. While Rachel laid out a homestead orange grove, her sons Alfred, Samuel, Lloyd, and Corrie expanded the family's economic base to include cattle, truck farming, and other investments. When Samuel Davis died in 1928, the local newspaper praised him as "an example of the success the colored man can attain." The sentiment extended locally to all of his siblings. As the family's evolution occurred, most members of the Davis clan accepted an AMEZ allegiance. Thus, Elder Warren C. Vesta would stand in to marry Samuel Davis and Matilda Shavers in 1891. Elder Joseph Sexton had united Corrie with Hattie Honors the same year, while Elder Oscar V. Jackson had acted similarly for Alfred Davis and Charlotte Hendry nine years earlier.[15]

Beyond these special social and economic spheres that surrounded and influenced AMEZ communities as they grew in the immediate post–Civil War years, additional industries and specialized opportunities arose in the late 1860s and 1870s that would carry implications for the church. At Pensacola, to cite an example, the timber industry came to the fore. It had constituted the principal regional industry prior to the Civil War, but a lack of rail transportation had impeded recovery and expansion immediately after the peace. This had come about even though a north-south rail line earlier had linked the town with Alabama's railroad system. Its connection had lain at Flomaton (earlier called Pensacola Junction and situated in Alabama just north of the Florida line), and the tie had offered Escambia and Santa Rosa residents and businessmen access to markets in the Upper South and Midwest. The road, unfortunately, had emerged from the Civil War as a casualty. In October 1868, though, work commenced on the line's complete reconstruction under a charter granted to the Pensacola & Louisville Railroad Company. "To-day the first rail, in the line of Railroad, soon to connect us with Chicago, via Louisville was laid," one newspaper noted. It added, "With the blessings of peace smiling upon our land, we see no further obstacles in the way of its speedy completion and of the rapid growth of our city."[16]

With the 1870 completion of the Pensacola & Louisville road, Pensacola quickly emerged as Florida's premier lumber town. Its port also became the most important point for lumber exports along the Gulf coast. A second and shorter line, which tied Pensacola with Perdido Bay to its west, buttressed the advances. By 1880 the town's population had doubled from its 1870 level. As one local man observed in 1869, however, the success came as no surprise. "It is impossible to estimate the extent of business these advantages will give Pensacola," he wrote. "Already, her unlimited supply of first class timber and lumber is creating a vast trade, which gives, in return for her forests, sterling exchange and the exchanges of the West Indies."[17]

While new or at least revived industry doubled Pensacola's size and created hundreds of industrial jobs for African Americans during the 1870s, two developments brought results just as remarkable at the AMEZ Church's first Florida home. As mentioned, the southwest peninsula's cattle trade had taken off after 1868 when revolution stirred in Cuba. The decade-long insurrection also spurred relocation of portions of that island's cigar industry to Key West's safer environs. "Monroe County, Florida, in which is situated the island of Key West, has the largest foreign-born population of any of the Florida counties," the *New York Daily Tribune* explained of the consequences in 1872. "Ever since the Cuban hegira from Havana in 1868," its article added, "Cubans have lived in Key West, and adopted that island as their home." A Methodist minister added his own observations two years later. "The city has grown rapidly within a few years," he began. "Indeed its population has doubled within a very short time," the minister continued. "Its increase has not been numerical alone; intelligence and wealth have increased at a greater rate than the population," he concluded. "The progress already made will give a broader ground for future prosperity, and it will not be long before the citizens of Key West will learn that Providence has placed within their grasp the power to control the commerce of every city encircling the Gulf of Mexico."[18]

While Key West's growing cigar industry opened good jobs to African American craftsmen such as James A. Roberts, the industry's expansion did not mark the only important influx of immigrants to the island during the period. From about 1872 Bahamians began arriving in larger numbers than previously, a dynamic that both enhanced the local AMEZ membership and helped to create local turmoil. In the former instance, many Bahamians had accustomed themselves to the Methodist church long before leaving their home islands. With Cornish Chapel offering the only thriving local black Methodist congregation, more than a few of the newcomers joined its rolls. Shadrack Hannibal, for instance, had begun life as a South Carolina slave, but in the mid-1800s he had seized his master's trading schooner and made for freedom at Nassau. In the early 1870s he had relocated his family to Key West where lucrative carpentry jobs awaited him and his sons. Shadrack returned to Nassau in 1882, but he, wife Matilda, and children James, Samuel, Jeremiah, Joseph, Purcilla, Eva, and Cecilia had ventured back to stay by the early 1890s. Methodists at Nassau, Hannibal family members naturally affiliated closely with Key West's Cornish Chapel.[19]

Unfortunately for AMEZ strength in Florida, the Key West Bahamian influx, although it provided recruitment potential for Cornish Chapel's pastor Thomas H. Darley, did not do so to the extent that might have appeared likely. The quandary stemmed from economics. As greater numbers of workers arrived from the Bahamas, they took jobs that local African Americans otherwise would have claimed by agreeing to work for lower wages. Resentment, not surprisingly, boiled within the community. Incidents of various kinds elevated tempers until, on election day in November 1874, a gun battle erupted in Key West's streets between the two factions. The violence persisted until federal troops managed to quell the tumult. Meager surviving accounts suggest that this incident and related acts turned some Bahamians who might otherwise have associated with local black churches such as Cornish Chapel to consideration of alternatives. Specifically, the circumstances led them, instead, to the Episcopal Church.[20]

In any event, because of the nature of the changes affecting the economies at Pensacola and Key West, the early 1870s witnessed an ongoing but partial reorientation of the Florida AMEZ Church away from a constituency dominated originally by relatively affluent city dwellers to an industry-based membership with rural connections. At Tampa, much the same thing occurred. Although the town grew little during the 1870s, its economy increasingly depended upon the cedar and cypress timber and milling industries. As will be considered again shortly at greater length, the Franco-Prussian War of 1870–71 disrupted the business, and the economic depression that followed the Panic of 1873 likewise carried a strong impact. Still, for a decade and one-half beginning about 1869 most Tampans, including many African Americans, supported themselves, either directly or indirectly, from timbering and sawmills.[21]

In light of the increasing prosperity and impressive growth at and near the church's centers of activity during the late 1860s and early 1870s, a question arises as to whether AMEZ leaders took proper advantage of the opportunities for expansion presented thereby. The answer? A qualified yes. The church reached out. But, when it did so, it acted only timidly. Moreover, when leaders took expansionist steps they sometimes moved in a haphazard fashion and without sufficient consideration of their decisions' implications. Careful reflection and planning, when it occurred, seemingly led to frustration and to surrender by the church of previous advances.

The first steps taken toward church expansion following the 1869 establishment of the Florida Conference had reflected a sense of purpose and optimism. This primarily involved a flurry of church building and enhancement. By way of illustration, in Tampa Elder Sexton and Deacon Williams stirred support for the erection of a fine sanctuary for Mt. Sinai. "The members of the A.M.E. Zion Church in this city, wishing to complete their church," reported the local newspaper in December, "propose to hold Fairs during the holidays, hoping to raise the necessary funds to enable them to do so." It added, "We hope they will meet with success." They did. As a result, contractor Samuel Bryant raised a "white, square wood structure" on land donated by his mother, Dorcas. At Milton, also, progress of the same nature resulted. On December 29 trustees Moses Patterson, Samuel Thornton, and James Brown claimed title to the land upon which Isaiah Chapel stood on Clara Street, allowing them to proceed with improvements of various kinds. Patterson, by the way, so influenced Milton and the community in which Isaiah Chapel stood that, to this day, the vicinity is known as Pattersontown.[22]

Warrington witnessed a happy transformation during the same period. As it turned out, the congregation had outgrown its home. "The colored Methodists had a large meeting on Sunday, celebrating some event" a report of July 16, 1869, observed, "their own place of meeting being too small they borrowed the use of the Baptist church, for the occasion." In November a large storm wreaked havoc in the neighborhood, likely damaging if not destroying the church. In the circumstances the congregation reorganized itself the next year at "New Warrington" and erected its sanctuary, Good Hope AMEZ Church, at the corner of Runyan and Hayne streets.[23]

By the time Good Hope opened its doors in 1870, the Florida church had begun to establish several new congregations. Pensacola's Mt. Moriah headed the list. "Methodist Zion Church is situated in the western portion of the city, near what is known as the Tan Yard," a local man later explained. He added, "The congregation worship in a small frame building." Sometimes called the Tan Yard church, Mt. Moriah eventually also bore the name Little Zion.[24]

In line with improvements elsewhere, "Big Zion"—that is to say Pensacola's principal church—could not long withstand the urge to upgrade itself following Little Zion's debut. On July 18, 1871, its trustees purchased for $750 a suitable lot on Bru Street, between Romana and Garden. "[It] is the largest and best furnished of all the colored churches," an 1890 description averred. "The church building is neatly painted," the account continued. "It has a belfry, and the property is kept in neat repair." After Samson Dunbar Talbot succeeded Joseph J. Clinton as bishop of the Florida Conference in 1872, the members of Big Zion and Elders Alexander C. Fisher and Warren C. Vesta dedicated their new sanctuary in his honor as Talbot Chapel.[25]

Other new congregations likely organized, as well. The optimistic spirit that had prompted establishment of Mt. Moriah and the building of Talbot Chapel may have pushed the church westward almost to the Alabama state line to the nascent community of Millview, on Perdido Bay. As noted earlier, a railroad completed in late 1872 linked Pensacola with the timber region along the Perdido River. Millview served as its western terminus, and, as early as mid-1869, reports had noted that workers laid off at War—

rington's Navy Yard were "erecting mills at Perdido." Some of them likely held membership in the Warrington AMEZ Church and, by the early 1870s if not earlier, urged Elder Alexander Fisher, in charge of the Pensacola church, to open a mission. Not until June 1878, though, would Elder Gabriel Sexton purchase a lot on Dauphin Street next to the Pensacola & Perdido Railroad tracks for the erection of a sanctuary.[26]

Some evidence for organized church outreach in the early 1870s, as illustrated by the Millview congregation, can also be seen in other actions taken during the period. In 1871, for example, leaders afforded the Florida church a toehold north of Tampa at Cedar Keys, a spot strategically positioned for future AMEZ penetration of the peninsula. Then a small community of prominence to a point that far exceeded its population, Cedar Keys (by the late 1870s, Cedar Key) served as the Gulf coast anchor for the state's only trans-peninsular railroad (its Atlantic terminus came at Fernandina). Otherwise, the cedar timber and milling trade provided the town's economic backbone. As a result the community maintained close ties with Tampa during the 1870s, and residents often relocated between the two places as circumstances required.[27]

The Cedar Keys initiative just might have stemmed more from a convergence of circumstances, though, than it did from any attempt at far-sighted planning. To begin with, Hillsborough County by 1871 probably could no longer support two AMEZ ministers. At the same time Cedar Keys desperately needed at least one. The economic slide that led to this situation began in the late summer of 1870 with the outbreak of the Franco-Prussian War. What was about to become Germany took honors as the largest customer for the cedar boards that Tampa and Cedar Keys produced. The local industry quickly collapsed. Within six months desperation grasped the region. "Times is hard hear no money," a Cedar Keys resident recorded in June 1871. "It looks like starvation with us."[28]

This was only the beginning. Spirits sagged even further when yellow fever beset the two towns in late summer accompanied by heavy rains that resulted in widespread flooding. By September 30 a Tampa report would declare that "quite a few persons have left town." Six weeks later, the place stood virtually deserted. Abandoning the islands of the Cedar Keys proved more difficult than escaping Tampa. "[After] the yelow fever Came to this plase 12 of the [citizens] died of it," the Cedar Keys resident informed her diary on October 9. "A sad time on the Island so much distress," she continued. "It looks like that the destroying angel Was abroad and [the sword] of Justis Was drawn over this place."[29]

As the tragedies unfolded, residents of Hillsborough County at least could find some solace in organized religion. Joseph Sexton particularly took care to place the AMEZ Church in the forefront of Tampa area work. Beginning in late September he announced a series of camp meetings to take place commencing in mid-October at Simmons Hammock, a place free of the fever threat. His announcements stressed that "all who wish, are invited to attend, especially the white ministers." Following the last gathering, a weeklong session held in mid-November, a local editor singled out the event for its "good results."[30]

Meanwhile, at Cedar Keys African Americans possessed few alternatives until the AMEZ Church entered the community. By late summer 1870, some individuals, reacting to sudden events of the past days and weeks, already had begun to "think that the Judgment day is Coming." One year later they heard a local white Methodist preacher blame the deepening troubles on local wickedness. The AME Church had yet to penetrate to the town and, if a Baptist church catered to the black community, its name and pastor are not known. It was in these circumstances that John G. Williams relocated to Cedar Keys from Tampa, where he had pastored at Mt. Sinai. Details of the mission remain hazy, but Deacon Williams's presence seems to have been welcomed. Local Republicans—most of whom were black—thought so much of him by December, in fact, that they had him named a justice of the peace. In that capacity Williams could perform marriages even though he would not receive ordination as an elder until about 1873. It does not appear that the young veteran erected a sanctuary. In 1873 the town built a "church house" to be used "by all denominations to preach," and it may be assumed that services convened there. If the number of marriages that Williams performed in Levy County is any indication, his congregation flourished little, perhaps reflecting the Florida Conference's inability to support the mission financially. Beginning in October 1874, the pastor earned his income as a full-time inspector of customs.[31]

Local economic crises thus effectively blunted a poorly planned and supported AMEZ foray into Levy County and the upper peninsula, and the same economic factors, coupled with a questionable episcopal decision, soon dealt almost-mortal blows to the church's outposts in Hillsborough and Polk. The facts were these. Joseph Sexton had taken up the pastorate of Tampa's Mt. Sinai upon Deacon Williams's departure. Sexton quickly acted to help revive the community's spirits in the midst of economic calamity. He enjoined friends to stage an elaborate "grand celebration" on

New Year's Day 1872 in honor of the ninth anniversary of the Emancipation Proclamation. "There was a splendid parade, speeches were made by
Peter Bryant, the orator of the day, the Rev. A. Sinclair [the Hernando
County Baptist minister], J. Sexton, and others," one account of the event
related, "and a bounteous feast was spread in Atzroth Grove." Despite
Tampa's critical need for just such leadership, Bishop Clinton soon perceived that Elder Sexton's talents could better be utilized elsewhere than
in a town with such depressing prospects. At the state conference meeting
held in April, the bishop reassigned Sexton to the church at Milton. Clinton
declined to name a successor of equivalent rank for the Tampa church, although by 1875 Bishop Talbot had dispatched the Alabama Conference's
young Israel Furby to the scene. In the meantime, a youth named Alexander Anderson may have acted as local pastor. Mt. Sinai thus survived the
bishop's actions, but the other churches founded by Sexton in eastern
Hillsborough and in Polk withered.[32]

The experiences of the churches in Monroe, Hillsborough, Polk, and
Levy counties vividly illustrate several additional points about AMEZ circumstances in Florida during the early 1870s. For one thing, along with
always-acute funding problems came a chronic shortage of trained preachers. The loss of a single experienced man dealt the church a severe blow. To
replace losses and to fill posts opened by expansion, bishops typically taxed
two sources. From the Alabama Conference came individuals such as Israel
Furby and Gabriel Sexton who looked upon their assignments as tempo-
rary—and not always desirable—sojourns, while from the local community came promising laymen without formal training of even a modest
nature. Santa Rosa and Escambia counties especially provided the church
with men who turned out to be fine preachers but whose erudition and
ability to offer leadership remained limited because the educational opportunities available to them remained limited. Joseph Lennox was one such
man. Born in South Carolina about 1831, he was living in Santa Rosa
County in 1867 and working in Escambia three years later. Accepting a call
to the ministry and with encouragement from Bishops Clinton and Talbot,
he had achieved ordination as an elder by 1874. Twenty-three-year-old
Vincent F. White, another recruit of the early 1870s, had come to Pensacola
from Alabama. He made his living in 1870 as a sailor. The same year Elder
Gabriel Sexton married White to Nancy Whitaker in Santa Rosa. Thereafter White apparently trained under Gabriel Sexton's personal tutelage, as
well as that of Joseph Sexton. White's ordination as an elder followed in
1876.[33]

Another obvious point derived from the experiences of the early 1870s concerned the central importance and occasionally unfortunate nature of episcopal decision making. Bishop Clinton and, after 1872, Bishop Talbot exercised responsibilities far broader than the Florida Conference. As a consequence, they could spend little time acquainting themselves with or otherwise supporting the poor, underpopulated, and remote Florida church. At best the bishop traveled to the state once each year for the annual conference. In the early years these gatherings seem to have been held either at Pensacola or Milton during April. Through his eight years of supervision over the Florida church, Bishop Clinton visited Key West only once, while Bishop Talbot compiled the same record during four years of service. If either visited Tampa or Cedar Keys, the fact failed to be recorded. As Florida churchmen well understood, the bishops' ability to discern underlying problems, conceive solutions, and understand the long-term implications of their actions remained extremely limited. The problem actually grew worse during Bishop Talbot's tenure. In the face of his church's strict philosophical opposition, he fell in love with and subsequently married a divorced woman. The ensuing scandal forced his retirement in 1876, consuming much of his time and energy in the meantime.[34]

In these circumstances numerous underlying problems that the Florida church urgently needed its bishops to understand—and to offer informed leadership regarding—went unaddressed. Importantly, AMEZ ministers found themselves struggling to compete in a state where the AME Church had risen to a position of immense social and political power (in Alabama and North Carolina, to cite two examples, the equation was reversed). Republican leader and journalist John Willis Menard summed up the situation in 1872. "Florida is destined to become the negro's new Jerusalem," he began. "The A.M.E. Church here is continually extending its lines; not only in religious matters, but in state affairs as well," Menard continued. He added, "The most influential men in the Legislature are Methodist ministers."[35]

Direct competition for the AMEZ with the AME Church had commenced by 1870. Months following the 1869 organizational session of the Florida AMEZ Conference, the Florida AME Conference had committed itself to missionary efforts in the southwestern peninsula. AME congregations opened at Brooksville, Tampa, and Key West by June. Interestingly, at Tampa and Key West the AME pastors quickly found themselves struggling for membership within an AMEZ-supportive environment. Still, direct competition between the two churches now had become a fact, offering another challenge to be faced by AMEZ leaders.[36]

This competition quickly focused, as well, at Milton and Pensacola. The same AME Conference that authorized missionary efforts in the south-western peninsula had created a Pensacola AME District. At the time, the Florida AMEZ Conference as a whole boasted no presiding elder. As at Tampa and Key West, though, the AME churches at Milton and Pensacola battled for existence within a religious environment dominated by the AMEZ and Baptist churches. As late as early 1874, a mere eighteen persons belonged to the Pensacola AME congregation. Then, a more vigorous re-cruitment effort bolstered the flock somewhat. "Though the sinners was before me, of the Zions on the one side and the Baptists on the other," the local AME pastor could report by August, "but having obtained help of God we continued to this day." To hone their competitive edge, AME lead-ers thereupon scheduled their annual conference for December 1874 at Pensacola.[37]

In the absence of on-the-scene leadership, however understandable the absence might have been, unprepared AMEZ ministers sometimes reeled from the competition and struggled to determine a proper response. On a personal level they mostly felt that fellow African Methodists should be welcomed in the spirit of brotherhood. Typically, when AME church builder Thomas W. Long joined Pastor Allen Dean at Key West in April 1871 for the dedication of Bethel AME Church, he could report, "I was invited by some of the good sisters of the Zion A.M.E. church to several suppers." At Milton, Gabriel Sexton welcomed his AME counterpart to AMEZ conferences. Some evidence suggests that at Pensacola Elder War-ren C. Vesta not only extended a hand of fellowship to John W. Wyatt but may have lent support for the construction of the AME sanctuary.[38]

On the level of competition between churches for local membership and influence on the other hand, the AMEZ preachers protected their home ground. Thus, as late as 1880 the AME Pensacola District found itself dispirited and defensive: "The work I am now engaged in was in a most discouraging condition," Presiding Elder Henry Call informed his superi-ors. He explained further, "In many portions of the district there were no permanent organizations of our church whatever." He added of his own need for determination, "I felt that the people had gone far enough in darkness."[39]

Some advocates of the AMEZ cause went so far in their quest to pre-serve and expand church presence and influence that they moved into ac-tivities that received less-than-enthusiastic support from the church, thus creating the potential for more intra-church problems. As mentioned in an earlier chapter, the Florida AMEZ Church mostly had refrained for a variety of reasons from direct involvement in politics at least insofar as its ministers seeking or serving in public office. The Colored Methodist Church (CME), founded in 1870 from the ME Church South, remained so small and weak in the state that its similar position mattered little. Far more significantly, AME policy aggressively pursued just such direct involvement. Given AME electoral successes, including the 1872 election of its candidate Ossian B. Hart as governor, its stance temporarily stirred far greater interest and enthusiasm than did the AMEZ position. An ardent Republican activist such as Tampa's Isaac Howard, a founder of Mt. Sinai AMEZ Church, could grow disenchanted enough to embrace the AME cause in 1870. Thus, he emerged also as a founder of St. Paul AME Church.[40]

At least two AMEZ preachers succumbed to the lure of public office, but, as they learned, they did so at their own peril. John G. Williams, as noted earlier, accepted appointment as a Levy County justice of the peace in late 1871. Two years later he successfully sought election to the Cedar Keys town council, serving additionally as mayor in 1874. By then, of course, Williams was seeking full-time government employment in the wake of his frustrated church-building experience. More importantly, in 1872 Alexander C. Fisher, who supervised all AMEZ activities in Escambia County, took a seat on the local county commission. Within seven months he abruptly resigned. The circumstances remain cloudy, but they could be interpreted to suggest that Fisher did so under orders from Bishop Clinton. Fisher's Florida tenure lasted a mere two years following the incident. In 1874 Bishop Talbot transferred him outside the state. Fisher's replacement at Talbot Chapel proved more reliable in the sense of eschewing political office. That individual, John M. Butler, fortunately possessed other impressive credentials and experience. Members of the Alabama Conference called him "the great organizer."[41]

Whatever actions individual AMEZ ministers or laymen took during the early 1870s, the passage of the years brought increased tensions and a movement away from the great optimism of 1869 and 1870. Racial violence and labor turmoil associated with Reconstruction played a role. Epidemics such as the 1871 yellow fever onset at Cedar Keys and Tampa and the plague's return in 1873 at Pensacola and Key West, in 1874 at Pensacola and Warrington, and in 1875 at Key West did as well. Added to plague came hurricanes. An 1873 storm lashed Key West, Tampa, Cedar Keys, and the panhandle, while the next year another gale devastated Tampa and Cedar Keys. In 1873 also, a depression known as the Panic of

1873 cast an economic pall over the entire nation that remained in place for years. So bent and buffeted, Florida's AMEZ leaders must have seen themselves and their church in the words of an 1875 Key West yellow fever report. "The city is in a state of panic," it declared. "The fever smites the natives as well as others." The report continued: "What the end is to be, none are able to forecast. We are so isolated—cut off—and now closely quarantined. Many who would leave, find no means of getting away."[42]

The tensions had touched Bishop Talbot as well as his ministers by 1875, with profound results for the church's future in Florida. At the seventh state conference held at Milton in April 1875, his temper boiled over. He chafed at the fact that, after more than one decade of labor in the state, his entire conference gathering consisted of only seven ordained ministers, two local deacons, and one local preacher, plus one trustee. When Milton AME pastor John Taylor sought admission to the conference's bar, Talbot let his feelings get away from him and angrily barred Taylor from the proceedings. The bishop then confronted Gabriel Sexton for having the temerity to welcome Taylor. Soon, he had lashed out at Warren C. Vesta for letting "such a knot build a church right over their heads in Pensacola." As months passed thereafter, though, and memories of Talbot's anger faded, the bishop mulled his next step. Had he not been consumed by the personal problems that soon were to deprive him of an active role in episcopal office, perhaps he would have thought better of his decision from the beginning. As it turned out, the church would labor with the consequences of his action for the remainder of the century.[43]

1. James Varick, the African Methodist Episcopal Zion Church's first superintendent. From Walls, *African Methodist Episcopal Zion Church*.

2. Zion Church, New York City, as it appeared after 1840. From Walls, *African Methodist Episcopal Zion Church*.

3. Superintendent Joseph Jackson Clinton, whose leadership brought the AMEZ Church to the Deep South as the Civil War neared its end. From Walls, *African Methodist Episcopal Zion Church*.

4. Map of Florida, showing principal towns and cities served by the AMEZ Church in the period 1864 to 1905. Collection of the authors.

5. Key West, as it appeared on the eve of the Civil War. Collection of the authors.

6. Cornish Chapel AMEZ Church cofounder Cataline B. Simmons. Courtesy Florida State Archives.

7. Sandy Cornish, benefactor and cofounder of Cornish Chapel
AMEZ Church. From Reid, *After the War*.

8. Army chaplain James H. Schneider.
From Tarbox, *Memoirs of James H.
Schneider*.

9. Florida's first ordained AMEZ clergyman, Wilbur Garrison Strong. From Walls, *African Methodist Episcopal Zion Church*.

10. One-time Tampa slave Dorcas Bryant helped to organize the congregation that became Mt. Sinai AMEZ Church. Collection of the authors.

11. Solomon Derry aided establishment of the AMEZ Church in the Pensacola area. From Hood, *One Hundred Years.*

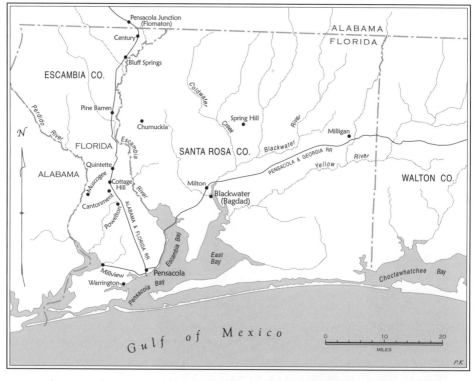

12. The Pensacola area especially welcomed the AMEZ Church. Collection of the authors.

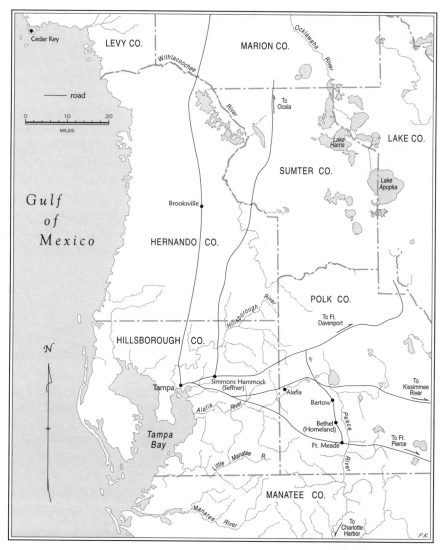

13. Early AMEZ outreach efforts centered, in part, on the Tampa Bay region. Collection of the authors.

14. U.S. Army veteran and Tampa AMEZ layman Aaron Bryant (*left*), Isaac Berry (*center*), and cowhunter and AMEZ layman Stephen Harvell (*right*). Courtesy University of Tampa Press.

15. Bishop James Walker Hood. Collection of the authors.

16. A view of Pensacola and its harbor taken in the 1870s. Courtesy Florida State Archives.

17. Corrie Davis, seen here, and Hattie Honors (*right*) were married by elder Joseph Sexton in 1891. Collection of the authors.

18. Hattie Honors Davis. Collection of the authors.

19. Cornish Chapel's Cecilia Hannibal Skinner. Collection of the authors; courtesy Robert W. Saunders Sr.

20. Talbot Chapel AMEZ Church (*bottom left, next to tree*), as it appeared in an 1885 bird's-eye view of Pensacola. Courtesy Florida State Archives.

21. Bishop Samson Dunbar Talbot. From Walls, *African Methodist Episcopal Zion Church*.

22. Bishop Joseph Pascal Thompson. From Walls, *African Methodist Episcopal Zion Church.*

23. Catherine Gilchrist Thompson, wife of Bishop Joseph Pascal Thompson. From Walls, *African Methodist Episcopal Zion Church.*

.

24. Attorney Peter W. Bryant participated actively in Tampa's Mt. Sinai AMEZ Church and Key West's Cornish Chapel. From *Pensacola Florida Sentinel,* 1895 special edition.

25. The courageous and inspiring career of Sojourner Truth reflected the prominent role played by women in AMEZ church affairs. From Walls, *African Methodist Episcopal Zion Church*.

26. Cornish Chapel AMEZ Church came to dominate a large portion of the Key West skyline, as evidenced by this 1890 photograph. Collection of the authors; courtesy Tom Hambright, Monroe County May Hill Russell Library.

4

CONSEQUENCES OF NEGLECT, 1875–1884

the enemies of the cause of God and goodness
are too strong and numerous

By the mid-1870s Florida's AMEZ Church had shifted from a time of optimism that had opened in the late 1860s to a period almost of despair. The denomination's members had suffered repeated visitations of natural and other disasters, and frustrated outreach initiatives had slowed church growth. Meanwhile, political turmoil raged as the region reeled from the impact of racial discord and national economic depression. Remarkably, the state, if not the Zion Church, continued to grow. Ongoing peninsular development soon would lead to the establishment of towns and the opening of new lands in a manner that bespoke what modern Florida could become. In these heady times of crisis and change, firm and farsighted institutional leadership—such as that promised by the kind of episcopal hierarchy embraced by the AMEZ Church—found its greatest need and responsibility. As it happened, Zion struggled to deliver.

The era opened with Florida's bishop Samson Dunbar Talbot seemingly frustrated at his conference's poor showing against the AME Church and concerned at AME encroachments on what had been considered AMEZ territory. Incidents occurring during the 1875 state conference sessions highlighted the problems. At the time, Talbot endured mounting scandal because of his marriage to a divorced woman. By June 1876 the controversy would compel the church's general conference to suspend his active episcopal service. The bishop chose simply to avoid the tumult, refusing to attend the general conference. Within two years, he had died.[1]

That Talbot walked away from the general conference did not mean that he had declined to exercise his authority in Florida during the previous months—quite the contrary. In April 1876 he probably shocked many of those gathered at the Florida Conference meeting by directing a counterinitiative aimed at the AME Church, a plan that he had formulated as he struggled with his other problems. At the same time, Talbot apparently announced a restructuring of the conference, although the action conceivably occurred one or two years later. Specifically, he aimed to establish an administrative structure that could bear the demands of his counterinitiative by creating two presiding elder districts, one centered at Pensacola and the other at Key West. Warren C. Vesta emerged as presiding elder at the former place, while Thomas H. Darley led in the latter.[2]

Talbot's expansionist initiative came with two prongs that addressed recent AME developments. One facet related to an 1873 AME decision to open a mission to the Bahamas. By 1875 five ministers of that denomination's Florida Conference labored in an Island District. They claimed 723 adherents and church properties valued at $3,500. This Island District, alone, appeared well on the way to exceeding the Florida AMEZ Conference in total membership. Talbot's decision not only recognized these developments but also the fact that, through Key West and its Cornish Chapel, AMEZ connections already reached deep into the Bahamas. Given the continuing movement of families back and forth, some Cornish Chapel members probably then resided in the British islands. Sensing opportunity to blunt the AME drive and to bolster his own conference's tattered ranks, Talbot ordered Elder Joseph Sexton, an experienced church builder, to Nassau to assist "in the organization of churches at that place." The bishop did so despite the fact that experienced pastors were still vitally needed in Florida. To replace Sexton at Milton and in Santa Rosa County, Talbot tapped the relatively inexperienced Vincent F. White.[3]

If Talbot's first action offered the hope of enhanced membership rolls for the Florida AMEZ Conference, justification for the second appears to have rested more on denominational resentment than upon a solid rationale. In this instance the bishop aimed his episcopal power far from the then-current centers of AMEZ activity. He focused instead on Jacksonville, located hundreds of miles distant in northeast Florida. True, at the time the growing city had started on the road to becoming Florida's financial capital as well as a center of its increasingly large winter tourism industry. More importantly for the bishop, though, Jacksonville offered the AME Church an informal headquarters for its Florida operations, with its role in that regard becoming formalized during 1877–78 by the establishment of an AME East Florida Conference centered there. Talbot knew that an AMEZ mission in Jacksonville would be seen as a challenge to the AME Church in the same manner that he had viewed AME initiatives at Pensacola, Key West, and Tampa. Whether the Florida AMEZ Conference could support such a distant mission remained a serious question, but Talbot eschewed caution. To spearhead his advance he named Alabama-trained preacher Israel Furby. In doing so he left Tampa's Mt. Sinai without a pastor.[4]

Having set his ministers in motion, Talbot thereupon departed the state with his successor yet to be determined. A well-chosen replacement could have reconsidered his predecessor's initiatives, shored up the church in Florida, and set a new course aimed at solid growth over time. Instead, the 1876 general conference placed little priority on remote and underpopulated Florida at a time when the region reeled from political and social crisis and the church scrambled to sustain its successes elsewhere. In those circumstances the delegates blundered insofar as the Florida Conference was concerned. Bishop Thomas Henry Lomax, who achieved election to episcopal rank at the same general conference, later explained subsequent events. "In 1876, the committee on districts gave five states to one Bishop: Georgia, Florida, Alabama, Mississippi, Louisiana," he began. "And he, a bishop who did not believe it was his duty to travel over the work, went and held the conferences and then returned to his home where he said he could make more money making pills." Lomax continued, "He said Bishops [Joseph J.] Clinton, [Singleton Thomas W.] Jones, and [James Walker] Hood were killing themselves traveling over the country, but he was not going to do it."[5]

Joseph Pascal Thompson, the man selected as bishop for Florida by the 1876 general conference, represented yet another church father little acquainted with the Reconstruction-era South. Born as a slave at Winchester, Virginia, on December 29, 1818, he had trained early as a blacksmith. At age sixteen, though, Thompson had fled bondage. He found a home "with a kind hearted man" at Williamsburg, Pennsylvania. There, the runaway received the basics of an education at night school and, through great good fortune, found the opportunity to study medicine under a physician who lived at Middle Point (now Matawan), New Jersey. Before completing his medical studies, however, Thompson received a call to the ministry. He had earned a license to preach by 1839. Two years later he joined the AMEZ Church, pastoring subsequently in New York and Canada. Finding that his medical training offered an important extra dimension to his ministry, Thompson eventually pursued a medical degree at Philadelphia's University of Medicine. He received his diploma in 1858, thereafter living and working in New York. A man of advanced years by 1876 when he accepted election as a bishop, Thompson enjoyed a comfortable life that included travel for pleasure coupled with the responsibilities of a longtime medical practice and pharmacy.[6]

Thompson's elevation as bishop—given his age, inclinations, and the distractions inherent in the lifestyle that he had chosen—could not have come at a worse time for the Deep South states of his district. Two of them, Florida and Louisiana, continued under Republican rule while white Democrats had not yet succeeded in quashing all black power in the others. As Thompson prepared to assume his ministry, campaigning ensued for fall elections that would be marked by direct and sometimes violent attempts at political intimidation and repression. In their aftermath a national crisis resulted that eventually left the presidency in Republican hands but effectively surrendered statewide political control in the South to the Democrats.[7]

As these momentous events occurred in Florida, long-standing AMEZ practice in the state mostly kept the church's preachers on the political sidelines or at least off the ballot. Typically, when the Hayes and Wheeler Club formed at Tampa in August 1876 to support the Republican presidential and vice presidential ticket, its leadership included prominent AMEZ laymen Peter W. Bryant, Aaron Bryant, and William Walker. The local AME minister, on the other hand, served as the organization's chaplain. Meanwhile, perhaps the most effective of Zion's Florida-based public advocates, Joseph Sexton, labored far from the state in the Bahamas. The denomination's rising star Israel Furby struggled, at the same time, in Jacksonville's extremely challenging religious climate. There, he labored to found the mission that eventually would be called St. Lukes AMEZ Church.[8]

It should be noted that, in 1876, the question of church involvement in politics burned hotly in Florida and other southern states and not simply in the house of Zion. Particularly within the politically powerful AME Church, divisions had emerged between those committed to the idea that the denomination should lead in political as well as religious matters and those who believed politics to be inherently corrupting and a diversion from the church's true mission. "Ministers cannot spare the time to enter the political field, because the enemies of the cause of God and goodness are too strong and numerous," one critic asserted in the 1880s, "our duty, as ministers, is to capture the world for Christ, and not for political purposes." Forces hostile to AME political involvements nearly had captured the state conference in 1875. They seemed to grow stronger each year thereafter.[9]

The real question, though, concerned where one drew the line between politics and the desirable and even imperative buttressing of virtue and morality. This proved not so easy to accomplish. The act of running for political office, many increasingly believed, clearly lay on the political side. Yet, some other efforts and initiatives, as shortly will be seen, appeared quite differently.

Significantly for this story, while attempting to capture the world for Christ, Florida's AMEZ ministers fervently embraced certain issues within a political context. They avoided running for office and committing the church on behalf of individual candidates for office, but they stood boldly forward when it came to contesting certain moral issues. "Almost all black leaders of the period, both secular and religious, advocated strong moral and spiritual codes of conduct as necessary for individual and racial self-improvement," Sandy Dwayne Martin explained. In particular, AMEZ preachers espoused the cause of temperance. They viewed alcohol and its abuse, and to a lesser extent tobacco use, as undermining racial progress and as a destroyer of men and families. They preached temperance and, eventually, abstinence.[10]

They also organized with others to battle this perceived evil in the public arena. The principal organizational vehicle for that contest in Florida consisted of the International Order of Good Templars based in the Grand Lodge of England of the Right Worthy Grand Lodge of the World. Not without a touch of irony, literally at the moment that Florida's political future lay in the balance in the fall of 1876, many AMEZ and AME preachers lent their energies to organizing the IOGT in Florida. This reflected not only circumstances in the state but within the AMEZ and AME churches generally. Bishop Joseph J. Clinton particularly exerted his great influence to commit Zion against the alcohol plague.[11]

Within that dynamic as it applied to the Florida AMEZ Church existed a very important linkage. The Key West IOGT chapter, known as the Oscar Carter Lodge, immediately and understandably stood out as one of the premier branches in Florida. The island city, after all, was by then the state's most populous municipality. Among the lodge's seventy-five original members could be found the names of many leaders in the African American community, including AMEZ members such as Matthew Shavers, Leila Bryant, and James A. and Theresa Roberts. One name, that of Thomas H. Darley, bears special mention. "Rev. Thomas Darley, presiding elder of the A.M.E.Z. Church, and Rev. Albert Davis, pastor in charge of the Baptist Church at this place," a local man related, "are two of the fathers of Temperance, having been among the first to introduce a temperance society among us." He added, "Both are Good Templars and are true and earnest workers in the cause."[12]

Darley's public prominence in the temperance movement and the IOGT's work carried extra significance because, in the leadership vacuum that formed during what would become the eight-year tenure of Bishop Thompson in Florida, Darley more than anyone else provided stability and direction for the Florida church. Bishop Clinton's son Joseph Newman Clinton went so far as to credit Darley with "[holding] Florida intact for Zion till [1889, when] Bishop T. H. Lomax D.D., came and held conferences among the orange groves near phosphate mines and in our pine barrens." Colleagues would remember the Key West native as "the Father of the Florida Conference" and as "the foremost man of the A.M.E. Zion Church in Florida." In that role Darley would bring about much good for his church, but he would direct its energies within the public arena to moral crusades rather than purely political ones.[13]

Unfortunately, during the first years of the post-Reconstruction period this philosophical and moral tack harmed efforts to bring the AMEZ Church to the positive attention of Florida's black community at large, where alarmed voices called for a different brand of leadership. Historian William E. Montgomery offered helpful context on the subject. "The eventual collapse of state governments set up under congressional direction after 1867, a process known as Redemption by most white southerners, was a disheartening experience for blacks," he wrote. "The illusion of a racially integrated society evaporated along with federal government support for the Republican state governments," Montgomery continued. "Blacks were on their own," he added. "They had their freedom and they possessed the franchise, and now they were expected to make the most of it." Whether many African Americans had possessed an illusion of a racially integrated society in Florida seems unlikely, but, for sure, they now mostly found themselves "on their own."[14]

To make the most of the situation "on their own," many African Americans in Florida sought strong and enlightened leadership that could offer practical direction in the midst of political peril, a function performed for them in good part by preachers since 1865. As they looked around, their eyes recognized some oncoming AME and Baptist ministers but not their AMEZ counterparts (the Colored Methodist Episcopal Church—owing to, in the words of Bishop L. H. Holsey, "strong opposition from colored people because of its relation to the M. E. Church South"—remained a negligible presence in the state). This situation appeared clearly in May 1877 when numerous leaders issued a public call for a "colored convention" to meet in Tallahassee. While the assemblage endorsed "the Southern Policy of the President," which tilted in favor of Democrats, it also backed a strong program for the future. "The platform called for liberty and equal rights through education, land ownership, and control of intoxi-cating drink," scholar Lee H. Warner observed. "It hoped that the race is-sue would pass away," he continued. "Instead, 'peace, order, confidence, more tolerance of opinion than ever before, and better protection to life, liberty and property' were the keys to prosperity."[15]

Whether a particular Floridian embraced the platform or not, he or she understood that someone was attempting to look out for African American interests. The question was who? In the convention's call and delibera-tions, no AMEZ minister's name ranked alongside those of numerous AME figures. A few AMEZ laymen attended as delegates, with James A. Roberts serving as the meeting's secretary. Yet the closest that the AMEZ clergy came to sharing the leadership spotlight involved the presence of Cataline B. Simmons, a cofounder of Key West's Cornish Chapel but, by then, a Baptist preacher at Jacksonville.[16]

The illustration offered by this convention saw its reflection in numer-ous other gatherings and contexts. The general population knew little if anything about Zion's ongoing and urgent efforts to secure personnel and financial resources sufficient to meet its commitments, but it did recognize in one public event after another that leaders of other denominations were the ones who stood out prominently. This likely reinforced for many a sense that the AMEZ Church held itself above or else did not care to associ-ate itself in such matters. To a very limited extent the dynamic received some national attention in early 1877 when a Florida delegation visited newly inaugurated president Rutherford B. Hayes, and subsequent news-paper reports inadvertently created from the incident the appearance of an AME initiative. In that instance the group (consisting of Tampa AMEZ member Peter W. Bryant, political leader and journalist John Willis Me-nard of Jacksonville, and one-time Radical advocate William U. Saunders of Fernandina) sought assurances concerning the security and future of the state's black population. The public at the time closely associated Menard —the first African American ever elected to the Congress (he was not seated), a former Lincoln administration official, and a one-time Florida state legislator—with the AME Church's political power, even though as a Key West resident he would affiliate later with Cornish Chapel. Bryant's religious preference went unmentioned and unknown to most, as did Saun-ders's apparent lack of religious association.[17]

Another implication of Zion's commitment to certain moral crusades at a time of political crisis, one that has to do with women, requires additional notice. The Florida church's practice regarding political participation by its ministers seems to have harmed its image more among men than among women, a fact that soon and quite naturally resulted in ever-greater involvement by women in AMEZ activities. This fact carried with it, as will be considered, discernible consequences of significance. The point is not, however, that other denominations such as the Baptists and Bethel's African Methodists did not experience growing proportions of women within their congregations. They did. Rather, it is to observe that women within Zion, at least Florida women, assumed a more influential role because of their greater relative numbers, the shortage of trained clergy and sometimes ineffective episcopal leadership, and important legacies of AMEZ heritage.[18]

Women had aided the cause in Florida, let it be remembered, literally from the church's advent in the state. After all, had not Lillah Cornish helped to welcome Wilbur G. Strong to Key West in 1864? By the same token, did not Dorcas Bryant present Joseph Sexton with a Tampa congregation in 1865? Even in the Pensacola vicinity, women had displayed similar activist spirit on Zion's behalf. Liza Wilkinson, Mary Davis, and Matilda Williams, after all, had formed close to a majority of the Navy Yard church that, in 1865, had awaited Bishop Clinton's coming from Alabama.[19]

Zion's women, of course, always had played strong roles in denominational affairs, perhaps more so than with any other black church. Pioneering (though not ordained) abolitionist missionaries such as Julia Foote had spread the AMEZ message while venturing courageously throughout the North and Midwest. Others, including Harriet Tubman and Sojourner Truth, literally had risked their lives to secure freedom for those held in bondage and later would help to press the cause of women's suffrage and rights. Their story, mostly neglected until recent years, deserves attention and respect for unheralded sacrifice and sustained contribution. One scholar of the subject, Florida A&M University's Chanta M. Haywood, recently examined the service of several early black women preachers, among them Julia Foote. "They knew for sure that they had been singled out by God and sent into that volatile world to perform religious acts that would change it," she discovered. "They risked their lives and disrupted their families' routines by leaving for months in order to act out their unshakable belief that they had been called to change the world." Haywood found the reality of these women's actions and daring to be personally inspiring despite the passage of more than a century after the events she described. "These women preachers have changed my life on a higher level," she related. "Their tenacity and even audacity have been inspiring and affirming."[20]

The active support provided to Zion by women extended to and expanded during the post–Civil War era, with results that placed the AMEZ connection in a unique position regarding the role of women in church affairs. Specifically, the 1876 general conference revised the church discipline to eliminate the pronoun "male" from its text. "This change allowed women to serve as delegates to the General Conference and in other capacities as well," explained one church historian. The reform came, he noted further, even though "[m]any conservative Zionites argued that such a broad modification of the discipline would effectively allow women to receive ordination to the orders of deacon, elder, and even bishop." The day of women actually serving as delegates or receiving ordination remained in the future in 1876, but within eight years Eliza Darley had represented Florida at a general conference as a delegate to the Ladies Home and Foreign Missionary Society.[21]

The growing influence of women within the AMEZ Church and its Florida Conference offers a subject for further discussion in chapters to come, but notice should be taken here that by the mid-1870s congregations increasingly consisted of women, and that fact influenced church direction and activities. For one thing since women tended to live longer than did men, they in time came to compose that core of supporters looked upon respectfully in each older congregation as the true elders. Thus, when in 1897 Emma Arnold was spoken of as "one of the oldest Zionites on the Alafia," the notice suggested that the Polk County woman likely commanded a voice in local church affairs greater than that of many of the men who worshiped alongside her. Similarly, when in 1892 Sampson Forrester's aged widow Rose Forrester took over as vice president of the South Florida Conference's Home and Foreign Missionary Society, the event hinted at more than a simple local election. The conference had turned to a trusted old hand who reflected the experience of years and church perspectives honed through challenge over time. Usually, such a voice could be expected to be a conservative one, keeping the church or one of its programs or agencies from venturing too far in new or disturbing directions, one often supportive of the ministers upon whom she had relied for decades.[22]

Relating closely to the first point, the tipping of the gender balance in favor of women (and to a degree greater than seen in Florida's AME churches at the time) played an important role in determining local church priorities in a manner that further edged Zion away from its Bethel counterpart. AMEZ-sponsored programs and activities reflected this. As noted, the church supported the temperance cause, the supporters of which included women in greater numbers than men. As might be expected, AMEZ congregations also focused on children and their needs within a mostly urban setting. Sometimes, as the following 1881 account from Key West illustrates, this especially could mean female children and could incorporate numerous influences wrought by women on the church. "The Sabbath School children of Rev. Thos. Darley's Church, under the lead of Mr. James A. Roberts, Supt., gave a May-Queen Exhibition on Tuesday last," the item began. It continued:

> Miss Georgiana Haley was chosen Queen, and Matilda Shavers and Mamie Menard chief maids, with some six others who assisted. The juvenile regal train marched to the church at 5 p.m. headed by the [Key West Cornet] band, and followed by a large crowd. After arriving at the church, the Queen and maids were escorted to the platform where after suitable singing, a beautiful gilded crown was placed on the Queen's head by one of the maids. This ceremony being over, the Superintendent, Mr. Roberts, delivered a fine address to the children. After which the children were formed in line, and marched with music and banners through the principal streets.
>
> In the evening, the children held an Exhibition at Good Templar Hall, which was packed to its utmost capacity. The May-Queen and maids recited an appropriate dialogue, which was performed to perfection. The Queen placed laurel wreaths on the heads of her principal maids after each one had spoken her part. The singing was grand, and each one performed her part admirably. The Queen and maids were dressed in white and pink, with spangles and other beautiful ornaments.
>
> The affair was the best we have seen of its kind in this place, and it reflected much credit on Mr. Roberts, the Supt., and Miss Alice Menard who practiced the children. After the May-Queen dialogue and singing were over, Miss Alice Menard read an Essay on "Women's Mission in the Sabbath School." The Essay was decidedly a good one, and was read in a deep, clear voice. The audience showed their appreciation with hearty cheers. The affair closed about 10 o'clock, and all went home highly delighted.[23]

Two last points, also concerning women and the experience of church membership in the 1870s and early 1880s, merit mention before turning to consideration of the specifics of Joseph Pascal Thompson's tenure as bishop of Florida. Although little evidence comes to hand on these subjects, churchgoing at AMEZ congregations surely felt and sounded differently than it otherwise would have had the gender balance stood more evenly. Arguably, women desired a different environment at church than did men, one that afforded stability, security, moral rectitude, warmth, and reassurance in large measure. The available record, for example, hints that congregations tended to be quite cohesive, and this may reflect the women's impact. "The colored Methodists of the Reserve are united and zealous, and in consequence are thriving," an early report from Warrington commented, "though not so numerous as the Baptists, they set them an example they would do well to imitate." This point about cohesion could be taken too far too quickly, though, as an 1880 Tampa incident makes clear. "A row occurred in Zion Church, Tampa, a few nights ago, between two of the colored sisters and a brother deacon," a newspaper reported, "in which the latter was carved with a razor." Elder Oscar V. Jackson subsequently found himself forced to press charges against congregation member Henry Hopkins for breach of the peace.[24]

The final thought concerns the way that services sounded to those in attendance at an AMEZ sanctuary. Countless writers have emphasized the importance of music to black congregations, although W.E.B. Du Bois may have stated the point most eloquently. "The music of Negro religion, despite caricature and defilement," he insisted in *The Souls of Black Folk*, "still remains one of the most original and beautiful expressions of human life and longing yet born on American soil." Historian William E. Montgomery, who singled out Du Bois's statement to punctuate his work *Under Their Own Vine and Fig Tree: The African-American Church in the South, 1865–1900*, added quite correctly, "Music contributed immensely to the excitement and the happiness of black worship services." Even whites often bowed to its beauty and significance. "Sunday was an extremely dull day," a Warrington man recorded in 1869, "save the singing and shouting emanating from the religiously disposed colored people of the Baptist and Methodist persuasions there was nothing to indicate its being Sunday."[25]

What is less well known is that in the post–Civil War era relatively few black churches boasted choirs, at least among the poorer congregations in the South. Florida's AMEZ churches, on the other hand, seem to have taken particular delight and pride in such organized and rehearsed presentations. Since congregations increasingly reflected a female personality, it must be assumed that as the 1870s and 1880s passed on, the choirs also contained larger percentages of women. Soprano voices thus eventually outnumbered bass ones, perhaps encouraging the early evolution from the performance of slave spirituals to standard denominational hymns that marked the regional African church experience during the period. So few accounts of Florida AMEZ religious services prior to the 1890s have survived that emphasis on the point is risky. One 1884 report from Key West, though, seems to buttress the case. "In a very few moments we found ourselves seated within [Cornish Chapel's] consecrated walls, surrounded by a most beautiful congregation," the visitor began. Following prayer, he observed, came the choir. "As we arose from our knees the choir burst forth in one of its delightful strains," he continued. "The house could not stand it--burst out the door and leaped through the windows bounded away out on the gulf until the angels caught the sound and wafted it home to the high courts of glory." The visitor concluded, "Thus ended one of the most delightful services we have ever witnessed."[26]

All of these dynamics and details combined to offer a backdrop to Bishop Thompson's Florida service, although most of the specific developments that would mark his tenure remained well open to question when he held his first conference in the state during April 1877. Minutes of these initial sessions have not been preserved, but certain of Thompson's actions may be discerned and seem to have been based in sound logic. For one thing, it quickly became apparent to him that several assignments required adjustment. In Santa Rosa County, for example, young and inexperienced Vincent F. White had found the going rough in a rich AMEZ territory where AME competition was stiffening. Thompson reassigned White to Jacksonville and substituted thirty-one-year-old Oscar V. Jackson, a Mississippi native. Israel Furby, released from Jacksonville mission work, departed Duval County for Levy at Thompson's direction to attempt revival of the almost moribund Cedar Keys church. Desperate for capable preachers, Thompson reached to the Bahamas for one of Joseph Sexton's discoveries, Robert N. Andrews. With Furby attempting to rekindle the flame at Cedar Keys, Andrews partnered with him at Tampa. John M. Butler, Warren C. Vesta, Gabriel Sexton, and Joseph Lennox remained at work in Escambia County, with Thomas H. Darley continuing to hold the fort at Key West.[27]

Thompson also looked ahead to formalizing an administrative structure for the Bahamas work. The 1876 general conference had authorized creation of a conference, and by April 1877 Joseph Sexton and Robert An-

drews could report sufficient progress for Thompson to schedule an organizational session. He specified a date in the following December for the
event.[28]

The gathering in the Bahamas did not come off quite as planned, perhaps an omen of future events. When Joseph Sexton and a few other ministers attempted to convene at Nassau on December 26, the bishop had yet
to arrive. The men then adjourned until January 4, 1878. When that date
rolled around, Thompson indeed had made it to the islands, along with
Alabama's Wilbur G. Strong and a few others. All told, fourteen ministers gathered for the occasion. Bishop William J. Walls later recorded that
among others present were Elders James R. Harris and D. L. Carr, plus
Deacons David Thomas, John A. Bain, and D. W. Martindell. Sexton reported a total of 206 members of the new conference, which, as a home
conference, would remain closely associated with its Florida parent. Existing and projected churches included ones at Nassau, Harbour Island, Tarpon Bay, Eleuthera, Governor's Harbour, Andros Island, Rock Sound, and
East Eleuthera.[29]

Other than a pleasant winter sojourn in a tropical island paradise, the
organizational conference must have been seen by Thompson mostly as a
justification for moving Joseph Sexton back to Florida where his services
were urgently needed. At the 1878 annual conference, the bishop transferred Sexton to Tampa and returned Andrews to Nassau. This event seemingly took place at Key West in February or early March, affording the
bishop his sole visit to that island city. At any rate, Sexton's return to his
old church saw him welcomed by eager and delighted friends. Although
Tampa's fortunes had ebbed and flowed during the decade, its black community had begun to prosper in an environment in which labor remained
scarce and commanded relatively high wages and the federal government
afforded customs service and other jobs to African Americans. Black farmers there also had enjoyed sufficient time for their homesteads to develop
and, more importantly, their citrus groves to mature. The local newspaper,
reporting Sexton's arrival from Nassau and Key West in March, observed,
"He visits Tampa for the purpose of having a church built for his people."
As it turned out, the preacher quickly regrasped the reins of community
leadership, pushing especially for the cause of education and the construction of a new grammar school. He had arrived in the town when Mt. Sinai
was endeavoring to survive, and when he departed the following year the
congregation was strong and vibrant.[30]

Sexton's Tampa experience highlights what a talented minister can accomplish but also illustrates every bishop's dilemma, the need to place the right man in the right position. This assumes, of course, that enough right men are available and that the bishop takes the time to assess their strengths, understand their weaknesses, and acquaint himself with the needs of the various charges. By the 1878 annual conference, unfortunately, Bishop Thompson's interest in the subject had almost run its course. Seemingly, Presiding Elder Darley now began guiding church appointments if he had not done so earlier. As a result, Bishop Thompson, if in name only, moved in 1878 especially to bolster the sagging Santa Rosa church. To aid Oscar V. Jackson, he dispatched Sexton's Tampa protégé Alexander Robinson to minister outside Milton. Robinson likely established a mission at Blackwater (later Bagdad), although a small congregation may have worshiped there previously. Soon, Thompson also directed George W. Maize, a twenty-year-old Alabama native, to assist Jackson and Robinson.[31]

A few other personnel actions also dotted the agenda in 1878. Bishop Thompson transferred Gabriel Sexton to Alabama, for example, although he allowed the now-senior clergyman to remain long enough to secure land for and construct a sanctuary at Millview. In Sexton's stead Allen Hartley commenced an Escambia County ministry. Apparently, Thompson also dismissed Cedar Keys's John G. Williams from the AMEZ clergy. Information remains hard to find on the subject, but Williams had suffered a run-in with the law in 1876, accused in the midst of the election campaign of attempting to defraud the United States in connection with his job as a customs inspector. He successfully defended against the charges and returned to Levy County. By 1878, though, Williams had decided to seek his fortune elsewhere, sold his home, and departed the county. In 1880 he was living at Savannah, Georgia, and working as a carpenter.[32]

In good part, the story of the remaining years of Bishop Thompson's tenure in Florida remained that of personnel changes, with frequent exchanges between Alabama and Florida remaining a constant. A few examples help to illustrate the point. Israel Furby and Talbot Chapel's John M. Butler returned to Alabama, in 1879 and 1880, respectively, with Warren C. Vesta taking Butler's place. No one filled Furby's Cedar Keys pulpit thereafter on a regular basis, and that congregation apparently disbanded about 1883. Edward Hunter arrived from Alabama in 1882 to assume the pastorate at Key West's Cornish Chapel. Joseph Sexton, meanwhile, attended to and quelled new local crises in several locations. He left Tampa the same year that Furby departed, for instance, in order to labor again in

Santa Rosa County. In 1881 Sexton journeyed from Milton back to Nassau where the Bahamas Conference had encountered rocky going (Robert N. Andrews, in turn, relocated from Nassau to Milton). Sexton then carried the AMEZ banner in 1882 to Jacksonville's always struggling St. Lukes. Oscar V. Jackson meanwhile took over the station at Tampa, where he worked to revive the eastern Hillsborough and Polk County churches of the "Tampa Circuit." In 1882–84 Jackson likely filled in for Sexton in the Bahamas, as he previously had done at Tampa.[33]

The single most significant personnel change came in 1882, with Thomas Darley's appointment to Pensacola's Talbot Chapel. This move cemented Darley's authority within the Florida Conference by placing him at the epicenter of AMEZ activity in the state. In that year the entire Florida Conference (exclusive of the Bahamas churches) consisted of only 1,037 members, and, as annual conference secretary Warren C. Vesta noted, "the most of the ministers are stationed in the extreme western part of the State." Presumably at the time of Darley's transfer if not before, Bishop Talbot's dual presiding eldership scheme was dropped. The conference thereafter boasted no presiding elder, but Thomas Darley effectively exercised the bishop's authority in his absence.[34]

Through these years and whatever his intentions, Darley proved unable to expand church operations significantly or to increase low membership totals. Only Cornish Chapel and Talbot Chapel came close to covering their own expenses, leaving the church dependent upon support from outside the state. With the bishop unwilling to focus his attention on securing that necessary funding, church initiatives rarely moved beyond the discussion stage. Some exceptions challenged the general rule, of course, although they usually involved a small congregation that essentially incorporated itself into the church. This had occurred, for instance, in 1874 at Escambia near Pensacola when St. Marks Chapel coalesced around a few believers. Two other Escambia County churches organized under similar circumstances during Bishop Thompson's tenure. Edwards Chapel sprang into life in 1879 at Pensacola thanks to the efforts of its local pastor Joshua Edwards. St. Paul Chapel at Muscogee followed prior to 1884.[35]

Just one foray outside of Escambia County during the early 1880s left any trace, and its details come in a form hazy at best. A letter from Gainesville's AME minister to his church newspaper, the *Christian Recorder*, constitutes the surviving record. In it M. A. Sturkes, who later would join the AMEZ clergy, observed during the summer of 1881 that "two ministers from the A.M.E. Zion Church joined us with their congregations on Sunday." He continued: "The Rev. Hill from the Zion A.M.E. is much liked and proves himself an earnest and able worker." The identity of the Reverend Hill remains a mystery. His associate likely was a thirty-five-year-old native of Great Britain named John A. Mulligan. Following the Civil War, Mulligan had ventured from Boston to Key West where he held a government job and may have attended Cornish Chapel, and during the 1870s he moved to Jacksonville to work as a teacher. In Florida Mulligan answered a call to the AMEZ ministry. By 1881 he likely taught school at Gainesville where he also preached. The two AMEZ churches there probably did not outlast the year, though. Mulligan removed to the Philadelphia and Baltimore Conference, eventually rising to the position of steward of the Allegheny Conference. No record of the subsequent activities of the Reverend Hill has come to light.[36]

The virtual lack of information about the Gainesville mission and its principal minister offers appropriate comment on the condition of the state AMEZ Conference as it moved into the 1880s. Even though Zion could boast benchmark successes in other locales outside the state, in Florida absentee and disinterested leadership, chronic funding problems, legacies of past missteps, and ever-present challenges from AME and Baptist competitors had left the church dependent upon a handful of capable and enterprising ministers to maintain its survival in the state much less to ensure its prosperous future. As Thomas Darley and Edward Hunter made their way in May 1884 to New York City to attend the Seventeenth General Conference, they must have yearned to discover some source for renewed optimism, for a national church commitment to their mission, and for the appointment of a bishop who would deliver upon the promise. The men, their conference, and their state needed something—anything—good to happen. Florida's government now lay in the hands of its former Confederate general governor. At the nation's capital exultant Democrats had not yet stopped celebrating the inauguration of President Grover Cleveland and the ouster of Republicans from power. Hundreds of miles to the north at New York City, Darley and Hunter must have reasoned, the news surely would resonate more positively and future prospects shine brightly yet again. Surely.[37]

THE REKINDLING OF SPIRIT, 1884–1888

————•·•————

our hearts were made
to feel glad

By the mid-1880s Florida's AMEZ Church was surviving, although it did so in good part by the power of inertia. An often-neglected child of the national church, its grand hopes appeared to have withered in a climate deprived of effective episcopal leadership, its hopeful plans frustrated by questionable judgment and continuing financial constraints. Meanwhile, political events had rendered difficult conditions for African Americans ever-worse in the state, region, and nation. Floridians especially suffered. Racial violence plagued the state as white officials ignored and sometimes encouraged the terror. Then, just at a time when the church needed to forge positive contributions, the clouds that had shrouded the AMEZ family parted. The problems of a denominational competitor provided an opportunity, and men of strong purpose stepped forward to direct the church accordingly. The long-awaited new day for Florida's AMEZ Church finally appeared about to dawn.

The Florida AMEZ Church in 1884 differed little from its condition one decade earlier, save that its ministers had grown weary as time had passed. Likely one-half of its one thousand or so members clustered in Escambia and Santa Rosa counties, where a number of small congregations and missions radiated out from Pensacola's Talbot Chapel and Isaiah Chapel at nearby Milton. The other AMEZ stronghold continued at Key West, still Florida's largest city. At Tampa, Mt. Sinai fared well and the eastern Hillsborough and Polk County mission churches established by Joseph Sexton in 1868 sputtered along, kept alive by occasional visitations from Mt. Sinai's pastor. One-time outposts at Brooksville, Cedar Keys, and Gainesville lay moribund. At Jacksonville's suburb of Hansontown, St. Lukes Church had come during Sexton's recent pastorate to enjoy some level of stability after years of local resistance. The conference's ties to the Bahama

Islands added one layer of membership on top of Florida's total, but the exciting promise of the organizational conference in 1878 had amounted over the years to little. A gifted preacher and administrator such as Sexton could bring its several congregations to life, but in the absence of such dynamic leadership the AMEZ spirit waned.[1]

While the Florida Conference had endured its trials and frustrations, the state had experienced changes of a dramatic nature, ones that set the stage for the new era to come. Population statistics offer context for understanding the magnitude and quality of dynamics then at play. The 1870 census reported fewer than 190,000 residents. One decade later the total had risen to almost 270,000, a jump of more than 40 percent. It required only five more years for another leap of comparable size. This resulted in a population figure in 1885 of about 340,000, almost twice that of fifteen years earlier.[2]

Percentage increases of black residents had not kept pace with the increases of whites. The numbers of black Floridians nonetheless had risen significantly. In 1870, for example, nearly one-half of all Floridians were identified as African Americans. Within ten years that figure had dropped slightly to 47 percent. The 1885 level stood even lower, at 44 percent. Where in 1870 the state had claimed nearly 92,000 black citizens, though, the statistic had risen to 147,000 by the mid-1880s.[3]

Importantly, the growth had not come evenly. This meant that the impact of growth in the areas most intensely affected carried a far heavier weight that the statewide totals might suggest. Basically, the state's Middle Florida heartland—the panhandle counties where Old South cotton plantations had reigned supreme and the majority of Florida's slaves had labored—now was losing ground relatively speaking to northeast Florida, the St. Johns River valley, and the central peninsula down to Tampa Bay. Where the Middle Florida counties of Jackson, Gadsden, Leon, Wakulla, Jefferson, Madison, Taylor, Lafayette, and Hamilton had contained about 70,000 residents in 1870, they had grown only about 25 percent to 89,000 during the subsequent fifteen years. Over the same period of time, the AMEZ counties of Duval, Escambia, Hillsborough, Monroe, Polk, and Santa Rosa bounded from 35,000 to 77,000, an advance of 120 percent. Monroe had managed to best even that impressive figure by growth at 166 percent, and Hillsborough bragged about an increase of 148 percent.[4]

These statistics fail to convey the whole story. The demographic changes of 1870–85 spoke directly to Florida's future as the South's most urban state. Interstate and intrastate immigrants were tending to relocate from rural areas to small towns and cities. Census totals for urban areas were not reported by the state in 1885, but figures for 1870 and 1890 tell the story well. Key West mushroomed from a town of 5,016 to a small city of 18,080. Jacksonville, the state's second city in 1890, now contained 17,201 persons as opposed to the 6,912 individuals who had called the place home twenty years earlier. The population of Pensacola grew from 3,347 to 11,750. Tampa, a mere village with 796 inhabitants in 1870, ranked as the fourth largest town two decades later with a population of 5,532. The state's capital, located in a region of declining prospects, had not fared so badly either. The town of about 2,000 persons in the immediate postwar era emerged as a community of almost 3,000 by 1890.[5]

The key to much of this growth involved transportation improvements, particularly the building of railroads. Through the 1870s, rail construction in Florida had remained stymied by a federal court injunction. This matter met with resolution in 1881 when the state paid off certain claims after selling Philadelphia industrialist Hamilton Disston four million acres of the peninsula at twenty-five cents per acre. Disston thereafter centered important elements of his drainage and development plans in the Kissimmee and upper St. Johns River valleys and the nearby town of Kissimmee. The Disston Purchase and the dismissal of the federal injunction freed the state to begin to subsidize railroad construction by granting large tracts of state lands for each mile of track completed.[6]

Two individuals in particular took advantage of opportunities afforded by the developments of 1881. In the western region of the panhandle, businessman William D. Chipley aimed to connect Pensacola at long last with the portion of Florida that ranged east of the Apalachicola River. His Pensacola & Atlantic Railroad (which later merged with the Louisville & Nashville Railroad) launched construction in August 1881. Trains were running through Milton eastward to a point sixty miles from Pensacola by August 1882 and would reach Sampson's Landing on the Apalachicola's west bank by March of the following year. When the line's Apalachicola River bridge opened in May, the steam engines could haul cargo and passengers from Pensacola to Sampson's Landing, across the river east to River Junction, then through to Jacksonville. Stations from Pensacola to River Junction included Bohemia, Bellevue, Escambia, Arcadia, Milton, Good Range, Holts, Chaffins, Crestview, Deer Island, Moss Head, Lake De Funiak (De Funiak Springs), Argyle, Ponce de Leon, Westville, Caryville, Bonifay, Chipley, Cottondale, Marianna, Cypress, and Sneads. Almost all of the sites represented new development sparked by Chipley's railroad.[7]

In northeast Florida and the peninsula, Henry Bradley Plant demonstrated initiative on an even-grander scale than did Chipley. A Connecticut native, Plant had come south in the 1850s to make his fortune in the express business, managing an extensive package forwarding operation. The Civil War having been kind to him, he found himself in a position following the peace to take control of numerous rail lines. By 1880 a Plant System had begun to take form based upon Plant's control of the only railroad tie between eastern Florida and Georgia. As the legislature moved to support line construction, Plant quickly expanded the railroad down the peninsula. His South Florida Railroad already had connected Orlando with points north by October 1, 1880. A link to Kissimmee followed in March 1882, with service to Tampa opened by early 1884. The Florida Southern Railroad, a line closely associated with Plant's other interests, meanwhile laid track down the peninsula's center through Polk and Manatee counties (later Hardee, De Soto, and Charlotte). Its trains were running to and from Punta Gorda at Charlotte Harbor by 1886.[8]

The new transportation links opened up development and encouraged further growth in any number of ways. The panhandle experienced, for instance, the beginning of what has become known as the Florida timber industry's fifty-year "bonanza era." As a result, the Port of Pensacola boomed. Eighty million board feet of lumber passed through its facilities in 1881 alone. That year a resident proclaimed, "There are very few men idle in Pensacola to-day." The prosperity found its way into the town's black, as well as its white, community. "The colored people of Pensacola are about as prosperous as any of their race in the South," reported a local man in 1884. "As laborers they are better paid, and their natural sociability leads them, having a goodly share of this world's goods, to place themselves in comfortably furnished homes far above the hovels peculiar to their people in other cities."[9]

Portions of the peninsula with access to navigable waterways and railroads likewise underwent transformation as newcomers flowed to the region. Specialized agriculture adapted to the local climate promised future wealth to all, even to many black settlers. "In twenty-five years the St. John's river will be built up like the Hudson," one African American community leader asserted in 1884. "One of the most encouraging things for us is where these booms are found, Ham is there with his orange groves and truck farms." In Duval County alone at mid-decade, black property owners held almost two hundred farms valued at over $400,000.[10]

Such an economic base helped to promote, at Jacksonville and in other regional towns, the development of a business and professional class. To cite one prominent example, John E. Onley—a Jacksonville contractor, builder, and investor—grossed the considerable sum of $20,000 annually from rents by 1884. The same year Frank P. Gadson, the "merchant prince of Ocala," operated one of Florida's pioneering department stores, catering to whites as well as to blacks. Black attorneys had achieved admission to the bar in the state as early as 1869. By 1882, at least two licensed and medical-school-trained physicians practiced their arts, Alexander H. Darnes at Jacksonville and William John Gunn at Tallahassee. Numerous other professionals followed in their wake.[11]

At Florida's southernmost reach of Key West, which lay distant from any railroad during the 1880s, industry and a busy port ensured prosperity as great as that seen anywhere in the state. During 1881, for example, the town's seventy-three licensed manufacturers turned out thirty-four million cigars, exporting almost six hundred thousand dollars worth of merchandise to foreign countries. "Key West, so long dormant, so long hidden from the American public by the apathy of her citizens," the *Jacksonville Florida Times-Union* observed in 1885, "is now drawing the attention of the whole country." The black community claimed at least a part of that attention. "Key West is the freest town in the South, not even Washington excepted," argued the *New York Age*.[12]

As it did at Key West, the tobacco industry also aided the renaissance of the Tampa Bay area once Henry Plant had gifted the vicinity with his railroad. "One of the largest cigar manufacturers in Key West intends to move his establishment to Tampa," a resident advised in October 1885. That man, Vicente Martinez Ybor, set out a company village two miles northeast of Tampa that he named Ybor City. After fire ravaged much of Key West in April 1886, others followed in Ybor's footsteps. By century's end, Tampa claimed position as "the leading center in the United States of high-quality, hand-rolled cigars." Elsewhere, as seen, prosperity had rested at least partially on the efforts of black residents who, in turn, enjoyed benefits of the good times. So, too, was the situation at Tampa. "The colored population . . . number about one-thousand, a majority of whom are industrious, thrifty and progressive," averred the *Tampa Journal* in 1887. "Many of them own their own homes," it continued. "They have churches, schools and several literary societies, and withal are respectable, orderly and peaceable."[13]

While Florida grew in the 1880s and certain areas began to prosper, the state's body politic experienced its own transformation in a manner that had an impact on the African American community and influenced the AMEZ and other churches. Democrats had grasped control of state government in 1877, but for years the potentially hard grip of the Democratic Party had rested softly on Republican shoulders. In 1884, however, when the nation elected Democrat Grover Cleveland as its president, Florida opted to hand the governor's chair to former Confederate general Edward A. Perry of Pensacola. Perry and his allies then called a constitutional convention and rewrote the state's 1868 charter to weaken state power, rein in state spending for certain Republican programs such as universal free public education, and consolidate their own control.[14]

Constitutional revision and the demographic changes mentioned earlier—coupled with various forms of intimidation and black disgust at politics and the corruption associated with it—in fact did ensure Democratic control of state government. Still, the issue had remained in doubt in the minds of many whites and blacks until 1884. Some had drawn hope, for instance, from two facts. First, one of Florida's two congressional seats rested until mid-decade in Republican hands. Second, as many African Americans sat in the state legislature in 1885 as had in 1868.[15]

The question of who ran municipal governments, though, constituted an entirely different matter from the issue of state government control. Many of Florida's towns and cities contained Republican majorities, and their citizens displayed sufficient respect for law and order that African Americans could continue to vote and serve in office in the 1880s. Although the tide that swept Cleveland and Perry into power suppressed that reality for several years at mid-decade, beginning in 1887 Republican control of municipal governments and black office holding soared. This resulted when activists combined with a national labor union, the Knights of Labor, to promote their mutual goals. In 1887 coalition tickets achieved major victories at Jacksonville, Key West, and Tampa. Important successes were registered, as well, in numerous other locales that year and during the years immediately following. The 1888 Monroe County election offers an especially striking example of the coalition's power. In the first contests held after the 1885 state constitution made most county posts elective rather than appointive, African Americans won the sheriff's and the county judge's contests. In the former instance, Cornish Chapel member Charles F. Dupont captured the sheriff's badge, while his friend James Dean (a future AME minister) assumed the judge's bench.[16]

As will be considered at greater length in chapter 6, Democrats looked upon Republican municipal control and black office holding with horror and in the decade's final years enacted legal restrictions of a type that Governor Perry had begun to pioneer at mid-decade aimed at severely restricting black urban political power. Perry's initiatives merit particular attention here, however, because they affected his hometown of Pensacola where Florida's AMEZ Church held firm to its strongest anchor. Before 1885 Pensacola had ranked as one of the state's strongest Republican towns. During 1883, for instance, African Americans had served it as city clerk, tax assessor, and marshal at a time when five of nine aldermen also were black. Perry and his hard-line allies chafed at the situation and moved quickly once in power to pass a law vacating the city charter. In its place, a new measure handed control over selection of local officials to the governor. The state supreme court, with a fresh majority recently appointed by Perry, went along with the change.[17]

In taking the steps that he did, Perry found some unlikely allies. AME minister and outspoken political leader George W. Witherspoon, for one, had relocated to Pensacola in the early 1880s after the Republican U.S. House of Representatives had opted to back a white Democrat by denying Witherspoon a seat that he probably had won in 1880. One of the strongest preachers in the state, Witherspoon also enjoyed lucrative employment in the customs service at Pensacola. Already furious at what he considered white Republican duplicity in his congressional loss and in the waning of Reconstruction advances, the renowned preacher and one-time state legislator found his attitudes reinforced as he witnessed up close the operations of town government.[18]

As his resentments built, Witherspoon decided to associate with others, including several individuals closely linked with the AMEZ Church, in a dramatic act. They joined a biracial reform coalition that nominated a "Citizens' and Democratic" ticket for the upcoming Pensacola elections. Witherspoon accepted the nomination for tax collector. In the face of his conference's unofficial but clearly understood practice to the contrary, Zion Elder Warren C. Vesta stood by Witherspoon as candidate for tax assessor. The appearance of AMEZ endorsement of the ticket seemed even stronger with the presence on it of Talbot Chapel member Augustus Dupont, a respected educator and experienced city and council official. Witherspoon failed to win election, but Vesta and Dupont took their races, ironically making the reformers two of the officials displaced by Perry's takeover. The governor thereupon stunned everyone by announcing that the AME Church's great crusader George W. Witherspoon had agreed to leave the Republican Party and accept appointment to serve as an alderman under the new regime.[19]

Along with the political turbulence of the mid- and late-1880s came the beginning efforts at legally enforced Jim Crow racial discrimination and a painful tide of racial violence. Residents today find it hard to believe that the vacation paradise of Florida has endured a history so stained with blood, but such truly has been the case. Racially motivated lynchings in the state mounted at such a rate during the 1880s and 1890s that, by 1900, Florida ranked on a per capita basis as the nation's leader in such crimes. The next three decades would see the state's rate exceed South Carolina's by a multiple of six and Alabama's by three. It doubled that of Mississippi, Georgia, and Louisiana.[20]

Little wonder that Floridians such as S. D. Jackson would lament the temper of the times. "What shall we do with the negro?" the Pensacolian rhetorically asked readers of one national newspaper. "Well, sir, I will tell you what they are doing with us down South," he continued. "They are shooting us down as so many partridges; don't allow editors to speak the truth always through their papers to the people; kicking us off of trains whenever they see fit to do so; distribute the school funds as their conscience directs, charging us very often as high as 24 percent. per annum for money when we are compelled to borrow it from them, and thousands of other things too numerous to mention." Expressing the frustration felt by many, Jackson added, "Too many of us wait too contentedly for our enemies to strike the first blow for us for liberty and recognition instead of striking it ourselves."[21]

In these circumstances more than a few Floridians cried out for leadership, for someone to blaze a path out of the seemingly endless wilderness. Another Pensacola man summed up the situation in that community for a New York newspaper's readers, and he did so in words that aired sentiments felt around the state. "Pensacola needs a leader for the colored people, as we are now entirely without leaders, except those who act in the capacity of preachers, straining every nerve to collect the dollars and cents for themselves and the wily and slippery politicians who care for nothing but to trade around and pocket all the money they can," he began. "The professional men huddle together, hold themselves almost entirely aloof from the ignorant masses, thereby letting ignorance and immorality reign supreme," the man expressed further. "There are plenty of good preachers, politicians and professional men here, but they have not the courage and interest in the race to lead the people right."[22]

In this climate of trepidation and yearning the AME Church blundered badly, as a consequence of which the AMEZ Church soon found itself in a position to offer effective competition in areas that previously had seemed off-limits. Reasons for the blunder were varied and complicated, including the chagrin of many black Republicans at George W. Witherspoon's seeming embrace of their political enemies. Bishop Daniel A. Payne, though, bore a good deal of the responsibility. Recognized in much of the world for his piety and intelligence, Payne from 1884 to 1888 served the Florida AME Church as its bishop. Earlier in the decade he had taken up winter residence at Jacksonville and over the years had come to feel a proprietary interest in the Florida church. Although Payne was a firebrand in his younger years, his attitudes toward political involvement by ministers and the church had evolved by the mid-1880s to a position of opposition. So, much of the still-powerful AME network in Florida stood on the sidelines as a Confederate general was elected governor, the Florida constitution was rewritten, Governor Perry seized Pensacola's municipal government, and Jim Crow laws debuted in the state. Payne eventually insisted that he had been misunderstood, but the damage had been done. Congregations throughout the old AME stronghold of North Florida found themselves in meltdown as the church turned for its survival to missionary work in the developing peninsula.[23]

The crisis fractured Florida's AME Church beyond its toll on membership. Denominational leaders who opposed political involvements began berating and, sometimes, condemning their colleagues who felt and acted otherwise, apparently with the bishop's acquiescence. Disgusted by the turn of events, a number of senior churchmen quit the denomination. Given a paucity of alternatives, some turned to the AMEZ Church for a new home even though that denomination also discouraged political involvements by its preachers. The years 1885–86 saw several such defections. Paul L. Cuyler, a Jefferson County native who had pastored Key West's AME church for several years, withdrew from the AME fold "under charges." After brief AMEZ service in Florida, he transferred elsewhere. To cap his distinguished career, Cuyler presided at New York City's "Mother Zion" Church. Similarly, experienced pastors J. W. Bowen and Auburn H. Erwin found a calling within the AMEZ family. Erwin had served as a delegate in the 1868 Florida constitutional convention, sat in the Florida house of representatives, and aided Duval County as a constable and justice of the peace.[24]

Foremost among the disaffected, however, came Robert Meacham. He was one of the state's principal leaders from 1867 to the early 1880s, and his adherence to the AMEZ banner amounted to a major coup for the church. The *New York Freeman* indicated as much in its coverage of the ministers in attendance at the Florida Conference's 1887 annual sessions at Pensacola. "Prominent among its members is the Hon. Robert Meacham," the paper's correspondent declared, "an ex-member of the Florida Conference of the A.M.E. Connection, ex-State Senator, the once acknowledged leader of Jefferson County, who used to be a gentleman of considerable local note."[25]

By the time Meacham reached his decision to take a place within AMEZ ranks, the Florida Conference had begun to evolve out of its lethargic condition of the late 1870s and early 1880s, although the progress of future years remained only in the beginning stages. The evolution had commenced at the church's Seventeenth Quadrennial Conference held at Mother Zion in New York City in May 1884. Bishop Joseph Pascal Thompson's uninspired supervision of Florida church affairs came to its end. At the gathering delegates transferred the Florida Conference from the Third Episcopal District to the Second. The new district also encompassed the Allegheny, Canada and Michigan, and South Carolina Conferences and was headed by Bishop Singleton Thomas Webster Jones. Delegates Thomas H. Darley and Edward Hunter, pastors respectively at Pensacola's Talbot Chapel and Key West's Cornish Chapel, likely breathed a great sigh of relief.[26]

The news, at least in a relative sense, certainly was good, but it was not as good as it could have been. Jones at the time was approaching his sixty-first birthday, and his district incorporated conferences widely scattered, with Florida lying farthest afield. Elected bishop in 1868, he brought with him the experience of years and a reputation as a conference organizer. His fellow bishop John J. Moore found much to praise in the man: "In his marvelous life he brought to his support the power of oratory, patience, forbearance, fortitude, boldness, courage, resignation in hardships, sacrificing comforts, battling frequently against formidable odds, but ever persistent in the strife." Florida required dynamic leadership, however, while its new bishop tended to a conservative course. "He was a fine and logical reasoner, and as a theologian he was entirely safe," Bishop James Walker Hood recalled. "He kept to the old beaten path of Methodism, but he was constantly bringing to view new beauties along that old path," Hood explained further. "We never knew him to make a theological utterance which seemed to us unsound." Moreover, Jones seemingly was ailing by the mid-1880s. The affliction would end his life on April 18, 1891.[27]

The change in leadership offered encouragement and inspired Elder Darley to take some tentative steps to reverse the tide that had left his church weak and isolated. In late 1884 or early 1885, for instance, he responded to AME missionary work in those areas of the peninsula that had been opened by railroad construction and Hamilton Disston–related development. Particularly, he dispatched one of his ministers, possibly James R. Harris, to establish a congregation at Kissimmee. St. James AMEZ Church resulted. At about the same time or within one or two years, the church also planted itself at the new town of Plant City, situated on the South Florida Railroad line twenty-five miles east of Tampa on the way to Kissimmee. There grew Little Zion AMEZ Church.[28]

These initiatives may have been planned at the 1885 Florida Conference held at St. Lukes Church, Jacksonville. Bishop Jones did not attend. Instead, Elder Darley in Jones's name authorized a new division of the conference into districts (possibly, this action came in 1886). In addition to the Key West (First) and Pensacola (Second) Districts that had existed earlier, the plan may have reincorporated the Bahamas Conference into its Florida parent conference by the addition of a Bahamas District headed by Joseph Sexton. St. Lukes again was struggling with internal problems and sagging membership rolls subsequent to Elder Joseph Sexton's 1884 departure, something that could not be hidden from firsthand inspection. Paul L. Cuyler first received assignment to the work. When he departed Florida during the fall, Elder Oscar V. Jackson stood in as his replacement.[29]

By then signs had begun to proliferate that a new day was dawning. Two 1885 Key West reports, to cite examples, expressed prosperity's impact and the first glimmers of a newfound sense of optimism that would grace church affairs in the not-too-distant future. The first report, written in January, welcomed AME pastor J. W. Bowen to Cornish Chapel's quarterly conference and recommended him for admission to Zion's Florida Conference. Pastor Edward Hunter and lay leaders James Hannibal and Romeo Dupont also announced progress toward payment on the church lot and in other fund-raising efforts. "The banner of King Emanuel is being unfurled in every valley and on every mountain top," Hunter proclaimed. Elder David Thomas of the Bahamas, the second report observed, joined Cornish Chapel's quarterly meeting at its next session. Two hundred fifty-seven children by then were attending its Sabbath school. Financial news continued to be positive, and a committee was appointed "to draw up plans and make suitable arrangements to build a parsonage." Dennis McGee, John Shavers, Romeo Dupont, David Mathews, William Johnson, Primos Daiz, and Alexander Tynes agreed to serve. At Sabbath services the next day, "the temple was filled with the presence of the Holy Ghost," while the Lord's Supper "was administered to 132 members." Hunter concluded, "The Lord acknowledged the work and our hearts were made to feel glad."[30]

As can be seen by the establishment of Kissimmee and Plant City churches, Elder Darley had determined to meet the AME challenge insofar as peninsular missions were concerned. He scheduled the February 1886 Florida Conference sessions in Tampa, a town bustling subsequent to the opening of Henry Plant's railroad and on the verge of growing even larger after the introduction of the cigar industry. Eager delegates arrived from the conference's far corners, including Thomas Lynn from the Bahamas, to see conditions in the emerging region firsthand. Local newspapers greeted them with feature stories on the city's glittering prospects. "Tampa, The Metropolis of the Gulf," one headline blared. In Bishop Jones's absence, his friend Bishop Moore presided, although he too suffered from poor health.[31]

Several decisions of consequence were taken at the Tampa gathering, and they did not come without sharp differences of opinion. The facts remain obscure, but Elder Oscar V. Jackson abruptly left the AMEZ Church the following month and associated with its AME competitors. After a one-year tenure at Starke, though, Jackson returned to the fold. In any event, the conference acted to further Darley's outreach plans as indicated by its acceptance of the invitation of a local preacher, J. S. Sims, to associate his congregation located at Center Hill in Sumter County. The body of worshipers emerged as Zion AMEZ Church.[32]

Bishop Moore, Elder Darley, and the conferees opted, as well, to reaffirm the AMEZ commitment to a Jacksonville outpost. The original decision to establish St. Lukes in the religiously hostile environment of the AME Church's Florida headquarters had dogged the conference subsequently, and the 1886 action likewise would set the stage for denominational challenge. But that fact could not be discerned in the heady days of 1886, so emboldened conferees dispatched James R. Harris to shore up the crumbling congregation. "On my arrival here from conference," he reported in March, "I found a large frame church building 60x25, in a beautiful location, also a parsonage with four rooms, on the same lot." He continued: "Our membership is small, also our congregation. The people here and their preacher could not get along last year, therefore the church is at low ebb." To counter the decline Harris scheduled a large camp meeting at nearby Pablo Beach for late September, to be held in cooperation not with local AME churches but with the Baptists. Bishop Jones proved unable to honor a commitment to attend, with Bishop Moore once more substituting. "Our camp was held right on the Atlantic Ocean, where we caught all the sweet breeze, and could behold as far as the eye sight would allow us the white caps of the mad ocean," Moore recorded. "Our camp lasted two weeks," he specified. "The first Sabbath of the camp-meeting we had a good turnout not withstanding the heavy rain and wind on that Sabbath." Bishop Moore's spirited sermons found a large audience, but the heavy rain and wind served as harbingers of troubled times yet to come in Jacksonville.[33]

Jacksonville problems notwithstanding and despite Bishop Jones's absence from Florida, modest progress was being made. The newly established churches would survive, and the conference's various pastors, save Oscar V. Jackson, sensed better times on the horizon. Minutes of the Key West District Conference held at Kissimmee on June 18, 1886, illustrate this fact. Edward Hunter, Auburn H. Erwin, and James R. Harris took leadership roles. "The subjects of education and temperance were ably discussed," Erwin related, "[and] the preaching by Elder[s] Hunter and Harris was instructive and was listened to with great earnestness by all." Erwin concluded, "There was great interest shown by the ministers and delegates on all the different subjects connected with our beloved Zion."[34]

The twelve months that separated the 1886 and 1887 state conferences turned out to be a time of terrible labor turmoil, a circumstance that, interestingly, redounded to the church's benefit. Virtually all AMEZ centers contained concentrations of industry and industrial workers, and many congregations reflected these local conditions. Thus, when the Knights of Labor organized at Pensacola in February 1886, AMEZ member Peter Davidson achieved election as the branch's worshipful master. Nationally, AMEZ leaders had decided to back the union, which had opened its ranks to blacks and whites alike. "Whatever may be said in criticism or denunciation of the Knights of Labor," the church's *Star of Zion* newspaper commented, "the fact remains that they are doing more to blot out color prejudice and recognize the equality of manhood in all the races than any organization in existence." It added, "Besides they are seeking to ennoble and dignify labor, the noblest of all professions and it is to be hoped that they will succeed in so worthy an effort." The Florida church quickly fell in line with the policy. Whatever reluctance it previously had evidenced with respect to political stances, it could not deny the truth of a Pensacola man's 1887 remarks. "Since the organization of the Knights of Labor in our District," he insisted, "the laboring masses have derived a greater benefit than they did from any other organization."[35]

At the time of the 1887 Florida Conference meetings, convened at Pensacola in February, the church's pro-labor position had only just begun to jell; yet Elder Darley already was preparing to take advantage of the popularity gained for the AMEZ cause as a result. Bishop Jones attended the sessions, thereby at last lending the power and credibility of his office to the plans approved. First, though, the bishop tightened the conference's organizational structure by proposing official adoption of a presiding eldership. Not only was the idea approved, but the choice of Darley to fill the position received unanimous approbation. "[He] deservedly holds respect, honor and confidence, alike of ministers and people, throughout the district," the bishop opined.[36]

Jones also issued a new schedule of appointments that reflected major shifts. Warren C. Vesta departed Pensacola for Key West, where he replaced Robert Meacham at Cornish Chapel. Meacham, in turn, headed for Punta Gorda to establish a church at the southern railhead of the Plant System. Dipping into the Tennessee Conference for talent, Jones assigned S. L. McDonald to substitute for Vesta at Talbot Chapel. Alexander Robinson returned to Tampa. One designation in particular hinted at Darley's ambitious plans. At his urging, Jones sent Deacon W. A. Bain eastward from Escambia County along the Pensacola & Atlantic Railroad tracks almost 150 miles to Middle Florida's Jackson County and the farming and timbering community of Cottondale. By August, McDonald had passed on word of Bain's success in establishing a toehold so deep into the panhandle. "Rev. W. A. Baine has put up a common church and is now getting ready to build another," he observed. "Sister Mollie L. Goodwin a worthy member of our church has donated the ground and as much timber as will be needed." McDonald added, "Would to God that we had a few more such sisters."[37]

The appointments telegraphed the beginnings of an ambitious expansion effort, but they did not constitute all of the ambitious plans the conference considered. At Pensacola a businessman proposed an arrangement that captured the AMEZ imagination at a time when Florida's AME Church prepared to begin construction at Jacksonville of its Divinity High School (later Edward Waters College). "A proposition coming from Mr. A. F. Randall of Tampa, Hillsborough county Florida, was sent to the Fla. conference . . . offering the conference, as a gift, 'College Hill and Park,' in a newly laid out town at that point, on certain conditions," Bishop Jones explained. The gift of land and a building for an AMEZ school rested upon important conditions, mainly that the church would undertake to sell a certain number of lots in the College Hill subdivision on Randall's behalf.

The idea caught fire with Darley, Jones, and others, who launched a sales campaign through the pages of the *Star of Zion*.[38]

These and other possibilities now filled the preachers with excitement. "The session was an agreeable one—said to have exceeded all others in harmony, instructiveness and hopeful promises," the bishop declared. "On the whole I am very favorably impressed with my experiences on my first visit to Florida." Successes at Punta Gorda and Cottondale buttressed expectations during the ensuing months. Knights of Labor victories added fuel to the fire, such as the election win at Tampa that saw Mt. Sinai member Joseph A. Walker elevated to the city council. Church construction projects arose to proclaim the rosy hue of the horizon. Tampa's Mt. Sinai congregation, for one, launched building of a new sanctuary in August. "They will have their bell high up," a newspaper reported, "where it will scare the devil and make the brethren flock in."[39]

At that point nature intervened to frustrate Presiding Elder Darley's carefully made plans. Yellow fever hit Key West, Tampa, Pensacola, and other points with a severity rarely experienced. Quarantines blocked commerce and travel as panic gripped residents. Potential buyers of College Hill lots evaporated with the wind, as did the possibility of a Tampa AMEZ school. Into December the plague raged. "Allow me to inform you that Zion is yet living in the land of flowers," S. L. McDonald wearily informed the *Star of Zion*'s readers in mid-November. "Our work is doing very well considering the great epidemic that has visited out city," he related. "It has taken several of the good citizens and among them some few of Zion's members." Searching for optimistic notes he added, "I have just received a letter from Deacon Bain, the West Florida pioneer, up at Cotton Dale, where he has stretched the borders of Zion to [Marianna] and bought a church for $250, which shows that all Zion needs in Florida is men to go out in the hedges and highways."[40]

Through the catastrophic months, Bishop Jones often joined his ministers in offering comfort and support. Although his term neared its end, he used the time to travel widely in the state. Some evidence suggests that he reached deep into the peninsula as far as Joseph Sexton's old Polk County mission churches before spending the Christmas and New Year's holidays at Pensacola. Quarantine restrictions kept him from venturing to Key West prior to mid-January 1888, but after the annual conference in February he made the trip. The travel took its toll, and the bishop succumbed to exhaustion. "On Sunday night after the sermon, the Bishop retired to his room, and was taken with a bilious attack, from which he suffered considerable until medical appliances gave him relief," Warren C. Vesta reported. He added: "He has made more visits this year, in the Florida work, than all the Bishops put together previously. A few more such trips as this made by our worthy Bishop, would soon plant Zion in all parts of this state."[41]

Before the Key West sojourn, as mentioned, Jones had presided over his final Florida Conference meeting. The attendees gathered at Milton's Isaiah Chapel for the occasion. As one newspaper put it, "many eminent colored divines [were] present." Presiding Elder Darley took advantage of the occasion to reorganize following the yellow fever attack. He oversaw development of outreach plans that would lead within the year to establishment of churches at Bartow (Star of Zion), Homeland (Mt. Olive), and Fort Myers in Polk and Lee counties, plus revival of the old Alafia and Simmons Hammock (Mt. Zion) congregations in Polk and Hillsborough. The plans also anticipated the building of a church at another point along the Pensacola & Atlantic tracks. This congregation, at Lake De Funiak (De Funiak Springs), would bear the name Friendship.[42]

Jones also informed the 1888 conferees of several pleasant developments. First, he welcomed Israel Furby back from Alabama and Oscar V. Jackson back from the AME Church. Then came a surprise that seemed to place the stamp of approval of the national church on the conference's bright hopes for its future. This had to do with the appointment of Franklin A. Clinton, the son of the late senior bishop Joseph J. Clinton, to the pulpit of Pensacola's Talbot Chapel (incumbent S. L. McDonald was hurried off to Jacksonville). Bishop Clinton had founded the Florida church in the 1860s, and AMEZ congregants nationwide revered his memory. Young Clinton had trained in Alabama under Wilbur G. Strong, who also claimed pioneering ties to the Florida Conference. In Alabama Clinton had grown close to educator Booker T. Washington, who had founded his Tuskegee Institute in the local AMEZ church. That a man with such strong prospects as Clinton would gamble his church career on Florida service seemed to promise glorious victories to come. The conference benefited as well from the fact that he possessed talents as a fine preacher. "It would be useless for me to attempt to describe the learned and easy manner in which the young divine addressed his audience," one Pensacola man recorded. "From the time that he arose until he took his seat nearly every eye was fixed upon him and his sermon was listened to with profound admiration."[43]

Jones neared the end of his tenure with feelings of satisfaction at the accomplishments of a few years. "Florida Conference presents a most cheering aspect," he informed delegates at the Eighteenth Quadrennial Session in New Bern, North Carolina, in May, "and its members are fully aroused in the interest of Zion." He added, "Hopeful progress has been made there also in new church buildings and new organizations, especially in the central and southern portions of that state."[44]

Despite the bishop's optimism, one series of events that occurred during the spring and summer of 1888 involving Jones, among others, raised a troubling question about what direction Florida's AMEZ Conference actually would take. With organic union between the AME and AMEZ churches again surfacing as a major issue for consideration, Jones found himself in a battle of words with the premier AME preacher in Florida, George W. Witherspoon. The exact nature of the quarrel has not come down to us, but, when it arose in April, Witherspoon still sat on Pensacola's city council and served as an AME presiding elder. Subsequent events hint that Jones singled out Witherspoon as emblematic of corruption within the black clergy, especially as the issue involved the participation of ministers in sinful conduct such as accepting political appointments and attending public entertainments. "*The Times* [a Pensacola newspaper] for the past two weeks has been filled with the Jones-Witherspoon controversy," the *New York Age* reported in early June. "In the last issue Mr. Peter Darley, the West End school teacher and son of the Rev. Thomas Darley of the A.M.E. Zion Church, came to Bishop Jones' defense in a lengthy letter."[45]

By then Jones had departed the state and surrendered his authority as bishop of Florida, but the controversy refused to die. F. A. Clinton attempted to quell the furor by extending a friendly hand of fellowship to Witherspoon, appearing with him at local functions such as the June cornerstone laying of Pensacola's Mt. Olive Baptist Church. Within days, though, "the noted negro evangelist" W. H. Sherwood, a former AME minister, arrived to aid Talbot Chapel's pastor in a revival. The fiery preacher stayed in town for months, carping at the sinful path taken by the AME Church and many of its clergymen. "[He] has knocked evil and evil-doers spasm-wise; whoever has fallen under his hammer has been beaten to cinders, and whatever has placed itself before him that assumes the complexion of sin has been swept away like chaff before a cyclone," one Pensacola clergyman related. Sherwood especially denounced "dancing, card-playing, and theatre going." In August he turned his guns on Witherspoon, pointing out the presiding elder's practice of attending the theater and insisting "if I was the Bishop I would kick him out." Sherwood thereupon piled even more charges upon his victim. They included "playing croquet, checkers, casino, visiting the opera, the theater, the circus, and saloons." Witherspoon countered with ferocious attacks of his own.[46]

The exchanges left Pensacola's black religious community badly divided and embittered, with both AME and AMEZ losing respect and credibility. Would this type of conflict and its disillusioning fallout dominate the AMEZ future in Florida, or would a different bishop take the church on a happier course? Months passed as other events bedeviled the state and brought misery and loss. Meanwhile, AMEZ ministers and members waited, anticipating hopefully the coming of a new leader.

6

BISHOP LOMAX AND THE GOSPEL HORSE, 1888–1893

———•◦•———

our hearts were made
to burn within us

For many years prior to the late 1880s, ministers and members of the Florida AMEZ Conference had longed for farsighted, energetic leadership that would guide the denomination to stability and growth. While Bishops John J. Moore and Singleton T. W. Jones had initiated processes during the middle years of the 1880s that promised a bright future of the kind desired, both men suffered from poor health and soon reached the limits of their ability to press Florida forward. Not until 1888 did the national church finally match the right man with the job. Once it did, the Florida church speedily reached out to grasp the chance for its long-awaited day in the sun.

The man who would dominate Florida church affairs in the late 1880s and for much of the 1890s was Bishop Thomas Henry Lomax. Born near Fayetteville, North Carolina, on January 15, 1832, Lomax boasted ties of a very distinguished nature. His grandfather William Lomax, a "native of the French Colony in Africa," had come to the United States in the 1770s along with the Marquis de Lafayette to fight in the American Revolution. Following the peace, William, now an honored veteran, settled in the Tarheel State where he joined the Methodist Church. His son Enoch later married Rachel Hammons, the daughter of Isaac and Dicy Hammons. The young couple then launched a large family of their own. Thomas Henry arrived as their seventh son. His future mentor, James Walker Hood, offered details of Lomax's younger days. "He is a self-educated man, comparatively speaking," Hood observed. "When quite a youth he employed himself in grubbing stumps at night to procure funds for his night schooling; in this way he learned to write, read, and cipher before the [Civil] war." Hood added in the mid-1890s, "From that time until now he has been a hard student." By trade a brick mason, Lomax early displayed skills as a businessman that led him as an adult to be considered "very wealthy and full of business."[1]

A strong head for business and a penchant for making money may have marked Lomax's adulthood, but those traits never led him to lose touch with the needs of those less fortunate or to a pursuit of worldly pleasure in lieu of spiritual fulfillment. He had joined the Methodist Church (Methodist Episcopal Church, South) by 1848 and acted as a class leader within two years thereafter. After Superintendent Joseph J. Clinton dispatched James Walker Hood to North Carolina in 1864 to help pioneer the AMEZ Church in the South, Lomax quickly fell under his influence. By 1867 Lomax had left the school that he then was conducting to accept from Hood a license to preach. It took a mere nine years for Lomax, with Hood's strong backing, to achieve election as the society's first southern-born bishop. The next twelve years saw him working successfully in Canada, Texas, Alabama, Louisiana, California, Missouri, Georgia, and South Carolina. The Eighteenth Quadrennial Conference, held at New Bern, North Carolina, in May 1888 presented Florida to the now-experienced bishop for inclusion in his Fifth Episcopal District.[2]

Although Lomax could claim fifty-six hard-lived years by the time he became bishop of Florida, he remained a man of high energy with a huge capacity for work and definite ideas about how to go about that work. He possessed remarkable gifts for assessing talents and needs and for nurturing personnel. "Bishop Lomax . . . is familiar with every part of the work, and thoroughly acquainted with all of his men; and therefore knows how to fit the man to the place," a Florida churchman commented in 1893. "This ability on the part of the Bishop has been the secret of his success," he continued. The churchman then added:

> He plainly and emphatically tells his men that each man must make his own appointment. If a pastor succeeds in a small appointment he gives evidence that he can succeed in a larger one and in due time will be promoted. If a man fails in a small appointment, he shows he lacks ability to improve a larger one and must needs wait for promotion until he has shown by his faithfulness over a few things his ability to be ruler over many. This is Bishop Lomax's idea about appointing men, and one which we believe should be carried out by every Bishop.[3]

Part of Lomax's genius involved the fact that he did not limit himself to men in staffing his churchly army. "The Bishop seems to have outstripped most of his colleagues in the plan of utilizing the help of mission-ary workers among the sisters . . . ," the man explained further. "This band of faithful women which he sent out brought in [substantial funds] which aided materially in meeting conference expenses, and relieved two churches that were in very embarrassing circumstances." He went on, "The force of workers in this new role was increased and all seemed delighted to know that they could do a work that was of such valuable help and felt much encouraged at the commendation which bishop and ministers alike be-stowed upon them."[4]

An additional point concerning Bishop Lomax, one that contributed greatly to his Florida successes, involved his personality. By way of con-text, at the time Lomax arrived in Florida the AME Church was reeling from troubling divisions of several kinds, but one of the most important dealt with the distance that had developed between Bishop Daniel A. Payne and his leadership cadre on the one hand and poor preachers and congrega-tion members on the other. To many, the higher-ups—who were increas-ingly college-educated—came to be considered "black princes" and were resented as such. Lomax, however, always retained the common touch and evidenced a determination to visit every region and every church under his charge, not only to inspire his preachers but also to offer friendship and comfort to the members of his flock. The church's people responded imme-diately, allowing Lomax to overcome obstacles by sharing enthusiasm. As one of his ministers commented, "Bishop Lomax is on deck now, and the outlook is truly encouraging."[5]

Florida's AMEZ family required the skills that the new bishop brought to the state in late 1888 far more even than had been anticipated, because his tenure began amid a crisis. The yellow fever plague that had ravaged much of coastal Florida in 1887 returned in 1888 to spread death far and wide. Tampa and Pensacola again suffered, but the yellow jack reached new targets as well. Talbot Chapel's Franklin A. Clinton and his family suffered along with the rest. The threat likely contributed to his decision that fall to leave for a ministry in Texas. Jacksonville's S. L. McDonald similarly fought for his life. "The yellow fever came and put my work to an end," he later reported, "and came very near putting an end to me." As had become a mainstay of the Zion ministry, the church reached out to the community during the time of trial. At Pensacola, for example, Elders Thomas Darley, F. A. Clinton, Israel Furby, Oscar V. Jackson, J. W. Bowen, and Joseph Len-nox joined Deacons Simon Brown and Joshua Edwards to sponsor a huge camp meeting at a place considered safe from the disease. "When the trumpeters of the Lord commenced to blow, I heard a mighty rumbling in his camp, some crying save me Jesus, others save Lord or I perish; and again here Lord I give myself to thee 'tis all that I can do," Darley recorded, "and about our second week of battle some 75 or 80 souls were singing thank God Almighty I am free at last." The presiding elder concluded, "All of these I am proud to say enlisted under the banner of Zion with few exceptions."[6]

Florida offered Lomax meaningful support to overcome whatever obstacles he faced, however. In the regions of greatest concern to him, the economy boomed. West Florida's timber industry thrived as "bonanza era" prosperity created jobs, fed payrolls, and spurred the growth of towns old and new. Even more significantly, peninsular settlement trends curved ever-upward in the wake of railroad construction and land sales at bargain prices. Added to the equation, the late 1880s saw the beginnings of commercial exploitation of vast phosphate deposits. As news spread of finds, a veritable gold-rush mentality brought hordes of newcomers to gamble that their piece of earthly heaven lay awaiting. "Gone Wild on Phosphates," an 1890 headline screamed. "Florida Sand Now Commanding Fabulous Prices."[7]

As it happened, Lomax became a firsthand witness to the phosphate industry boom when he visited the very region where its impact came most profoundly. This happened because the 1888 Florida Conference had mandated—likely owing to Elder Joseph Sexton's influence—that its next meeting take place at the Polk County seat of Bartow, where the Star of Zion Church recently had been established close to the site of Sexton's boyhood home and the missionary churches he had founded in 1868. Once at the town in February 1889, Lomax and his fellow churchmen perceived possibilities for the area and the race.[8]

Those possibilities, in fact, astounded the clergymen. Warren C. Vesta attempted to offer a sense of the wonder the men felt as they beheld the Polk County scene during those February days at the decade's close. In doing so the Florida Conference pioneer advised the readers of the church newspaper *The Star of Zion* to look southward. "This indeed is the most favorable as well as the most convenient country for the poor man to come and make his home," Vesta began. He continued:

> Here land is cheap, the climate is mild and December is as pleasant as May. The country is lately being settled up, and those who rush in now, will come up with the country. The land abounds with lakes, creeks and rivers, whose waters are thronged with all kind of fish. The forest is rich with game of most any kind you wish, so that living is

cheap and easy. Railroads are running in most every direction and more are being constructed. Truck farming and fruit growing are being carried on with very successful results. . . . Bartow is the place for our people to go to as fast as they can, as that County, which is Polk, as well as [De Soto], the adjacent County, abounds with phosphate mines. . . . The white people of the section are kind and friendly to the colored people, wishing them to emmigrate and come among them. A good number are already there, but not enough to supply the demands of them.

Vesta concluded, "It is passing strange how our people can content themselves in the States of Georgia, South Carolina and North Carolina working for $6 to $10 per month when the happy gates of golden opportunities stand open night and day in South Florida, where they can come and build themselves up and accumulate something to leave their children when they have gone to the other world."[9]

Bishop Lomax desired to take some time to get better acquainted with his charge before deciding exactly how the church should take advantage of the magnificent opportunities, but he moved nonetheless at the Bartow conference to set the stage for further action by an administrative reorganization. The conference had been divided for several years into two districts, both under the supervision of Presiding Elder Thomas H. Darley at Pensacola. Now, Lomax put teeth into the arrangement by affording each district a more distinct authority. He accomplished that purpose by naming a presiding elder in each case. Darley stepped into the position of conference steward, while retaining the pastorate of Pensacola's Talbot Chapel. For the new First District, headquartered at the same town, Lomax placed S. L. McDonald in charge. Meanwhile, the bishop transferred Joseph Sexton back from Nassau to Key West and named him presiding elder of the Second (or South Florida) District. Lomax specifically included authority over the Nassau District (what remained of the old Bahamas Conference) for Sexton, with local responsibility seconded to David Thomas.[10]

Although the entire Florida Conference then consisted of but fifteen elders and five deacons, and all of peninsular Florida below Jacksonville contained only six AMEZ churches, Lomax delayed the beginning of any organized outreach effort. Two exceptions require mention. First, he allowed Pastor Vesta at Key West's Cornish Chapel to launch a mission to the island's Cuban community under Deacon B. B. Bonner. Also, he permitted Elder W. A. Bain at Bartow to respond to a request from two AMEZ members—then living at Orange Bend in Lake County but formerly of

Lancaster, South Carolina—to organize a congregation for them and one friend, W. J. Barrett. W. J. Sanders and his wife, A. B. Sanders, who had made the request, took on responsibility for the charge. W. J. Sanders acted at first as local preacher, launching a successful ministerial career within the AMEZ fold. The Orange Bend congregation grew slowly, but it would serve as a base for expansion in the fast-growing central peninsula.[11]

In the aftermath of the Bartow conference, the bishop commenced the travels that would allow him to get to know his charge and its people with visits to Tampa and Key West. Impressed with Tampa, he, Darley, and Vesta looked upon the city as "destined to be the Chicago of the South." At Key West, Florida's largest city, Lomax elevated his prevailing state of delight. Key West entranced him. Cornish Chapel member Charles F. Dupont had just taken office as sheriff, with James Dean assuming the county judgeship. Frank Adams presided as tax assessor, with several black men holding seats on the board of aldermen. Lemuel W. Livingston of the Douglass School recently had penned an article for the *New York Age*, one that Lomax almost certainly had seen, in which he insisted that "the freest town in the South" could be found on the island. "There are no attempts at bulldozing and intimidation during campaigns and at elections here," Livingston wrote. "No Negroes are murdered here in cold blood, and there are no gross miscarriages of justice against them as is so frequently seen throughout the South, to her everlasting shame and disgrace. In public places colored people experience better treatment than they get in Washington, and Washington is far ahead of other Southern states." Livingston concluded, "For this state of affairs both the colored and white people are entitled to credit." As Vesta put it, "Here the Bishop met with objects that it had not been his pleasure to see before, I mean curious and strange scenes."[12]

At the island city Lomax shared with Darley the conference steward's old pulpit with results that offer a textbook example of Lomax's impact on local congregations and in local communities, particularly the bishop's ability to motivate women to greater efforts on the church's behalf. "Space will not allow me to detail what he said," Vesta related, "but let me tell you [that he] carried the church out and stood her on the Sea of Glass and you might imagine what grandeur she appeared." He then picked up the story at the sermon's conclusion. "It might be truly said that the Bishop was carried out in the spirit in the Lord's day," he began. "The sermon had the effect to [so] familiarize the Bishop to the people that on Monday night the officers and teachers of the Sabbath School made up a surprise party for the Bishop [and] presented to him sweet songs and melodies, led by Mrs. Lela Bryant, Mary McGee, Mary Rodgers, Flora Harris, Easter Vickers, Sarah Matthews, Ellen Papall, Tenner Flemming, Matilda Hannibal, Celia Barten, Sarah Shavers, Susan Ambriste, Rosa Harris, Anna Bryant, Delia Joseph, Anna Roberts, Mary Tynes, Susan Matthews, Mrs. Carolina Portlock, Amelia McGee, Mary E. Roberts, Misses Elizabeth Kelly, James A. Hannibal, the superintendent of the Sunday School, Isaac Murry, Samuel Hannibal, William Mickens, Alfred Bustian, Anthony Bronson, Alex Gabriel, Rev. [R. W.] Butler, of the A.M.E. Church, Rev. [S. A.] Huger of the M. E. Church, Dr. Livingstone, principal of the public school, Rev. T. Darley and wife, your writer and wife, and many others."[13]

The series of events not only inspirited Cornish's women leaders, they also cemented relationships that served Lomax as a platform for the development of his plans. This eventuality began to grow apparent within days, as Darley, Vesta, and Key West's powerful and influential black leaders commenced lining up behind the new bishop. "I like to forgot to mention the grand entertainment given by the officers of the church for the enjoyment of the Bishop," Vesta recounted. "Rev. T. Darley and myself were invited on Tuesday night to escort the Bishop to the nice two story building, owned by Mr. Frank Shavers," he explained further. "Here we were conducted upstairs where we found the table loaded down with the delicacies of the season," Vesta added. "By request of the trustees and leaders here we met the faces of the officials," he concluded. "We took our seats and engaged in the history of the past, meditated on that of the present and then joined in and sung one of Zion's sweet songs, and like the Paul of old, we all bowed and the Bishop invoked the throne of grace, after which we enjoyed the goodies."[14]

One of the goodies that surfaced at the session likely concerned the idea of separating the church in South Florida and the Bahama Islands from direct ties to the panhandle congregations and allowing the church there to grow along with the developing semitropical region. As the year proceeded and the bishop grew ever-more familiar with his Florida church, he, too, came to embrace the suggestion. Decades of conservative practice and chronic funding problems had left West Florida leaders timid about expansion. The passionate oratory of AMEZ evangelist W. H. Sherwood and its fallout, as discussed in chapter 5, also had left them divided, wary, and questioning the church's direction. In the circumstances Lomax may have come to see that the desires of South Florida contained within them a solution to panhandle maladies. If he pushed creation of a new conference, he could set the two Florida bodies in healthy competition with one another. Before he could act, of course, he needed to resolve the matter of Sherwood. Details of what transpired between the bishop and the preacher remain unavailable, but records reveal that in December Sherwood presented his credentials to the Florida AME Conference annual meeting and petitioned successfully for admission on trial to its clergy.[15]

Soon thereafter, Lomax revealed his plans. On February 12, 1890, the twenty-first session of the Florida Annual AMEZ Conference convened at Clinton Chapel, Pensacola, amid rumors of important developments pending. Reportedly, "nearly every delegate was found present." The bishop must have anticipated substantial resistance from some West Florida preachers and laymen. As a result and among others, he had brought with him Alabama's Wilbur G. Strong for support, and the old warhorse of pioneer days in the meeting's opening hours aided in perfecting conference organization in the manner desired. That night Lomax scheduled Joseph Sexton to preach on the topic "My time is in thy hands," intended to instruct those present on "the duties of ministers and members." It was, Presiding Elder S. L. McDonald commented, "one of the grandest efforts of his life." For four days thereafter speaker after speaker, many of them imported from Alabama where conference division had occurred years before, delivered "lively" addresses following Sexton's lead.[16]

On Monday, February 18, Lomax finally came to the point everyone had awaited. Now, while echoing Sexton's earlier message, he informed those gathered that he intended for the church to set out boldly with a renewed spirit and firmer sense of direction. "He took up the work of the ministry, in which he gave such noble instruction that the conference was made to feel greatly benefitted," McDonald commented, "for he told what a minister must be to make a success." The elder continued: "Then talking of things in general, taking in the Negro Problem, and solved it in God's way." At that point Joseph Sexton stood and moved the division of the conference. The act quickly stirred "a lively debate," but the gathering eventually concurred with the bishop's desire by "set[ting] off another conference called the South Florida conference, from Jacksonville to Key West, leaving Jacksonville in the Western district." Lomax in short order named Warren C. Vesta as steward for South Florida with Thomas H. Darley continuing to occupy the position in West Florida. McDonald concluded, "This was said to be the finest conference ever held in Florida."[17]

Assuming that Bishop Lomax's plans were meant to create healthy competition as a spur to church outreach, they produced immediate results. The listless West Florida church sprang to life in an unparalleled fashion. First District Presiding Elder S. L. McDonald took the lead. "I have traveled over a great deal of the state this year where there never was a Zion preacher known," he reported in early 1891. "From River Junction to Jacksonville . . . ," he added, "and not a Zion church in all the plains." Interestingly, in line with the bishop's emphasis on incorporation of women into church ministries, McDonald seems to have relied upon a Mrs. L. Bradley to aid his efforts. In any event, AMEZ preachers, some brought in from Alabama and others recruited locally, claimed outposts during the year in Washington County at Caryville (New Hope), in present-day Okaloosa County at Milligan, and in Walton at Mossy Head and Point Washington (Thomas' Chapel). Two additional chapels (Pine Barren and Pine Orchard) now graced Escambia County, and a mission church operated in Duval County outside Jacksonville. One report claimed that, by year's end, the district contained twenty-three congregations with a total of 6,246 members.[18]

South Florida determined not to be left behind. Assuaging an embarrassing setback of previous years, its leaders unfurled the AMEZ banner once more in the Central Florida county of Alachua. The first location for church building appears to have been at Orange Heights, where a lot had been secured by August. In October, Elder B. F. Stevens also organized at Gainesville, where the congregation eventually came to be known as Harris Chapel. A few miles to the south at Evinston in Marion County, Jones Chapel AMEZ Church emerged. From Orange Bend in Lake County, the AMEZ advocates reached out, as well, to the county seat of Leesburg and westward to Sanford. At Tampa they ventured into the Cuban, Spanish, and Italian cigar community of Ybor City. Quickly, church reports disclosed that 8,545 members belonged to the future South Florida Conference. This figure cannot be independently substantiated, however. Congregations claimed for Manatee, Orange, Osceola, St. Johns, and Putnam counties but not otherwise reported apparently represented optimistic plans rather than hard facts.[19]

Optimism certainly marked the day when the South Florida Conference organized at Cornish Chapel on January 14, 1891. "The Presiding Elder and some of the pastors made their reports which were very good, showing improvements on all the lines," conference reporter J. M. Sims recorded, "that that year's time had been properly employed and great good had been accomplished." Elder Sexton, Bishop Lomax, and others fanned the fires of excitement. Lomax chose as his principal text "I am doing a great work so that I cannot come down." Of the message Sims observed, "We need not say that he did well for this he never fails to do, but we can say for him that he mastered the subject to the satisfaction of his audience." Sims added, "May he live long to preach the gospel." The bishop's initial appointments for the South Florida Conference were Joseph Sexton, presiding elder; W C. Vesta, Key West station; G. W. Maize, Tampa station; James R. Harris, Sanford station; W. A. Bain, Kissimmee; R. R. Frederick, Simmons Hammock; W. J. Sanders, Bartow; James D. Dudley, Ybor City; A. L. Higgs, Key West mission; H. E. Jones, Nassau; D. A. Forbes, Homeland; R. W. Ballard, Gainesville; J. H. Jordan, Evinston; and J. M. Sims, Leesburg.[20]

One month afterward but with the same atmosphere prevailing, the reworked Florida Conference (already being called the West Florida Conference by some) gathered at Milton. Its thirty members far overshadowed the thirteen who had assembled in January at Cornish Chapel. Having helped to midwife Florida's new organizational structure, Thomas H. Darley stepped down as conference steward to enjoy a well-earned rest and to aid in reviving the troubled St. Lukes Church at Jacksonville. Otherwise, the sessions proceeded smoothly. "A very pleasant and harmonious experience," concluded one observer. The presiding elder summed up the sense of the gathering in words written prior to its opening ceremonies. "Many are the cheering reports from the brethren throughout the connection for Zion, and if Florida is behind we are coming to the front," S. L. McDonald asserted. "Look for us after awhile; the South Florida boys are making rapid strides building churches, gathering in members and lifting the flag of Zion, with Elder [Joseph] Sexton as P. E. and a worker for good church government and a self-made man." He added, "The Florida conference is moving slowly on, and we are striving by the help of God to get to the mark of the high calling."[21]

Personnel matters naturally constituted a significant portion of the business conducted. Of note, veteran Oscar V. Jackson accepted transfer to the South Florida Conference for assignment at Nassau. Otherwise, the first appointments for the redrawn Florida Conference included S. L. McDonald, presiding elder; W. H. Smith, Pensacola station; Israel Furby, Tanyard Church and Warrington; Henry Taylor, Edwards Chapel, Escambia; M. S. Arnold, Millview and Pine Orchard; B. F. Stevens, Milton and Blackwater (Bagdad); W. A. Neal, Thompson Chapel and Point Washington; to be supplied, Marianna, Cottondale, and Cypress; Alex Robinson, Jacksonville station; Joshua Edwards, Pensacola mission; Louis Johnson, Caryville, Mossy Head, and Lake De Funiak; Simon Brown, Powelton and

Muscogee; J. L. Cook, Pine Barren mission; Alfred Ponder, Redding and Hancox; Wilson Perry, Live Oak mission; and G. G. Hornsby, Milligan. Churches at Tallahassee, Monticello, and Lake City were "to be supplied," when possible.[22]

As the appointments suggest, the Florida Conference anticipated further expansion in 1891 while the South Florida Conference intended to use the time to consolidate gains. This is exactly what happened. New panhandle churches grew at several locations although none appear to have arisen in the peninsula. Cypress in Jackson County numbered among new spots, as did Marianna. Thompson Chapel opened in Walton with missionary work conducted through the old North Florida heartland of the AME Church. That body had continued to experience disenchantment and waning enthusiasm among many of its members, and the Zion leadership figured to take advantage if it could. Accordingly, the county seats of Monticello (Jefferson), Lake City (Columbia), and Live Oak (Suwannee) greeted AMEZ preachers on what amounted to exploratory forays. Perhaps offering the greatest opportunity and prestige, the denomination established Pleasant Valley Church at the state capital of Tallahassee.[23]

Suffice it to say that the experiences of these years brought elation to Zion adherents in both conferences. Men who were previously calm and conservative emerged as firebrands for God. Milton's Priscilla Parren conveyed a sense of the changeover in describing her pastor's efforts on one occasion in 1891 at Isaiah Chapel. B. F. Stevens, through a series of sermons during Sabbath services, reached ever-greater peaks of religious intensity. "He rode out on the Gospel horse and our hearts were made to burn within us," she declared. "God bless our pastor and may he live long to preach the gospel." Record-breaking crowds began to frequent church gatherings in both conferences. Up to 1,200 persons at a time now crowded into Talbot Chapel, to offer one example.[24]

Revivals touched even greater numbers. Of one series of such events held at Pensacola, Talbot Chapel's pastor W. H. Smith noted, "These meetings have been largely attended during the day at each service and at night we had no church in the city large enough to accommodate the anxious crowds coming to hear this message of God." He added in conclusion: "Nightly we've seen hundreds holding up their hands and some standing asking for prayers. While few have been captured outright from sin and satan (15 or 20), we feel safe to say the good done among our people cannot be estimated, and probably will not be known until the flooded light of eternity shall roll the mist away and reveal the truth."[25]

Having come so far, the Florida conferences then ran upon the shoals of a serious problem. There simply were not enough preachers, ordained or otherwise, available from any source sufficient to fill any more new pulpits. "If I can only get the brethren with the missionary spirit we can plant Zion all through Middle Florida," S. L. McDonald already had moaned in early 1891. This lack of available talent may account for the South Florida Conference's decision that year not to expand its reach. So far as is known, only one church premiered in either conference the following year. This was St. Lukes of Pensacola, and its sanctuary did not rise until 1893.[26]

The shortage encouraged the advancement of women into the pulpit. As mentioned earlier and in line with Bishop Lomax's preferences, women had begun to take an ever-more active role in Florida church affairs. This included missionary work and, to a very limited extent, preaching. They did so in the early 1890s, it should be emphasized, without benefit of ordination. The first such action by an AMEZ conference did not occur until 1894 when Bishop James Walker Hood ordained Julia Foote a deacon of the New York Annual Conference, although, even at that late date, the act placed Zion in the forefront of efforts to encourage ministries by women. In Florida, as noted, Mrs. L. Bradley apparently assisted Presiding Elder McDonald in 1891. By the next year the Florida Conference had designated Mary V. Anderson as official conference missionary and placed her in charge of the Jacksonville mission. The minutes from the 1892 annual meeting noted, "Sister Mary Anderson, conference missionary, offered petitions to a throne of mercy, asking for wisdom upon the executive head, and strength to the members of the conference that their work may be pleasing to God and beneficial to man." Born in Mississippi in February 1863 and widowed during the 1880s, Anderson supported herself as a grocer, at least in later years. After one year at Jacksonville, though, she seemingly took a five-year hiatus from the ministry. She would return to it, quite successfully as will be seen, just before the end of the century.[27]

Anderson's departure opened the door for the designation in 1893 of another woman, Mary Frances Green, as her replacement. The wife of George B. Green of Pensacola, Mary Green had been born in Alabama about 1863. "Mrs. Mary Francis Green, noted for her originality and easy flow of language in public recitation and debate, who was complimented so highly by the Editor of The Star [of Zion] as Zion's gifted elocutionist and a lady of whom the race may well be proud; returned from Milton, Fla., where she has been in constant attendance at the bedside of an aged and afflicted mother," a Pensacola colleague expressed in the *Star of Zion*'s pages during the spring of 1893. "Mrs. Green is now making arrangements for an extended tour in the interest of the missionary department of our church."[28]

Surviving records fail to reveal if Green's appointment lasted beyond 1894, but her continued involvement in church affairs appears clear. She attended the Twentieth Quadrennial Conference and earned praise for her participation. "Among the lay delegates who sat in the General Conference of 1896 and participated actively and helpfully in its deliberations was Mrs. Mary Francis Green, of Pensacola, Florida," the necrology of the 1900 quadrennial session observed. "Some of us present remember her familiar face and call to mind her clear voice and forceful words as she stood upon the floor of State Street Church, Mobile, Alabama, to utter sentiments which were shared by a majority of those who composed the great General Conference of 1896." The item added: "She, too, has laid down the cross and taken up the crown. Truly has the poet said: 'Death moves on every passing breeze and lurks in every flower.'"[29]

The important contributions of Bradley, Anderson, and Green notwithstanding, the Florida churches found themselves looking high and low for suitable preachers. Other conferences naturally offered themselves as recruiting territories for Lomax and his Florida colleagues. The Alabama jurisdictions long had supplied reinforcements for the Florida clergy, and the time-tested tradition proved itself again. Thus, in 1893 Harmon McKinney joined the Florida Conference from West Alabama. Of greater significance, the renowned Wilbur G. Strong had arrived from the same state the previous year to fill the South Florida pulpit at Cornish Chapel. Such contributions helped, but they did not begin to fill the need. So, leaders now cast their nets further afield. The South Florida Conference sent in 1892 to South Carolina for S. W. Cunningham, for instance. Its parent conference reached as far as Tennessee the next year for E. J. Carter.[30]

A separate source, the clergy of other churches, proved both helpful and controversial. As discussed in chapter 5, the sagging fortunes of Florida's AME Church had led beginning in the mid-1880s to a slow migration from that denomination to Zion. This movement kept up in the 1890s, gifting AMEZ conferences with men such as M. A. Sturkes and A. Jackson. Given the high standards of behavior to which AME clergymen then were being held, crossovers came at times with the baggage of charges hanging over their heads. This fact did not sit well with some AMEZ veterans. "Men are continually coming to us from our sister churches, and are looked upon as being gentlemen, when they could not stay in their own church on account of their misdeeds," B. F. Stevens explained. "They are recommended by some of the ministers and are received and given appointments, and if they don't get the best Zion has in that conference, they will say that they are going to quit," he continued. "Now I say that they ought to be showed the place the carpenter cut, and if he did not get, take him up and throw him out, for they will set the connection on fire."[31]

The specific object of Stevens's ire is not otherwise identified, but the most controversial crossover of the early 1890s was and is known very well. Joseph Newman Clinton, another of Bishop J. J. Clinton's sons, was born at Pittsburgh on November 19, 1854. A precocious young man, he graduated from Lincoln University by age nineteen. Clinton then taught at Philadelphia for three years before relocating to Gainesville, Florida, in 1876 where a government land office job and a political career awaited him. He held local office honorably at Gainesville, represented Alachua County in the Florida House of Representatives during its 1885 session, and stood out through the 1880s as a Republican Party stalwart. Clinton also lived at Pensacola in the late 1880s while he served there as an inspector of customs. He joined the AME clergy about the same time. His ordination as a deacon followed in 1891.[32]

While Joe Clinton had favored the AME Church with his talents (no AMEZ church had operated at Gainesville during his residence there), he soon saw that the fortunes of the times and his personal connections best lent themselves to AMEZ service. Accordingly, within months after his ordination he contacted Lomax concerning possibilities. The bishop responded by inviting Clinton to serve beginning in February 1892 as presiding elder of the Florida Conference's Pensacola District. Among those infuriated by the dramatic action was Clinton's immediate predecessor, S. L. McDonald. That longtime clergyman not only suffered deposition but was transferred to Jacksonville to clean up the shambles of the church there, problems that had persisted during his watch as presiding elder. If B. F. Stevens's comments, quoted above, concerned the Clinton crossover, the new presiding elder's political activities and the favoritism evidenced by the appointment—rather than any moral charge—likely constituted the grounds for criticism and disapproval.[33]

The entire question of ministerial recruitment would not have posed so great a problem in a state with an ever-increasing pool of talented young men had the church been able to organize a system for proper training. Typical AMEZ efforts through the early 1890s were touched upon in an 1891 report by Warren C. Vesta regarding neophyte A. L. Higgs. Following Presiding Elder Joseph Sexton's praise for Higgs's work in the *Star of*

Zion's columns, Vesta amplified the words of his longtime colleague in a telling manner. "Referring to the work on this island, he said Key West is still marching on to victory under the leadership of Rev. A. L. Higgs," he first observed. Vesta then continued, "The assertion . . . refers to a very energetic young preacher, we are trying to rear up in this city." He concluded, "He was ordained a deacon last session of the conference, and has charge of the mission work of this city, and so far is doing a good work, adding to his charge weekly, and if continued will soon be another strong Zion church on this island."[34]

Other denominations had not been slow to recognize the need for systematic training for its clergy recruits, and they were not alone in offering solid educational foundations for the state's promising African American students. The Baptists had acted by the early 1880s with the establishment of Live Oak's Florida Institute, and by late in the decade the AME Church after several frustrated attempts had addressed the same concerns with the opening of Jacksonville's Florida Normal and Divinity High School (as of 1891, Edward Waters College). Other Jacksonville facilities such as the ME Church–sponsored Cookman Institute (a forerunner of Bethune-Cookman College) also created praiseworthy opportunities for schooling. Plus, in 1887 the State Normal College for Colored Students (now Florida Agricultural and Mechanical University) had opened its doors as Florida's first public institution for higher education of African Americans.[35]

Denominational pride and the need for specialized recruitment, nurturing, and training called for AMEZ educational initiatives, but listless leadership and constant financial shortages had forestalled progress through the 1880s. Not that many church advocates did not recognize the need. In 1891 S. L. McDonald expressed what many churchmen thought. "Educational matters are becoming very interesting in Fla.," he commented. "Several graduates have been turned out from the schools in the city of Jacksonville, and some from the Normal School at Tallahassee." McDonald then turned directly to his concern. "I am sorry to say that very few . . . are Zionites," he began. "Zion must have a high school, and Zion will have a high school; this we pray for, hope for and will have, God being our helper."[36]

Following the disappointing failure of the 1887 College Hill proposal at Tampa, momentum began building in 1890 for a denominational high school. That July the West Florida District considered a proposal to "build a high school in Pensacola, Fla., having at its head as professors and teachers some of Zion's sons and daughters." Bishop Lomax, conference steward

Darley, South Florida presiding elder Sexton, and their associate Warren C. Vesta had other ideas. They had become convinced that Bartow and Polk County, then at the height of the phosphate boom, offered Zion more potential than did any comparable place in the state. In September 1890 Lomax, Darley, and Vesta carried their enthusiasm to the point of buying a large tract of Bartow land for residential development. They then successfully encouraged the South Florida Conference in January 1891 to call for a joint effort with the Florida Conference in furtherance of a high school. The latter body reluctantly concurred in February. The plan called for a committee to decide upon location. It first met at Tampa in July and consisted of Darley, as chairman, with Sexton, Vesta, S. L. McDonald, and George W. Maize. Not too surprisingly, they accepted the bishop's offer to donate Bartow lots for the school and specified that town as the institution's site. McDonald and Sexton, as presiding elders, accepted responsibility to lead fund-raising efforts. Meanwhile, excitement built that the AMEZ Church soon would boast its own institution of higher learning.[37]

All things considered, in 1892 and 1893 church fathers (and mothers) found much cause for celebration. By the creation of the South Florida Conference, Zion finally had trumped Bethel (its South Florida Conference would not organize until 1893). Spectacular growth had added to the cheer. By 1892, for instance, the fifteen-member South Florida Conference had grown to forty-three. The conference claimed a solid fifteen hundred adult members and ordained twenty-two new preachers to minister to them. That year both conferences split into presiding elder districts. Joseph Newman Clinton, as mentioned, headed the (West) Florida Conference's Pensacola District, with M. A. Sturkes presiding over its Jacksonville counterpart. The South Florida Conference acted similarly, creating a missionary district with the presiding eldership to be filled later and leaving Joseph Sexton in charge of the remainder. Later the same year a proud bishop could report nineteen circuits and stations in the Florida Conference and twenty-five in the South Florida. "The general condition of the work is good," he proclaimed.[38]

Spirits remained high when the 1893 annual meetings rolled around. Forty-five ministers now worked the South Florida Conference, including twenty-one elders, sixteen deacons, and eight traveling preachers. Twelve new churches had been built since 1890, plus extensive reconstruction at Cornish Chapel and Mt. Sinai. The twenty-fourth session of the Florida Conference likewise glowed with satisfaction, even though the bishop found it necessary to chide his male preachers on missing fund-raising goals. "He warned the brethren that they must either show themselves adequate to the demands of their position or stand aside and let the willing and efficient sisters come in and do the work," an onlooker recorded. The tone overall sounded pleasant, though, as delegates departed with memories of the "excellent singing" by visiting clergyman James H. Manley with the conference choir "which delighted large audiences which thronged the church at evening's services."[39]

Sadly, the happy celebrations were about to end suddenly in calamity. In light of the memories about to take hold, the church's leaders and adherents doubtlessly came to reconsider over time the gentle words that Bishop Lomax, to whom much credit for the successes rightfully belonged, had shared with them early in 1893. "God created us for a great and grand purpose, hence we should be honest in all our dealings with mankind, and strive to get the unity of the Spirit, as no man can succeed without the Spirit of God," he said to them. "Some men go to build churches without the Spirit of God, hence a failure," Lomax continued. "No chain is stronger than its weakest link, and where there is no principle, there can be no religion." The bishop concluded, "Again religion is more important than spirit and a feeling; it should be both spiritual and profitable."[40]

7

AFFLICTIONS OF MAN AND GOD, 1893–1900

——•◦•——

awaiting his command
to swoop down upon us

During the seven-year period that commenced in 1893 and ended at the turn of the century, Florida's AMEZ Church found itself pummeled by forces often difficult to perceive, much less to understand. After a period of remarkable connectional success, the denomination, its churchmen, and its members now stepped aboard a roller coaster of fate. As time passed, visitations into regions of despair only occasionally found themselves punctuated by tantalizing but elusive glimpses of a happier future. Meanwhile, the state, region, and nation evolved in a manner that served to usher out old hopes and promises only to replace them with prospects of a far-less agreeable nature. A generation of leaders grew tired of their struggles, and new men came forward to chart paths in new directions. The hand of man and of God lay heavily upon the AMEZ family.

Omens of the difficult times that lay ahead first showed themselves to Florida's AMEZ adherents during the final two months of 1892. In November Democrat Grover Cleveland recaptured the presidency from Republican Benjamin Harrison, while archconservative lawyer and one-time Confederate officer Henry L. Mitchell of Tampa claimed Florida's highest executive office. Both victories, coming in the face of fevered opposition by the People's (or Populist) and Republican parties, represented clear defeats for national reform and signaled a further turning away by government from the needs and concerns of African Americans. The next month a more significant event for the state's AMEZ followers occurred when the denomination lost its Jacksonville sanctuary because of nonpayment of debt. Deposed presiding elder S. L. McDonald, then pastoring at St. Lukes, opted to move the congregation into humbler surroundings by occupying a nearby structure known as Noah's Ark. The year's last day

brought a local newspaper notice that deepened the church's embarrassment. "The pastor of the Noah's Ark A.M.E. Zion church has been working
very hard repairing the church," it advised, "and not a member or trustee
has given him any help." The item concluded, "May the Lord bless them."[1]

The real troubles began in 1893, though, the year in which Mitchell and
Cleveland took up their offices. First and of paramount importance, the
nation entered one of the most serious economic depressions that it had
experienced. The Panic of 1893, as it is known, officially began on May 4,
but economic tremors had been rippling through the South, especially in
its timber and agricultural industries, for several years. Historian C. Vann
Woodward explained. "The Panic of 1893 did not mark the beginning of
the depression in the South, for there the proportion of failures was exactly the same in 1891 that it was two years later," he observed. "The panic,
however, did bring home to the cities and industrial towns of the South as
never before the distress that had gripped the surrounding countryside for
years."[2]

Florida's towns and small cities, which constituted the AMEZ centers of
activity in the state, previously had resisted the economic malaise, but the
calamity of 1893 hit them hard and its effects lasted for years. Pensacola
and its vicinity, where the church enjoyed its greatest concentration of
congregations, experienced particular damage because an outbreak of yellow fever attacked the community within weeks after the Panic's onset.
"God rolled out one of his war chariots of fever and let slip from it two
arrows in quick succession and quickly hurried two out of our midst and
his chariot stood suspended above our city while the dust of his feet and his
nostrils swung round about it, apparently awaiting his command to swoop
down upon us," Talbot Chapel pastor W. H. Smith recorded. Five thousand
persons reportedly had fled the city by early August. Quarantines soon
isolated those who remained within the plague-ridden territory. Smith,
Thomas H. Darley, and several other AMEZ ministers comforted the sick
and dying. "We are now passing through a crisis of which we have never
witnessed before in all our lives," Smith lamented. "The church is trying to
rally her broken forces and present a stubborn front with God as leader."
He concluded, "We ask the prayers of the whole church."[3]

The yellow fever crisis opened a different kind of sore that had been
festering for more than one year in a manner that rent the church and its
clergy. As mentioned in chapter 6, Bishop Thomas Henry Lomax in 1892
suddenly had named Bishop J. J. Clinton's son Joseph Newman Clinton as
the presiding elder of the Pensacola District. Although a man of distinction

and accomplishment, Clinton at the time had served the ministry but a few years and had attained ordination as a deacon only in 1891. To make matters worse, Clinton stood out as a Republican Party activist in a Florida church that frowned upon direct involvement of its clergy in politics. He also had pursued his call to the ministry not within the family of Zion but within that of Bethel. Further, upon his arrival at Pensacola Clinton had pursued a well-paid position in the U.S. Customs Service. This employment not only took time away from his church responsibilities but, during the yellow fever crisis, it kept him away from Pensacola in the seemingly safer environs of a nearby federal island enclave.[4]

Clinton then compounded his already controversial position within the local church by appearing to be insensitive to the suffering at Pensacola. He did so by informing readers of the church's *Star of Zion* that he had "spent the summer on Santa Rosa Island, better known as the Quarantine Station for the Port of Pensacola, inhaling the gentle Zephyrs sweeping over the placid waters of the Gulf, as they rolled up and dashed themselves into spray, kissing wave after wave upon the sandy beach, receding and returning again making sweet music to break the monotony of the oppressive stillness that surrounded." Many began to believe that, so far as Clinton was concerned, the epidemic's worst aspect involved money. "The depression of business and the yellow fever scare in the month of August," the elder declared, "has materially affected our collections." Some previously wary colleagues turned bitter. "Our presiding elder is over at the quarantine station attending to 'Uncle Sam's' business as he has been for three months and may be there for three more," Pastor Smith angrily commented to the *Star of Zion*. "That is right; 'go it' while you can; while others are getting a slice, take one too." He later would add, "This whole district has suffered and been hindered by want of attention of those who were appointed to overlook it heretofore."[5]

Naturally, Clinton's partisans defended their man and attacked Smith and his allies. B. F. Stevens, then of Milton's Isaiah Chapel, helped to lead the charge. He lambasted Smith for running up a debt at Talbot Chapel and alleged the preacher's shameless self-promotion in promising to erect a brick church for his pastorate if the congregation helped him to retain the post. Talbot member Robert Dudley, among others, challenged Stevens. "Any church in any connection may be proud of him," Dudley insisted of Smith. By late 1894 the feud had broken into the *Star of Zion*'s columns, bringing even greater embarrassment.[6]

The situation grew so out of hand by early 1894 that Bishop Lomax felt constrained to take decisive action. In his mind, Clinton had failed to discharge his new responsibilities properly. On the other hand, the presiding elder was the son of a revered bishop and a leading man in Florida's African American community. Lomax's solution was to separate the man from the problem by transferring Clinton to the South Florida Conference and replacing him as presiding elder of the Pensacola District with W. H. Smith. Not to place too high a premium on Smith's behavior, the bishop also reinstalled Darley as conference steward in order to provide close oversight.[7]

That left Lomax with the question of what to do with Clinton after the transfer. He met the challenge by shifting all of the northeast Florida churches from the Florida Conference to the South Florida Conference and then reorganizing the jurisdiction into three new districts: a first district centered at Gainesville; a second headquartered at Bartow; and a third focused on Jacksonville. The bishop designated Clinton as presiding elder of the Gainesville District, which located him conveniently in his hometown where his wife and children still lived but away from the more-prestigious seats of the conference. Lomax gifted the Bartow District to Warren C. Vesta and its Jacksonville counterpart to M. A. Sturkes.[8]

Lomax's maneuver quieted, but did not eliminate, the divisions within the Florida Conference and may have set that body temporarily at odds with the South Florida Conference. Information on the subject remains spotty, but at its January 1894 annual meeting some delegates joined Pensacola Zionites to push the creation of an Escambia High School. This institution presumably would have enjoyed area backing to the detriment of the Zion high school planned for Bartow and for which funds were being raised. Clinton's friends, too, desired to prolong the conflict. When in May the salary of Presiding Elder Smith came under discussion at a district conference held at Muscogee, the question "brought on a hot discussion."[9]

All things considered, on the other hand, both conferences in 1894 were weathering the various storms of the present and recent past. "Money has been scarce," B. F. Stevens acknowledged in November, "but despite the hard times [Talbot Chapel's new pastor E. J. Carter has been reducing its debt]." Finances generally suffered, but numerous locales anticipated church building. Simon Brown managed to lay the cornerstone for a new sanctuary at Pensacola's Tanyard in July, while A. L. Green planned a new Isaiah Chapel for Milton. In the South Florida Conference, conditions fared even better. F. R. McIntyre announced prospects for building a church at Orlando "soon," while a large-scale reconstruction and enlargement of Cornish Chapel began at Key West. The weight of construction news coming from spots such as Orange Bend, Gainesville, Micanopy, Leesburg, and Grandin helped further to tip the balance away from the bad news.[10]

As the construction news suggests, both conferences managed during the difficult times to expand by the establishment of at least a few new congregations. A smaller number, not surprisingly, opened in the Florida Conference than in the South Florida Conference. In the former case Quintette in Escambia County and Spring Hill in Santa Rosa welcomed AMEZ missionaries. In the northeast Florida and peninsular counties of the South Florida Conference, the same could be said for Hawthorne and Micanopy (Alachua); White Springs (Hamilton); Greenville (Madison); Orlando (Orange); Georgetown, Grandin, Putnam Hall, and Satsuma (Putnam); and St. Augustine (St. Johns). At least three additional missions appeared by 1895. They touched Titusville (Brevard), Palatka (Putnam), and Seville (Philips Chapel) in Volusia.[11]

That so much progress could be made against the prevailing tide of woe stood, among other things, as a victory for Bishop Lomax's policy of utilizing women in church endeavors. At Joseph Clinton's farewell Pensacola services in May 1894, for example, "Miss Minnie Jordan read the welcome address." It was said that "her speech and pen proved to be equal to her performance on the [organ]." When the Gainesville District convened at Leesburg in August 1894, women likewise provided staunch support. "We had a band of sisters such as sister Martha Jones, Eliza Horton, Amelia Williams and others, who conducted the evening prayer meetings which gave impetus to the work," reported W. J. Sanders. Similarly, at Plant City Blanche Secenger (or Seconder), Idella Clayton, Mamie Secenger, Ida Simmons, and Mt. Sinai pioneer Samuel Bryant's daughter Charlotte Bryant proved mainstays of the Sunday school program and assisted pastor C. H. Miles in numerous additional ways. Fund-raising, of course, remained one of them. While E. J. Carter could claim credit for reducing Talbot Chapel's debt, women such as Mary Frances Green, Minnie Jordan, Georgia A. Edwards, and Minnie L. Gaskin actually raised most of the cash.[12]

They often did so by stressing church events of particular interest to other women. In the circumstances, programs such as Children's Day took on special significance. The healthy sum of $26 resulted, for instance, from Talbot Chapel's Children's Day services of June 24, 1894. Sermons and addresses by men punctuated the occasion, but hearts and spirits rose with "the lovely music" offered primarily by women. "Promptly at the hour appointed," Mary Green recalled, "the music pealed forth from the sweet voices of the choir according to the order laid down on the program." Children played their role, as well, adding to the event's meaning for mothers. "The little girls who read tend to show what Zion will be in days to come," Green reflected tellingly. She then added, "Each little boy was very ready in speaking and had a happy way of saying his part." Donors opened their pockets eagerly thereafter. "Children's Day was made more important than ever," Green concluded.[13]

In a similar vein, beginning in 1896 women contributed greatly to the work of the church's Varick Christian Endeavor (VCE) Society. Based upon the Christian Endeavor Society created in 1881 by the Reverend Francis E. Clark of Portland, Maine, the organization aimed particularly at the development and education of young people. As approved by the 1896 general conference, the VCE plan called for a local society to be organized in each church. The movement soon spread in Florida, at least in the larger congregations. From Plant City in 1897, for example, C. H. Miles could report, "We organized last year under the pastorate of Rev. R. R. Frederick a fine V.C.E. Society which is now second to none in the State." He added, "We are arranging for the V.C.E. Convention which is to meet in this town." Central to the local VCE activities, Miles noted in a fashion typical of such reports, were "our officers: Miss Ida W. Simmons, President; Mrs. Rose Lifridge, Vice-President; James G. Gooden, Secretary; Mrs. Mary C. L. Brown, A. P. M.; J. S. Hicks and I. H. Lifridge, L. C."[14]

Shortly before the VCE societies offered women this new outlet for church contributions, other events occurred that dealt major blows to the church and necessitated that all such AMEZ supporters redouble their efforts. One occurrence especially brought disastrous consequences. February 1895 is remembered sadly within the African American community for the death of the great Zion hero Frederick Douglass, who passed away at Washington, D.C., on the twentieth, but in Florida the month brought an event far more tragic. The Great Freeze of 1895 inflicted its terrible damage during February 7–10. A lighter freeze had preceded it in December, but warm weather thereafter had lulled residents into believing that nothing but balmy days lay ahead. Then, for four successive nights temperatures in the peninsula dropped well below freezing. No similar event of Florida's modern era permits easy comparison. The citrus industry was virtually destroyed, as were most farm and garden crops. Trees and plants were killed to the roots. The economy was in shambles. As one man put it, "It is at best a serious disaster." When the South Florida Conference gathered at Bartow on the eleventh, the destruction could not be denied. The peninsular boom had gone bust. Fittingly, on the twelfth Bishop Lomax and Warren C. Vesta sold their investments in Bartow property. Hopes for a connectional high school there, while technically remaining alive, essentially had evaporated.[15]

Several measures permit an assessment of the freeze's impact on the AMEZ Church. Conference steward collections offer one of them. In 1894 Florida Conference Steward Darley raised $292.65, a sum already low due to the problems discussed earlier in this chapter. The next year his proceeds dropped 30 percent. By 1896 they had plummeted to $135.75, a total decrease of 54 percent overall. South Florida Conference figures for 1896 are not available, but between 1894 and 1895 Warren C. Vesta's collections slipped 16 percent from $270.54 to $228.35.[16]

The Jacksonville District's experience offers another indication of the damage. In the months immediately following the freeze, Presiding Elder M. A. Sturkes retained some sense of optimism. "In the midst of the hard times my brethren are building churches in my district," he reported proudly. The following months brought different tidings entirely. By February 1896 a jurisdiction that had claimed almost two dozen stations and missions the previous year had collapsed. Sturkes's successor S. L. McDonald discovered that he supervised only "6 preachers, 60 members, one elder, and two deacons."[17]

Reports from individual churches and pastors reflected the pain, as well. "The delegate from Tampa reported Tampa as not being in as good condition as it was in the past," an 1895 item observed. At that city in May, the community's black pastors joined to form a pastors' union. "By the help of the Lord we mean to gain strength sufficient to support us," they proclaimed, "for united we stand, but divided we fall." Membership rolls quickly announced flight from congregations. "During these panic stricken times," Joseph N. Clinton recorded soon after the freeze, "[South Florida Conference membership has dropped to] only one thousand members." Tallahassee's J. C. Lee believed that he could take pride simply in his ability to boast "Zion is alive in this town."[18]

The Florida churches thus entered the AMEZ "Year of Jubilee," its 1896 centennial celebration, faced with devastation at most every hand. Its frustrated and belabored bishop sought to ameliorate conditions in advance of the national quadrennial convention scheduled for May in Mobile, Alabama. His only available tools consisted of personnel shifts. As mentioned, he dropped M. A. Sturkes as presiding elder of the South Florida Conference's Jacksonville District in favor of a man he earlier had fired from essentially the same position, S. L. McDonald. George W. Maize now substituted for Warren C. Vesta as Bartow District presiding elder, except that the district now centered in Tampa rather than Bartow. Joe Clinton, who had redeemed himself in the bishop's eyes by laboring doggedly to hold his charge together, remained as Gainesville District head.[19]

The Florida Conference drew the bishop's attention, as well. He divided it into a Pensacola District and a Cottondale (Jackson County) District and provided entirely new leadership for each. At Pensacola he installed the erudite Dr. C. O. H. Thomas, who then was serving as a presiding elder of the Alabama Conference. Fillmore R. Smith had arrived from New Jersey in 1895 to pastor at Tampa's Mt. Sinai in order that Wilbur G. Strong could return to Alabama to head its Mobile District in anticipation of the quadrennial conference. Lomax now transferred Smith to the Florida Conference to preside over the Cottondale District.[20]

The times, added to the paucity of his resources, created an even-more-difficult situation for Lomax. The previous September Booker T. Washington, a race leader who maintained close ties with Zion, had issued at Atlanta's Cotton States Exhibition a ringing call for turning away from the questions of political and social equality for African Americans in favor of economic security. "Essentially, he counseled blacks to be wary of constant agitation for political rights and focus instead on economic self-help," Sandy Dwayne Martin explained, "emphasized industrial skills over the acquisition of literary and liberal arts education, stressed self-help and racial solidarity over efforts to achieve 'social' integration with whites, and strongly advocated a view of southern whites as friends rather than adversaries (as he advised whites to regard blacks in the same fashion)." Washington's approach, while practical, offered little to lift spirits in troubled times. Quite the contrary, it came as a bitter pill for many. Within the year the U.S. Supreme Court added to the sense of crisis. Particularly, echoing the shame of its 1883 Civil Rights Cases decisions, the panel declared approval of the "separate but equal" doctrine in *Plessy v. Ferguson,* a decision that would usher in a new and even-harder era of legally mandated racial discrimination. "The court had officially vanquished for the next half-century," a historian observed, "the antislavery vision of an instrumental rule of law sensitive to higher law principles."[21]

Judicial actions such as these, coupled with lax law enforcement practices by white officials, meanwhile were setting the stage for rates of racial terrorism even higher than previously had been the case, a fact that added to leadership burdens faced by men such as Lomax. Earlier chapters have touched upon Florida's violent race relations patterns, ones that placed the state in the lead for lynchings per capita by the century's end. Admittedly, the buildup of racial violence plagued the entire southern region, but the fact that white people would lynch ninety black men between 1900 and 1917 in sparsely settled Florida deserves attention. Rare indeed were lawmen who effectively withstood lynching threats, as did Monroe County Sheriff Charles F. Dupont, a Cornish Chapel member. In 1891 he outwitted a Key West mob believed to number about one thousand persons in order to save his prisoner's life.[22]

Contrary to Sheriff Dupont's example, law enforcement personnel sometimes perpetrated violence upon black men and women. The case of Robert Meacham offers an interesting illustration. The respected political and religious leader had departed the AME clergy in the mid-1880s for the AMEZ Church. Having pastored at Key West and founded congregations at Punta Gorda and Fort Myers, Meacham had left the ministry in 1890 to accept Punta Gorda's postmastership. When that employment ended, he associated with the "colored conference" of the ME Church. On February 12, 1896, Meacham found himself at Tampa just as the sixth session of the AMEZ South Florida Conference was convening at Mt. Sinai. Before the day was over, he lay near death from gunshot wounds at the hands of policeman Thomas Milton, who had acted from "blind rage" as a result of a misunderstanding. Meacham survived. Unusually, authorities prosecuted his assailant. This probably occurred because Milton, too, was black.[23]

It may easily be seen, given all of these events and circumstances, that Florida's bishop and delegates approached the Twentieth Quadrennial Conference feeling buffeted and uneasy. Ministers Simon Brown, H. P. Shuford, J. M. Sims, A. L. Green, J. M. Simons, and B. J. Arnold, with lay participants G. V. Irby and Mary Green, represented the Florida Conference. Its South Florida counterpart sent Warren C. Vesta, Joseph N. Clinton, Thomas H. Darley, George W. Maize, Fillmore R. Smith, and laymen Solomon Sally and John Shavers. They reported sagging membership totals that, in themselves, likely reflected a too-rosy estimate: 1,370 for the South Florida Conference, and about 1,000 to 1,200 for the Florida Conference. The Floridians' expectations for the gathering are unknown, but its outcome likely surprised them. The South Florida Conference received a new leader, while Lomax continued in charge of the Florida Conference where he had struggled so recently.[24]

The inclusion of the South Florida Conference in Bishop Cicero Richardson Harris's Fourth Episcopal District brought to the state a leader who represented a younger generation than did Florida's previous bishops. Born in Fayetteville, North Carolina, on August 25, 1844, Harris by age six was living with his widowed mother and siblings in Ohio. As a high school graduate he returned to the South, to Fayetteville, in 1866 to teach. Associating closely with Elder (later Bishop) James Walker Hood, Harris joined the AMEZ Church in 1867 and within five years had asked for a license to preach. His rise in the church hierarchy proceeded rapidly. A deacon by January 1874, he received ordination as an elder before year's end. He aided the founding of Livingston College (originally Zion Wesley Institute) in 1879, teaching mathematics on its faculty for years thereafter. Beginning in 1880 he served also as business manager of the *Star of Zion* and as the church's general steward. Harris's election as bishop came eight years later.[25]

Florida's new bishop was a man of particular qualities, ones that would influence the state's church greatly in years to come. Bishop William J. Walls observed of him, "His traits of Christian character were always unquestionable, and his life of usefulness, in the schoolroom, the general office, and the bishopric, endeared him to all who knew him."[26] Harris's mentor Hood added his own thoughts. "[He] is essentially a logician, preferring the a priori method of reasoning and always leaving his arguments so well supported that there remains no loophole for a would-be antagonist or contestant," Hood offered. The veteran churchman continued:

In fact, his discussions beam with such a flood of sincerity that one hesitates to take issue with him, lest the opponent should be regarded as callous. The bishop's mind is systematic and forceful, never losing confidence in the power of "the word." As a Methodist he is strictly orthodox, and believes in evangelical religion pure and simple.[27]

Harris's orthodoxy suggests the deep conservatism of his approach to life and church affairs. Especially, he embraced the practical or down-to-earth approach espoused by Booker T. Washington. "His sermons from time to time," minister M. Edward Church later would record, "have convinced the white people of Florida that he is the most conservative Bishop of the Negro race." Church added, "He is one of the most conservative Bishops of the race." Harris evidenced, as well, a deep concern for the church's rank and file. "America can boast with pride of her Washington who gained the independence of this country; her Lincoln to free it, and the South Florida Conference can point with pride to her Bishop Harris who brought her from a three-sided fight to the land of peace and reconciliation," Church continued. "He is fatherly in his ruling and feels that the humblest member has rights that ought to be respected."[28]

Sometimes Harris's conservatism went so far as to provoke his colleagues to response. This occurred, for example, at the 1896 general convention when Harris declared that "intelligent and morally upright black ministers working in the South should have no fear about lynchings and other acts of brutality." On that occasion, a prominent church historian has noted, "a minister, a bishop, and a prominent layman rose to dispute the belief that these acts were things of the past and confined to lower-class white perpetrators and immoral black victims."[29]

Harris brought with him to Florida, besides his conservative philosophy, a remarkable reservoir of energy and a determination to reverse the ill tide that had washed upon the peninsular church. Immediately he established the practice of extended visitations through the conference prior to its annual meeting. In 1897 the bishop commenced his travels at Key West in January before proceeding to Polk, Hillsborough, Marion, Alachua, and Osceola counties. "He has visited more churches in the State in two weeks than all other Bishops in as many years," Joe Clinton related. "In the vicinity of Phosphate Mines, near Wade, Florida, the name and face of Bishop Harris are familiar to the hard toilers and laboring men who love to worship Zion," he added. "On the little Alafia and at Ft. Meade and Homeland as well as along the banks of the beautiful Alachua Lake, the dear Bishop and the mission preacher could be seen wending their way to some little backwoods chapel where never the foot of a Bishop had trod; while women and children looked and wondered as they saw for the first time a living active Zion Bishop."[30]

By his first conference meeting, held at Kissimmee on February 10, 1897, Harris already had begun to offer new inspiration to his preachers. "The Bishop is particularly fitted and best adapted to build up this Florida work," one of them proclaimed. Adding fuel to churchly fires, Harris resurrected the conference high school idea, except that his vision anticipated something greater, "a mechanical and collegiate institute" along the lines being pioneered at Tuskegee by his friend Booker T. Washington. Joseph N. Clinton, for one, could not help but be impressed, although he evidenced a degree of skepticism. "The indefatigable Bishop Harris, who would, if possible, have a college built and operated in every conference in Zion, and who can think out and lay more plans for industrial educational in one day than can be executed in a century, breaks the record of all predecessors in Florida," the presiding elder observed.[31]

Clinton's skepticism hit close to the mark. The industrial and collegiate institute died aborning, and the bishop endured greater resistance and experienced far more frustration during his first term in the state than he could have believed possible in 1896. The South Florida Conference four years later claimed fewer members than it had previously. The bishop laid out the situation succinctly for the 1900 general conference delegates:

> This is the smallest Conference in the District, numbering but little over 1,000 members. It is almost entirely a missionary district, the chief Churches being at Key West and Tampa. It extends from Jacksonville to Key West over five hundred miles and from Port Tampa to Nassau, N. P., one of the Bahama Islands, a distance as traveled by water of another five hundred miles. This entails heavy traveling expenses for the Bishop and Presiding Elder, hence while the work was barely sufficient to support one Presiding Elder, three were required until last Conference, when the number was reduced to two. Hampered as we are for lack of mission money, we have made little headway here, though the General Fund reported in February, 1896, was $296.64 with 1,370 members in 1900, same month, $314.00 and 909 members. Yellow fever, however, during much of the past year, doubtless caused a decrease in the collections at Key West and Nassau.[32]

Harris's lack of success could not be attributed to any want of effort on his part, and, although he may have contributed inadvertently to the conference's problems, his labors likely forestalled even greater setbacks given the impact of the 1895 freeze and that of persistent poor weather conditions over the next several years. His inadvertent contribution to the problems arguably came from his unwillingness to stand up for better treatment for the race during the Spanish-American War of 1898. Key West and Tampa emerged during the conflict as centers for war-related activity, and troops found themselves stationed in numerous other spots including Polk County's Lakeland. Several regiments of black troops joined their white counterparts, and trouble soon brewed between them in the sweltering heat. "Prejudice reigns supreme here against the colored troops," one soldier wrote from Tampa, while another found Lakeland "a hotbed of rebels." Gunfire broke out at Lakeland on May 16, and a disturbance sometimes called the Tampa Riot rocked that city on June 6. Arrests of black troopers resulted, and criticism mounted nationally in African American circles of the failures of local and military leadership and law enforcement.

As it turned out, the prisoners' fellow soldiers solved the immediate problem. Upon their return from Cuba, the men seized the prisoners from custody and carried them safely out of state.[33]

Whether he should have acted more forthrightly in the soldiers' cases or stood out more forcefully against the march of Jim Crow, Harris strove as hard as could have been expected to make a go of his charge. The reshuffling of his leadership team offered him his best option for bringing about change, and he rearranged its personnel and the district lines as circumstances required or permitted. In 1897, for example, he abolished the Gainesville District and placed Joseph N. Clinton in charge of an enhanced Second (Tampa) District. George W. Maize, in turn, moved to a new Key West (or First) District. S. L. McDonald remained atop the Jacksonville District until James R. Harris replaced him in 1898. As he reported to the 1900 general conference, Harris had reduced the three districts to two (Key West headed by Joseph Sexton and Tampa by George W. Maize) earlier the same year. Increasingly he relied on the talents of veteran Florida preachers to help him stem the still-flowing and still-unfortunate tide. Joseph Sexton and Wiley Walker accordingly assisted as conference missionaries from 1898 to 1899 with James R. Harris and John W. Cox following them in 1900.[34]

All the while, the bishop endeavored to stem not only the tide of membership loss but also that of clerical loss, especially among veteran churchmen. Joseph N. Clinton retired from the ministry in 1898, by way of illustration, in order to accept appointment by Republican president William McKinley as deputy federal collector of internal revenue for Florida in charge of the Tampa District. Death took others. To name one, a passing train killed S. W. Cunningham at Tampa in 1899 shortly before he was to assume the pastorate of Mt. Sinai. Thomas H. Darley, blind now for several years, died months later in the same city. The pioneer churchman's wife, Eliza, had predeceased him by less than one month. Tightened standards demanded by the national church eliminated others. A. L. Higgs discovered as much in 1897 when he suffered suspension "until he filled the requirements of the Discipline." Recruits from many of the church's other conferences or from the AME Church stepped in to take the place of absent veterans, but they could not offer Harris the knowledge of place and people that years of experience had taught those who were now gone or about to retire.[35]

While Harris could not boast large new missionary fields, enhanced membership rolls, or munificent collections, he had won the loyalty and affection of his clergy while setting the stage for new initiatives during a second term. "The whole of South Florida, all the churches, both white and black, recognize him as one of the greatest Negro men and churchmen in America," insisted George W. Maize. The bishop had trained his ministers and streamlined their organization. Surviving congregations had been buttressed, a few new mission seeds had been planted, the downbeat attitude and minor squabbles of past years had been washed away, and a reworked spirit not of grandiose hopes but of practical progress had been imparted to clergy and lay members. Meriah Elizabeth Gion Harris, the bishop's wife, took pride during March 1900 in sharing with *Star of Zion* readers a sense of the changes. "The work of the Conference was conducted in a careful, pleasant and agreeable manner," she wrote of the South Florida Conference gathering at Leesburg. "It is composed of an orderly and Christian set of men who are struggling to build up what might be termed a Missionary Conference," she continued. "If the brethren continue to improve in the business-like manner that they now seem to be gaining in so short time they will be able to expedite business more rapidly and be classed among the best Conferences of the Connection."[36]

Meanwhile, Bishop Lomax enjoyed marginally more progress in the Florida (or West Florida) Conference. In four years he raised membership rolls by perhaps 10 or 15 percent to thirteen hundred persons. The bishop also collected more than $4,000 for new church construction and renovations. Mt. Moriah at Pensacola, Milton's Isaiah Chapel, and Caryville each claimed a new sanctuary, while Tallahasseeans worshiped in two. The gem in the construction crown, though, was Pensacola's new Talbot Chapel. As race riots rocked Tampa in June 1898, Lomax laid its cornerstone while admiring Florida's first brick AMEZ church. He credited Pastor George W. Gaines for the accomplishment in a personally penned letter to the *Star of Zion*. "Saturday, July 10th, we rode down to the spot where the church building stood and to my amazement I found a new brick building 108x40 feet with press brick front elevation, an all-round, up-to-date, first-class job," he wrote. "The building when completed will cost about $4,000, and will be numbered among the best class of church buildings in this city," he continued. "It will be remembered that when Rev. G. W. Gains was appointed to this charge from the Conference on the 10th of last February, there was not a dollar in the treasury to begin this work; but trusting in God, he called the trustees to his assistance and they promised to stand by him." Lomax concluded, "The church will be completed for dedication on the first Sabbath in September."[37]

Without question, the dedication ceremonies for Talbot Chapel proved to be the highlight of Lomax's term and, maybe, of his tenure in Florida. They offered a shining symbol of AMEZ success and resurgence (a rare commodity, indeed) and, as such, deserve a closer look. The gala events, which extended over a four-day period, drew dignitaries from church and state alike. Naturally, Pastor Gaines and trustees G. B. Green, James Frederick, W. E. Plummer, J. P. Patterson, A. Oliver, James Brown Sr., Robert Ridley, Charles Bradley, David Allen, and T. W. Milton took leading roles throughout the festivities. One-time Talbot minister-in-charge J. H. Manley, the "sweet singer of Zion," returned from his new post at the prestigious Old Ship Church in Montgomery, Alabama. The AMEZ general steward John Wesley Alstork, just two years away from his election as bishop, attended as well. The Talbot choir under Mrs. L. Bradley and Mary F. Green repeatedly thrilled crowds, while Minnie L. Gaspin "captivated the audience" with her "brilliant paper on the history of Talbot Chapel." The emotional peak resulted at Sabbath services when "the pastor and trustee board presented the building and keys to the Bishop who proceeded to solemnly dedicate it." It was said that, following Alstork's subsequent sermon, "the whole church was on fire with the Holy Ghost."[38]

Harris's overall success resulted from an administrative reorganization that allowed him to push the cause of missionary work more effectively through the panhandle region. When the term commenced in 1896, two districts had divided the conference. The first, a Pensacola District, was headed by Dr. C. O. H. Thomas, and a counterpart centered on the Jackson County farming community of Cottondale under Fillmore R. Smith's superintendence. In 1898 this scheme gave way to a three-unit plan that kept the Pensacola District but created in place of Cottondale two districts headquartered at Milton and at Tallahassee. Dr. Thomas, having bristled at the bishop's leadership, had returned to Alabama and was replaced at Pensacola by pioneer preacher Simon Brown. B. F. Stevens took the Milton charge, with another pioneer, Solomon Derry, recently transferred from the Alabama Conference, taking over at the state capital. This team remained in place until 1899 or 1900, when T. L. Holt superseded Stevens.[39]

As the reorganization suggests, Lomax stressed mission work outside the old heartland of Escambia and Santa Rosa counties and, instead, pointed to the timber milling and farming communities that stretched eastward toward Tallahassee and beyond. This region comprised the AME Church's historic homeland in the state, but economic misery and lay disenchantment had weakened the denomination's hold considerably. By early 1898

Presiding Elder Stevens was planning ten new mission points within his Cottondale District alone. "For years in this part of the country Zion has been only in name," C. Frances Sams reported from Tallahassee a few months later. "Thank God, we now have a church edifice and nearly 40 members." Missions, albeit only tentative ones in some cases, crept into Franklin, Wakulla, and Jefferson counties. Meanwhile, labor violence swept Escambia and Santa Rosa counties during 1899–1900, causing interruption of church services at times as well as impeding progress with missionary work elsewhere. Still, the century ended with Lomax's legion of three or four dozen preachers energetically proclaiming, "We are workers for Zion."[40]

As also was true in South Florida for Cicero R. Harris, Bishop Lomax faced the seemingly never-ending problem of where to find enough "workers for Zion." The same dynamics that were sapping the South Florida Conference of its veteran strength and limiting the bishop's ability to expand missionary efforts touched heavily in the panhandle also. The May 1899 passing of pioneer Harrison Williams—"the aged patriarch"— in Escambia County may have driven the point home to the conference's leadership with poignancy. "Our greatest need in the State is more good men," Fillmore Smith already was asserting in 1897. "Brethren, you who want work, come down South," he continued. "We have room for all good men," Smith added. "The harvest truly is ready, but the laborers are few." Shortfalls in funding, low compensation, and a desire to upgrade clerical standards added to the weight of the problem.[41]

By way of encouraging volunteers, Lomax in 1898 delineated for *Star of Zion* readers an explanation of just what he was looking for but was having such difficulty finding. "We need now men possessing three grand qualities," he wrote. "First, they should be devoted followers of Jesus and His Church; secondly, they should love their Connection beyond self-agrandizement and do to all men as they desire them to treat them in all their dealings in Church or State, and do nothing without considering what the end will be; thirdly they should make no promise unless they can see their way clear to fulfil their obligations." The bishop continued, "They should never do or say anything against a man or minister that would have the least tendency to impede his religious work in the Church of God."[42]

Always running short of men of the type that he sought, the bishop grew evermore committed to a greater role for women in church affairs. Bishop Harris approved of what he would refer to as "the high place accorded the woman in the A.M.E. Zion Church," but Lomax went further to champion the cause. "If the women will preach," he insisted, "let them have a chance as well as the men." He voiced the sentiments especially loudly in 1898 as the church endured a national crisis over the ordination of Mary J. Small as an elder. Following two years of intense controversy, Zion would emerge from its 1900 general conference as a leader within the U.S. Christian community in placing women securely in the pulpit.[43]

Thanks to Lomax, Florida did not lag far behind, despite some gentle ribbing. The teasing came from the *Florida Baptist Herald*, which noted in August 1898 that "the question of ordaining women to the gospel ministry has created quite a breezy controversy between leading brethren of the A.M.E. Zion connection." The item added, "We Baptists have settled that matter too long ago to talk about." Baptist opposition to women preachers notwithstanding, Lomax would not be forestalled. Available records fail to provide specific information, but the bishop may have ordained Mary V. Anderson an elder as early as 1898. If not, he likely ordained her a deacon at that time with elder's rank coming within a few years. At any rate, Lomax offered a regular appointment to Anderson at the 1898 Florida Conference annual meeting. It was for Santa Rosa County's Bagdad Mission. After serving during 1900–1902 as conference missionary, Anderson would go on to preside at Warrington's historic Navy Yard Church in 1902. Three years afterward she held the pastorate of Milton's Isaiah Chapel, one of the conference's principal and prestigious posts. Lomax furthered the ministerial career of Mrs. G. V. Irby, as well. Not later than 1900 he had named her "conference evangelist" of the Florida Conference.[44]

The close of the nineteenth century, as seen, found Florida's AMEZ churches finally managing to breathe more easily following the challenges of the previous seven years. Few grand advances could be totaled, but the hemorrhaging of earlier years had been stemmed, and renewed hope, thanks to the leadership of Bishops Harris and Lomax, permitted an optimistic anticipation of the new century. Winds of change in church, society, and state were circulating, though. Meanwhile, members of Florida's AMEZ family certainly joined others in pondering just what those changes portended. The answers were not long in coming.

27. Tampa remained little more than a village in the 1870s. Collection of the authors.

28. The Reverend Edward Hunter. From *Charlotte (N.C.) Star of Zion*, November 28, 1901.

29. The Reverend John A. Mulligan. From *A.M.E.Z. Church Quarterly*, January 1891.

30. The beautiful St. Johns River valley attracted tens of thousands of settlers in the 1870s and 1880s. Courtesy Florida State Archives.

31. Judge James Dean of Monroe County. From *Pensacola Florida Sentinel,* 1912 annual edition.

32. The Reverend Paul L. Cuyler. From *Charlotte (N.C.) Star of Zion*, January 10, 1901.

33. Bishop Singleton Thomas Webster Jones. From Walls, *African Methodist Episcopal Zion Church.*

34. Mary Jane Talbert Jones, wife of Bishop Singleton Thomas Webster Jones. From Walls, *African Methodist Episcopal Zion Church.*

35. Bishop John Jamison Moore. From Walls, *African Methodist Episcopal Zion Church.*

36. Bishop Thomas Henry Lomax. From Walls, *African Methodist Episcopal Zion Church.*

37. Elizabeth Lomax, wife of Bishop Thomas Henry Lomax. From Hood, *One Hundred Years.*

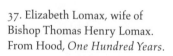

38. Bartow's Main Street as it appeared in 1888, just before the discovery of phosphate deposits set off a veritable gold rush in the region. The Polk County courthouse appears to the left. Collection of the authors.

39. Dr. Lemuel Walter Livingston served as U.S. consul in Haiti after presiding as principal of Key West's Douglass School. From *Washington (D.C.) Colored American*, December 9, 1899.

40. Cornish Chapel AMEZ Church, Key West, as photographed about 1936. Collection of the authors; courtesy Tom Hambright, Monroe County May Hill Russell Library.

41. Joseph Newman Clinton, AMEZ presiding elder and son of Bishop Joseph
Jackson Clinton. Courtesy Florida State Archives.

42. The Reverend James H. Manley. From *Indianapolis Freeman*, May 26, 1906.

43. The Great Freeze of 1895 devastated citrus crops and groves through much of peninsular Florida, as this Polk County family discovered in its aftermath. Collection of the authors.

44. The Reverend Robert Meacham. Collection of the authors;
courtesy Luther Alexander and Rowena Ferrell Brady.

45. Stella Meacham, wife of Robert
Meacham. Collection of the authors;
courtesy Luther Alexander and
Rowena Ferrell Brady.

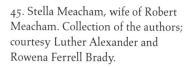

46. Bishop Cicero Richardson Harris.
From Walls, *African Methodist
Episcopal Zion Church.*

47. Meriah Elizabeth Gion Harris, wife
of Bishop Cicero Richardson Harris.
From *Charlotte (N.C.) Star of Zion*,
February 11, 1897.

48. Bishop John Wesley Alstork. From
Charlotte (N.C.) Star of Zion, January
3, 1901.

49. Developer Henry Flagler's exotic Ponce de Leon Hotel, St. Augustine, soon after its opening. Courtesy Florida State Archives.

50. Attorney Isaac L. Purcell helped to fight the advance of Jim Crow racial discrimination in Florida. From *Colored American Magazine,* September 1905.

51. and 52. (*Left*) Bishop Isom Caleb Clinton. From Walls, *African Methodist Episcopal Zion Church*. (*Right*) Annie Kimball Clinton, second wife of Bishop Isom Caleb Clinton. From Hood, *One Hundred Years*.

53. and 54. (*Left*) Bishop Alexander Walters. From *Washington (D.C.) Colored American*, May 19, 1900. (*Right*) Katie Knox Walters, wife of Bishop Alexander Walters. From Hood, *One Hundred Years*.

CLIMBING TO THE MOUNTAINTOP, 1900–1905

I don't mean to leave
a wheel unturned

The twentieth century's early years offered something like an Indian summer for Florida's African American residents and for its AMEZ Church. In certain respects the community and the institution reached post–Civil War peaks of advancement, but they did so in a state altered dramatically since General Grant had accepted Confederate surrender at Appomattox Courthouse. During this supposedly progressive period, the peninsular state would turn yet another unfortunate corner in race relations policies and practices. Generations would be condemned thereby to poverty and second-class citizenship. Some, of course, cried out against the twentieth century's increasingly threatening aspect, but Zion leaders concentrated instead on extending their reach in order to bring needed comfort and solace as opposed to political relief. By the midpoint of the new century's first decade, those leaders had achieved their goal and could behold a church grander than could have been dreamed within recent memory. The view from the mountaintop proved chimerical, though. Indian summer soon surrendered to fall, and the ripples of time's passage presaged chilling winter winds to come.

Florida at the twentieth century's dawn truly offered a different guise than it had three or four decades earlier. The poor, isolated frontier state had begun to give way to the modern leisure mecca taken for granted by millions upon millions of residents and tourists today. The changes owed credit to many fathers, but none more so than to William D. Chipley, Henry B. Plant, and Henry Flagler. Beginning in the late 1870s and for decades thereafter, they had pioneered railroad construction in a fashion that had cut isolation and offered easy access to Florida's treasure-house of natural resources. Importantly, Plant and Flagler had integrated their transportation empires with efforts to provide accommodation and recreation to upscale visitors flush with cash and time to spend. Plant's Tampa Bay Hotel at Tampa and Flagler's Ponce de Leon Hotel at St. Augustine set new marks for luxurious living, bringing fine dining, golf, and tennis to the amenities for which Florida already was growing famous. Where these accessions had remained little known outside upper-crust circles until 1898, international coverage of the Spanish-American War had brought the world's attention to the exotic semitropical world that Plant and Flagler were attempting to create.[1]

Chipley and Plant have commanded attention in earlier chapters, but Flagler deserves a closer look here. His Florida career came a few years later than did those of his two colleagues, but his mark remains the most visible to modern eyes. Whereas Chipley concentrated in West Florida and Plant in Central and southwest Florida, Flagler remade the state's Atlantic coast from St. Augustine southward. His magnificent Ponce de Leon Hotel opened in the nation's oldest city on January 10, 1888. The next year his railroad line—eventually known as the Florida East Coast Railway—sparked life into Ormond and Daytona beaches and in 1892 stretched farther south to New Smyrna. Flagler's steel rails then touched Brevard County's Titusville in 1893 before passing down to Lake Worth, where Flagler launched the towns of Palm Beach and West Palm Beach. Other developments followed as the tracks crept ever southward until the magnate reached the remote village of Miami in 1896. There he erected one of the pearl's of his resort chain, the Royal Palm Hotel. Although his coastal resorts and their towns would not see breathtaking growth until the twentieth century, Flagler by 1900 virtually had created a new Florida.[2]

Census figures illustrate the impressive impact that Flagler-sparked development brought to the Atlantic coast. Jacksonville, the region's anchor city, jumped 25 percent in population from 1900 to 1905, giving it 35,000 residents. Daytona registered a 30 percent gain during the same period, with Titusville tallying 25 percent. West Palm Beach meanwhile leapt over 125 percent, with Miami nearing 200 percent growth. Florida as a whole expanded, too, but not on so grand a scale. The new century's first five years saw the state experience over 16 percent growth to 614,902 persons. Peninsular cities thrived at the expense of the state's old panhandle population center. Tampa climbed 44 percent to 22,823. Tallahassee, on the other hand, claimed only an 11 percent increase. The capital city's county of Leon—the state's most populous in 1860–slipped from 19,887 inhabitants to only 18,883.[3]

This flowering of new and established peninsular towns and cities courtesy of railroad and resort construction brought with it a significant impact on the African American community. Railroads, resorts, and auxiliary businesses required a dependable supply of labor. In return, they paid livable wages (or close to that mark) at set rates and on regular schedules. In these circumstances Florida's black population rose from 230,000 in 1900 to almost 266,000 five years later. As the overall total grew, the share remained at 43 percent. This fact pointed to another and easily understandable dynamic at play. As conditions deteriorated in Florida's old panhandle agricultural areas, individuals and families were relocating to towns and cities in search of better times. To cite a few examples, by 1905 African Americans made up almost 60 percent of Jacksonville's population, half of Pensacola's, and over one-third at Orlando and Sanford. At Tallahassee on the other hand, a 60 percent black community in 1870 now stood at 56 percent African American even though it, too, was growing with the new century.[4]

Those white men who held the reins of Florida political power astutely grasped the demographic trend and what it portended for the future. Although African Americans were blocked by legal measures adopted in the late 1880s from any meaningful statewide electoral power, they maintained influence in just the type of cities and towns that were prospering in the peninsula. At the century's turn, black men retained positions on the governing authorities of Fernandina, Jacksonville, St. Augustine, Palatka, Daytona, Cedar Key (the name changed from Cedar Keys in 1878), and Key West, while they contested seats regularly in other locales. The persistence of black office holding and the potential for increased black voting in urban areas heightened white fears and helped to encourage the adoption in 1905 by the legislature of a mandatory whites-only primary for the Democratic Party. Since many municipalities avoided partisan contests, they increasingly found themselves following a similar but somewhat different path. Instead of whites-only Democratic primaries, they hosted with legislative approval whites-only municipal parties. Tampa, for example, took this course during the century's first decade.[5]

This tightening of Jim Crow electoral restrictions, while finding roots in local circumstances, nonetheless reflected regional and national trends. The historian C. Vann Woodward, among others, has traced the hardening of racial segregation practices during the period, as the tentacles of the racism monster spread into most aspects of public life. "The South's adoption of extreme racism was due not so much to a conversion as it was to a relaxation of the opposition," Woodward explained. He added, "Just as the Negro gained his emancipation and new rights through a falling out between white men, he now stood to lose his rights through the reconciliation of white men." The *Orlando Sentinel-Reporter*, while commenting upon the 1900 election of "Progressive" William S. Jennings as governor, alluded to the same point. "He was the choice of an undivided party," it observed, "and he assumes office with the question of the right of the white man to rule, which has distracted the South so many years, forever settled." Woodward offered further explanation. "In the early years of the twentieth century, it was becoming clear that the Negro would be effectively disfranchised throughout the South, that he would be firmly relegated to the lower rungs of the economic ladder, and that neither equality nor aspirations for equality in any department of life were for him," the historian wrote. "The public symbols and constant reminders of his inferior position were the segregation statutes, or 'Jim Crow' laws."[6]

Many African Americans, taking their cue from the militant stance of W.E.B. Du Bois instead of the less confrontational and more practical philosophy of Booker T. Washington, fought these encroachments on freedoms guaranteed by the U.S. Constitution. In 1905, for instance, black plaintiffs sued a major railway to invalidate state-required race separation on trains. Their lawyer John Wallace, a Civil War veteran, had served in Florida's senate for eight years before penning the state's first history of the Reconstruction era. Attorneys Judson Douglas Wetmore and Isaac L. Purcell similarly and successfully attacked a companion measure relating to streetcars and trolleys. Black leaders protested at Jacksonville the same year when the city council segregated streetcars and then litigated the matter when violators suffered arrest.[7]

Fundamental changes thus were afoot as the twentieth century began to claim Floridians' attention. As this occurred the AMEZ Church responded to them in certain ways and, in turn, was affected by them. Rather than expend its energies and resources on broader political questions, however, the church and its leaders, with certain exceptions to be discussed, maintained their traditional avoidance of direct political involvements and channeled resources instead toward expansion. In the short term, gains came quickly. With the church having foresworn any role in the larger battle against Jim Crow, though, the question of whether the gains would prove permanent remained an open one.

The South Florida Conference's experience is illustrative. The Twenty-first Quadrennial Session of 1900 had allowed Bishop Cicero R. Harris to return to the region for a second four-year term. Already, Harris had begun laying plans for expansion down the Atlantic coast and into other growth areas. His intentions evidenced themselves during the February 1901 annual conference meeting held at Gainesville. Harris revamped the conference's modest two-district organization into a wide-ranging five district scheme. Tampa, Jacksonville, and Gainesville districts (led, respectively, by George W. Maize, L. A. Patrick, and W. A. Bain) were to tend areas in which earlier missionary work had borne fruit or to service new communities within those areas such as St. Petersburg, Dunnellon, and Clearwater. The bishop also added a new Cuban District headed by C. A. Mayo to work the Key West and Florida Keys Latin communities.[8]

Most significantly, Harris redrew the Key West District to reach out to burgeoning communities at New Smyrna, Titusville, Jupiter, West Palm Beach, Coconut Grove, and Miami. Presiding Elder Joseph Sexton's charge included, as well, enhanced efforts in the Bahama Islands at Nassau, Fox Hill, Baintown, New Road, Harbour Island, and Andros Island. Sexton, for one, wondered whether Harris's plans could work out given limited financial and personnel resources. Remarks made in June alluded to the less-than-rosy picture perceived by the veteran churchman. "I have only two churches in my district, the Key West church, and the church at Nassau, N. P.," he commented. "We think in the near future we will have a Zion church in Miami, Fla.," the longtime church builder continued. "I don't mean to leave a wheel unturned, though some parts of my district look doubtful."[9]

The hesitation voiced by some experienced ministers such as Sexton at the bishop's grand plans carried valid notes of caution that Harris should have considered. M. Edward Church in August 1902 addressed the matter from his station at St. Petersburg. "I was appointed here by Bishop C. R. Harris, April 22, 1902," he began. "On my arrival here I did not find one Zion member to say welcome," he continued. "You may know that I was at a loss for a starting point; [far] from home without a member or a place of worship." Competition from AME, CME, and Baptist churches—their missionaries often having arrived earlier than AMEZ preachers—confronted men such as Church with serious roadblocks. After noting that the South Florida Conference contained only one self-supporting congregation (Cornish Chapel at Key West), Church got to the heart of another, and even greater, problem. "It is believed by some that all Florida needs is strong preachers," he declared. "It is a mistake; the preachers of the South Florida Conference will compare favorably with any other set of men in

Zion." He added: "It is a piece of injustice to the preachers and a burning shame on a Church so great as Zion to continue to send men out in the face of strong opposition to build churches without one cent of mission or Church Extension money."[10]

The bishop likely would have sympathized with Church's point. He probably first would have reminded his colleague that all the nation's black churches, including Zion, continually dealt with shortages of funds to meet day-to-day commitments, much less for missionary work. Then, he would have argued that, in any event, zeal, determination, and God's guiding hand could more than overcome mere financial obstacles. In that regard no man committed himself more than did Harris. Accustomed to traveling his district, the bishop now set off on tours even more extensive and demanding. Prior to the 1901 conference meeting, for example, he had ranged from Nassau and Miami to Kissimmee, Bartow, Alafia, Leesburg, Evinston, High Springs, Gainesville, and Fernandina. The next year he took in several of the same locations plus Jacksonville, Cedar Key, Putnam Hall, Plant City, Seffner, Tampa, and Key West. He maintained the same pace for the remainder of his term, and it carried effect. "The Bishop is gone to other points South," J. R. Montgomery reported in 1902, "but left a lasting impressive for Zion in Gainesville."[11]

Montgomery was correct. Harris's indefatigable exertions paid off. The Bahamas work seemed so promising by 1902 that a Bahamas District, with A. Jackson as presiding elder, replaced its Key West predecessor. At Nassau in February 1903 the bishop heard reports of at least tentative successes at Baintown, Crooked Island, Abaco Island, Fox Hill, and other places. Meanwhile, at Miami the bishop delighted in the first stirs of Harris Chapel AMEZ Church. He attended a reception there in January at which the cream of local African American society cheered him. By summer a newspaper could report, "The A.M.E. Zion Church is known in Miami, Florida, as never before." The article continued: "She is now worshiping in her new church, all within five months. With men possessing missionary spirit, all of [Florida's] East Coast will soon know her as never before." The journal concluded: "Brother L. J. Hobbs is now sent to pastor Coconut Grove mission. Bro. Hobbs is a good man, and is a worker in deed and in truth."[12]

At that point Bishop Harris's spirited initiative ran out of steam. By summer 1903 churches operated at Miami, Coconut Grove, and Deerfield on the Atlantic seaboard and at Nassau, East Nassau, Baintown, Fox Hill, and Abaco in the Bahamas. Presiding Elder A. Jackson pleaded for reinforcements that would permit him to sustain and continue the work. "I have places on the East coast for men who would like to come," he urged in the *Star of Zion*. "The door is open," he continued. "You can build up a church and at the same time get from $1.25 to $3 per day for labor and mason's work." Jackson ended by asking, "Why stand ye idle all the day long when the harvest is so great and the laborers so few?"[13]

Not only did few new laborers step forward, but many already working laid down their charges from lack of support. M. Edward Church, as reporter for the conference's 1904 annual meeting, tried to put a good face on matters. "The pastors reported Thursday which showed marked increase on all lines," he related from Tampa's Mt. Sinai Church. "It was a source of joy to see a band of hard working preachers returning from the battlefield with victory inscribed on their banners." Church added, "All were well dressed and represented our Zion in every sense of the word." The facts were otherwise, however, and what a different face the bishop's appointments put on affairs. He collapsed the conference's five districts back to two, eliminating the Bahamas, Cuban Mission, and Gainesville districts. The Bahamas commanded but two designations (R. P. Perry to Nassau station and Ed Dean to Nassau mission). The Atlantic coast received pastors only at Miami (F. A. Hamilton) and West Palm Beach (W. P. Pickens). The same degree of drastic cutbacks carried across the remainder of the peninsula, as well. From nearly sixty appointments made or anticipated in 1902, Harris now had cut the total to thirty.[14]

As it turned out, Harris's problems only were beginning. He had raised expectations high with his original expansion plans, and he found the going difficult in explaining why they had failed and could not be pursued further. Word of the bishop's intentions had circulated prior to the annual meeting. An unnamed conference member, apparently an individual whose opinions were taken seriously, subsequently called for what amounted to secession from the South Florida Conference. Angered by the temerity, Harris lashed back through the *Star of Zion*. "A supernumerary preacher of the South Florida Conference suggests the setting apart of another mission conference from that Conference," he exclaimed. Harris continued:

If he may be taken as a specimen of the preachers who would supply the appointments of the new conference, it would be a laughing stock of the other churches in Florida. He deserted his appointment last year and failed to put in his appearance at the last annual conference. The church he left, consisting of five or six members failed to give proper encouragement or support to two or three preachers which were sent to it, and now he finds a voice in the STAR to complain of being without a pastor. To make mission work succeed these days we need able and self-sacrificing pastors whom the Connection can aid from its mission fund while they labor for the unbuilding of the work.[15]

The intra-church feud left conference members shaking their heads in frustration. Louisa Vaughn of Homeland put the sentiment into words for many others even before the bishop's words found print. "Pray the time will come," she wrote, "when our South Florida ministers will take as much interest in the mission work as they do in the other States."[16]

Interestingly, as Harris's outreach plan disintegrated in 1903 and 1904, he found voice to enter the political arena, at least to the extent of commenting publicly on the race relations dilemma. The bishop, as mentioned, inclined to conservatism and embraced Booker T. Washington's practical and economics-based platform over the more radical and political stance espoused by W.E.B. Du Bois. This fact was more than a matter of passing interest in 1903 because, on April 18 of that year, Du Bois's now-classic *The Souls of Black Folk* reached publication. In its pages the eminent sociologist and race leader directly attacked Washington and his philosophy. Harris's comments would have been understood as relating to the feud. Effectively, they also placed the South Florida Conference in the position of having endorsed Washington over Du Bois while validating Du Bois's approach of public engagement on political matters of importance to the race.[17]

What Harris intended was a defense of the race, although his words probably appeared to some as an attempt to downplay the culpability of white Democrats at the expense of white Republicans. "Education and Enfranchisement have been employed, the one by the friends of the Negro without regard to party, and the other by the Republican party," he declared in a letter to the *Star of Zion* from High Springs. "Had the party preferred the welfare of the Negro to its own self-aggrandizement, Congress would have passed the Blair Educational Bill and the bill to reimburse the depositors of the Freedmen's Savings Bank who were losers by reason of the implicit confidence in the party which appears to be the only friend of the Negro."[18]

The bishop continued his remarks by noting Secretary of State Elihu Root's recent comments that "declared Negro enfranchisement a failure." This, he reasoned, went too far. "To my mind, the attempt to saddle the comparative failure of Negro enfranchisement upon the Negro, is both cowardly and foolish," Harris insisted. "Cowardly, because it claims that the party has failed to do what it might to make enfranchisement a success, and now fails to acknowledge its delinquency; and foolish, because it is utter folly to ask of the Negro, just freed and still living among its former masters, to maintain his rights with a bit of paper against the heavy odds of racial prejudice and a combination of political training, which has proved a master of Northern whites, before the war, together with other forms of education, the possession of wealth, of property, and of business ability." The bishop concluded: "These were arrayed against the Negro and his political ally, the Republican party. What could have been expected, but defeat, especially when aided by pro-slavery constructions of the United States Constitution by the Supreme Court?"[19]

The problem with Harris's remarks related not so much to their content or to the fact that the bishop had entered the political arena but to the lack of any follow-through. Surviving minutes of the 1903 and 1904 annual conference meetings offer little hint of a continuing interest in the matter, which was, after all, of considerable importance to the race.[20] The closest reference came at the 1904 session. "The first order of business of the second day's session . . . ," the minutes revealed, "was the reading of the Bishop's Episcopal address to the Conference." The account continued, "It was quite an elaborate address, showing the pressing needs of our people educationally, morally, financially and otherwise." Was then the church to serve as a leader for the race to resolve these issues in the public arena? No mention was made of the subject. Instead, Harris chose to avoid that question and responsibility for the failure of his expansion plans by implying criticism of his clergy and the church's effectiveness and viability as a separate entity:

> He said it has come when we need an educated ministry in the true sense of the word. He spoke of the proposed appropriation from the general fund for the support of the Hood Theological Seminary connected with Livingston college at Salisbury, N.C. He spoke briefly upon the organic union of the A.M.E. Zion and C.M.E. churches showing the great power in union. He said if all colored Methodist churches were united, so terrible would be the foe against sin that vice, immorality, ignorance and prejudice would be driven from the face of the earth. He reviewed the work accomplished this quadrennium and concluded, thanking the brethren for their hearty cooperation in the work.[21]

What Harris accomplished by these remarks and his other actions of 1903 and 1904 was to sow seeds of disunion rather than to sell the merits of union. Not only did some of his ministers desire to secede from the South Florida Conference, but they began feuding among themselves. This took its most public form when conference reporter M. Edward Church and one-time Presiding Elder W. A. Bain began hurling insults at each other in the pages of the *Star of Zion*. As a part of the exchange Church articulated a personal admission that reflected a broader state of affairs. "I have always preferred silent contempt, but some men take great delight in misrepresenting me," he wrote. "Conceit does not seem to tell them that [I] have feeling," Church added. "I am tired [of] it. I shall hereafter take advantage of an[y] opportunity to resent all misleading statements concerning me from friend or foe."[22]

Comparatively speaking, affairs of the Florida Conference meanwhile had proceeded placidly. The 1900 general conference officially had changed its name to the West Florida Conference and had assigned to it a replacement for longtime Bishop Thomas Henry Lomax in the person of Bishop Isom Caleb Clinton. Then seventy years of age, Clinton had been born in Lancaster County, South Carolina, on May 22, 1830. His owner Irvin Clinton, a lawyer, had permitted the slave to learn to read and write. Clinton accepted a call to the ministry while still a slave. Soon after the end of the Civil War he organized Mount Carmel Church near Lancaster and also opened a school. There, AMEZ Bishop J. J. Clinton—who was not related—discovered the preaching teacher, ordaining him a deacon and elder on March 24, 1867. Election as bishop did not come for Isom C. Clinton until one-quarter century thereafter, although he had fulfilled honorably a series of positions within the national church organization. "Before his promotion he had been a successful pastor and organizer," a friend observed. "He had been a consistent friend of the poor and keeper of the needy, and known for his philanthropic deeds." Bishop William J. Walls added, "This godly nobleman . . . was one of the most beloved men of our church, the first citizen of his home town and county, and [the] ideal man of the race wherever he was known."[23]

Unfortunately, Bishop Clinton already was feeling the weight of his years when he received assignment to Florida, a condition that would result in his death on October 18, 1904. As a result he depended greatly on Bishop Lomax to assist in the execution of his episcopal duties. Thus, Lomax stood by his colleague in Pensacola's Talbot Chapel on February 27, 1901, when Clinton greeted his new flock. The impression made was a good one. "The bishop delivered his annual address which was a master-piece of thought, reason and logic," reporter J. W. Murray related. "In it he referred to all the departments of the Church and the Connection's inter-ests," Murray continued. "Under his wise and energetic management of the deliberations of the Conference, the ministers and members have de-veloped a lively vigor, and it is safe to say that during his administration of affairs this activity will swell with each passing year, as he possesses that organizing spirit, comprehensiveness of mind, executive ability that char-acterize the most successful dignitaries of the age." The reporter added, "With this wise counsellor, able and impartial executive officer, a born leader and Christian giant to lead, the West Florida Conference will ex-plore fields and regions of accomplishment and power such as has never yet been known in the history of the Conference."[24]

Bishop Clinton would undertake to explore "fields and regions of ac-complishment and power such as has never yet been known in the history of the Conference," but circumstances compelled him to do so in a manner different from that of Bishop Harris. The elderly man simply could not endure the kinds of conference tours and one-on-one church-building ef-forts that his South Florida colleague routinely scheduled. This left some churchmen yearning for direct support. "We want to see our Bishop I. C. Clinton," Acting Pastor T. J. Smith of Tallahassee's Pleasant Valley Church declared late in 1901. "Rev. S. Derry, P. E., talks so much about him," Smith stated further. "God bless our Bishop. We hope he will come to see us."[25]

Instead of addressing that yearning for direct support, Clinton began carefully preparing the conference for improvement and sustained, if modest, growth. He did so in at least two important ways. First, the bishop reserved one year to assess his charge. He then reorganized it in the inter-est of efficiency and felicitous utilization of personnel. The three districts that he inherited (Pensacola, Milton, and Tallahassee) shrank to two: Pen-sacola and Tallahassee (soon changed to Milton). T. L. Holt, the Pensacola District's capable presiding elder, remained at his station until 1904 when Clinton placed the Milton District in his charge. The Milton District's 1901 supervisor, pioneer churchman Simon Brown, retired the next year to the pastorate of Pensacola's Mt. Moriah (Tanyard) Church, while Tallahassee District presiding elder Solomon Derry, another veteran nearing retire-ment age, accepted appointment as conference missionary. Clinton re-placed them with a younger and more energetic J. C. Lee. When T. L. Holt moved into Lee's position in 1904, Lee took Holt's in return. By then Clinton's leadership team had been in place for two years, and its composition of young, vigorous churchmen compensated well for the bishop's weaknesses of age and body.[26]

Closely associated with these administrative changes was a determined effort at recruitment of clergy, both skilled veterans and untrained recruits. As to skilled veterans, Clinton's actions concerning the conference's flagship church, Pensacola's Talbot Chapel, help to make the point. Pastor George W. Gaines had arrived in Florida to take over Talbot in 1898 as a seasoned preacher and administrator of the West Alabama Conference. Although Gaines was described as "a model preacher," his drive had diminished by 1902. While his action did not please many Talbot congregants, Clinton in the situation reached to the Western North Carolina Conference for H. S. McMullen as a dynamic replacement. Gaines, in turn, departed resignedly for Hickory, North Carolina, to take up McMullen's old station."[27]

Sometimes, of course, dependence upon newly arrived but dynamic outsiders caused problems for leaders such as Clinton, but the bishop proved to possess an excellent sense of his subordinates' abilities. Again, the example of H. S. McMullen helps to make the point. True to Clinton's expectations, the North Carolina pastor quickly displayed his dynamism. In the process, controversy ensued as McMullen blasted away at his beloved predecessor. "By request of Rt. Rev. I. C. Clinton, D. D., we entered this new field on March 30, 1902; but my! my! what a general state of confusion the church was in," he exclaimed in an August number of the *Star of Zion*. "The tide of oppression had already been turned against us even before our feet struck the western sand," he observed further. "Seemingly the devil and his agents met us on our arrival, and for quite awhile we were at sea." McMullen added:

> But thank God, we went on land. Mark my word, somebody will be held responsible to God for the state of affairs with which we were confronted. The plain truth of the matter relative to the condition of our church in Pensacola, Fla., is that the people have been badly misled by some would be know all big little fellow. Some of our brother ministers will never get far on the highway of the Christian life until they have learned to do right. A hint to the wise is sufficient.[28]

Confronted with this type of public airing of conference laundry, Bishop Harris had proved incapable of quieting the furor, but Bishop Clinton apparently exerted more-effective control. The tone of Pastor McMullen's communications abruptly changed direction. Suddenly, his joy at

Pensacola and its church respected no bounds while negative words completely escaped him. "The good work of Tolbert chapel A.M.E. Zion church of Pensacola, Fla., still goes on," he insisted by March 1903. "Our Zion in Pensacola is sweeping rapidly onward and is abreast with the times." Now, praise replaced criticism. "We don't believe it to be any harm to commend a man, especially when he has done commendable work. Do you?" he asked. He found opportunity as well to express in a lighthearted manner his delight in living among his former antagonists. "By the way, since we have learned to eat oysters, fish, chowder, gumbo, etc., we are spreading [forth] a little," the pastor commented. "You see us. In a few days we will be called up to 'Jerusalem' to answer at the roll call." His change of attitude helped avert divisions within the conference, and it also won McMullen the respect of his congregation. "He is getting along very well with his church paying off each note as they fall due," T. L. Holt reported by October. "He truly is doing well, when you consider all things as you ought, and what he met here when he came," the presiding elder argued, "and aside from all the opposition he is marching as a Christian minister and is carrying things at will."[29]

Besides recruiting and molding experienced churchmen such as McMullen, Clinton pressed his presiding elders to recruit young men to be trained for clerical service within the conference. Year by year enough replacements came forward to fill conference ranks, a signal success in a region with rapidly aging preachers and a declining population. The 1904 annual meeting evidenced the results. That year West Florida lost R. P. Perry to the South Florida Conference and E. J. McKenzie and J. D. Peterson to disciplinary action. On the other hand, H. Maige, R. B. Bury, E. J. George, and J. R. Long joined the conference. Additionally, J. W. Anderson, H. P. Farris, A. Shinn, C. J. Powell, F. J. Smith, P. W. Wilkens, and J. H. Wheeler qualified for ordination as deacons. R. W. Houser and W. K. Killingsworth also achieved elder status. S. Allen returned from the Alabama Conference and W. M. Witherspoon arrived from its Palmetto State counterpart. Clearly, by then the West Florida Conference, at least so long as it remained under Clinton's guiding hand, could sustain itself and perhaps expand its reach without fear of failure from personnel shortage and resultant disharmonies such as those experienced in the South Florida Conference.[30]

Whatever plans Bishop Clinton may have anticipated implementing for conference expansion had not yet been executed when he passed away late in 1904; still, he had achieved significant results for West Florida. Within two years following his death the conference's twenty-four stations and missions had grown by 50 percent to thirty-six. Exact totals for membership growth during his tenure remain less clear. The conference had approximately 1,300 members in 1900, with "marked improvement" being noted "on all lines" just prior to Clinton's death. Two years afterward depopulating West Florida claimed 1,602 congregants, while the booming peninsula's South Florida Conference held but 1,650. It was said in 1908 that the West Florida trend continued. "The numerical strength of this conference," T. R. Gains then insisted, "is steadily increasing year by year."[31]

A sense of the hope with which Clinton gifted the conference, its ministers, and its members flows through T. L. Holt's late 1903 report on his Pensacola District. Having noted charge after charge "doing well" and "in good order," he turned to a new development that looked forward to future progress. "The district is truly improving," he wrote. "We have only one church in the West Florida Conference that can give a pastor a support, Big Zion or Talbot chapel, Pensacola, of which Rev. H. S. McMullen is pastor," he continued, "but on October 4, 1903, we organized a new A.M.E. Zion church in a very popular part of the city known as Clinton chapel church." Holt concluded: "This church will equal any in the future. With our leading church here with G. B. Green and W. E. Plummer as the founders and backbone of the church from a financial stand and some other strong men . . . we will bring this church to the front."[32]

His problems notwithstanding Bishop Harris, too, had accomplished some solid results as the decade's midpoint approached. Although his mission work had not resulted as hoped, several new stations graced the conference by 1904 and 1905. E. D. Wood commented, for instance, on the new Lakeland District in 1903. "The pastors' reports as a whole were very encouraging, showing improvement throughout the district," he averred. "Space will not permit me to speak separately of all reports, but we must speak of the good work being done at Lakeland by Rev. W. A. Bain who, among the pervading influence of opposition, has managed to buy such property that will place Zion on a solid foundation in the future at that place." Especially, the conference's premier churches thrived. Mt. Sinai pastor James C. Thompson, a Central Alabama Conference transfer, was "fast bringing that church back to the mark." Across the gulf from Tampa at Key West spirits lifted even higher. "Three months today I landed on this island and took charge of Cornish chapel," G. W. Johnson had reported as early as 1901. "I found a mortgage of $3,000 with a balance of $385 on the interest due, and I am proud to say that my grand rally on the fourth

Sunday in May was a great success in which we raised $1,400 and paid on the mortgage $1,385, and reduced it to $2,000." Johnson explained further, "We have also added 26 members to the church and raised a total for all purposes during the three months $1,861.15." He concluded, "God be praised."[33]

Good news such as Wood's and Johnson's found eager ears in Florida as the midpoint of the new century's first decade neared, partly because most sensed that times of difficult trials were approaching just as an era was ending for the state's AMEZ Church. One minister had pointed to that sense in late 1903, describing "the grave condition of affairs" what with "lynching, mob violence, anarchy, etc." Just who would lead and what that would mean for the race remained an open question. The year 1904 witnessed a presidential election and, in Florida, a contest for the governor's chair. President Theodore Roosevelt's re-election victory offered hope. Meanwhile, the success of Governor Napoleon Bonaparte Broward in Florida sent chills through the African American community because of his racist language, criticisms of education for African Americans, and support for transporting all blacks to Africa. The church, too, anticipated new leadership. Following Bishop Clinton's 1904 death, Bishop John Wesley Alstork picked up the reins of the West Florida Conference, while the 1904 general convention named Alexander Walters to succeed Cicero R. Harris in South Florida. These were men of an entirely new generation from their predecessors. Their advent marked the waning of the pioneer churchmen, and the loss of knowledge built up of the failures and successes of almost half a century.[34]

Offering in symbolic form the era's longings, tensions, and evolutions, Pensacolians gathered twice during January 1904. On the first day of the month, as had become their custom, they celebrated Emancipation Day and expressed their hopes for an uncertain future. Talbot Chapel AMEZ Church hosted the large and excited gathering of "'Ebony's' sons and daughters." Lawyer Isaac Purcell's recitation of the Emancipation Proclamation, an onlooker declared, "was replete, unique and aroused the spirit of patriotism in the bosom of all true lovers of the cause of freedom and liberty." R. T. Thomas then delivered a "gem" of an address on "the progress of the Negroes of Pensacola." The onlooker commented, "This young man is a thinker and writer of the first water." One-time state representative John Sunday's twelve-year-old grandson thereupon recited the proclamation in his own way. It was said that "the lad walked off with the cake."[35]

At the second event, also conducted at Talbot Chapel, the speaker juxtaposed young Sunday's evocation of an uncertain but hopeful future with a rich and comforting visit to the past. "Rev. Joseph Sexton preached two powerful sermons at Talbert chapel A.M.E.Z. church on the 17th inst.," a report noted. "The Reverend gentleman informs us that he has passed his 72d mile-stone; but my! my! he preaches as though he was just fixing to preach." The sun was setting, though, on the pioneer church that Sexton had helped to found. "His hosts of friends are sure indeed glad to see him again," the reporter assured. He added, "We are still, by the help of God forging our way on and getting ready to go up to Jerusalem."[36]

AFTERWORD

———•◦•———

Zion is still showing
her colors in the state

Although Florida's African Methodist Episcopal Zion Church failed to attract a membership of more than a few thousand during its first four decades in the state, the church proudly flies its banner yet today at historic denominational outposts such as Key West's Cornish Chapel, Tampa's Mt. Sinai, and Kissimmee's St. James. Not only do those posts represent legacies of the AMEZ presence, but so, too, does the continuing commitment to good schools and broad-based education within the African American communities served by the church since the late 1860s and early 1870s; to the African church as a key component of urban life in a once-rural state; and to the overthrow of Jim Crow thanks, in part, to the dedication, contributions, and sacrifices of Zion members and clergy reaching well back into the nineteenth century.

This presence remains the fact even though Florida's boom-and-bust economy, combined with other factors, dealt serious blows to the state's AMEZ family in the twentieth century. On the eve of World War I, 113 congregations offered welcome to 11,496 members. Within only a few years after the conflict's end, though, totals of both congregations and members had plummeted, a dynamic already witnessed on several occasions during the previous century's final decades. "The Florida conference is thin in membership," a correspondent noted by 1922, "and scarce in preachers."[1]

The Reverend G. H. Miles attempted to offer insight into the decline in a letter penned in 1923 following the annual meeting of the Florida Conference at Pensacola. "Nowhere in our Zion field have we lost ground as we have in Florida," he began. "Here in this land of flowers we have lost more than one half of our points, and many churches have gone from us by bad management." Miles continued:

> Each year sees Zion growing smaller in Florida. The men of the conference seemed discouraged and are actually asleep with a few exceptions. Our churches are located around Pensacola. Once we could boast of five good churches in this city, while now we can not claim one first class building in Pensacola. Our leading church here now is Talbot chapel. This church claims a membership of 500. They have a fine brick church started, which, when finished, would equal any church in Zion. [But,] the work on the new church is at a standstill. There is no roof on the building. This leaves the woodwork exposed to the weather and more than $2,500 worth of lumber is now decaying. Zion is to be pitied.[2]

Miles then explored specific reasons for the decline that he had witnessed. "In the country we have lost out in the same manner . . . ," he explained. "The recent migration from this state has shut up some of our churches altogether," the minister continued. "Many of the rural churches were built at places where large saw mills once operated. But these mills have moved and the people have gone also." Miles concluded with a plea to the national church organization. "It is well to build and buy great churches in the north to house our people who are leaving the south," he asserted, "but we must not 'Rob Peter to pay Paul.'" He added: "The night is dark indeed but can't outlast the morning. We need men and money." The response came, though, in the form of transfers, as bishops relocated senior clergymen to more promising locales and replaced them with junior recruits "from neighboring conferences." W. M. McGee put the dynamic into words about the same time as Miles's letter was published in the *Star of Zion*. "The personnel of the South Florida conference," he wrote, "registers the effect of the Methodist transfer system."[3]

The peninsula church fared better for a time than did the panhandle conference, but, there too, decline marked the passage of the early 1900s. By 1920 a report from Jacksonville noted "discouraging and adverse circumstances." The discouragement seemed quickly to beset most places. Another 1923 report, this one from Tampa, illustrated the point. "When Rev. W. M. Wilson came to us last January, 1922, he found things in bad shape," an unidentified layman recorded. "Members were scattered and less than one dollar in the treasury," he described further. The man went on to declare: "The church was in a shameful state of decay. The people had lost confidence and had become discouraged." Where energetic and skilled ministers such as Wilson found opportunity to work, church fortunes often rebounded as they did at Mt. Sinai. Unfortunately, as time passed such men became harder and harder to secure, and lapsed or struggling congregations disappeared forever.[4]

Its struggles and decline notwithstanding, the Florida AMEZ Church has exercised influence on a grander scale than its size would suggest, and its story permits insight into numerous facets of the black church experience, institutional development, and the evolution of the African American community in the post–Civil War era. Especially, intra-church impediments to AMEZ growth and the nature of its rivalry with the AME Church point out aspects and dynamics of the mid- and late-nineteenth century black experience that merit reflection and attention.

Numerous complications arose out of the intra-church impediments to AMEZ growth. The church's struggle to address the dual mission that stemmed from its attempt to appeal to widely divergent interests within its principal congregations appeared large among them. The church's leadership found its initial mission among urban dwellers who eventually would rise to become the state's black middle class. Within a matter of only a few years, however, its host towns emerged as industrial centers. This change led the AMEZ leadership to outreach aimed at a more diversified membership. Unfortunately, the interests of the two groups often clashed, with the church reluctant to express a position that could fully satisfy either body. It thus found itself unable to sustain much enthusiasm for its mission outside the circle of individuals and families whose loyalty had been won previously.

By the same token, internal factors limited the AMEZ ability to reach out into the state at large. It commenced as an urban church in a rural state. A conservative approach evidenced by an unwillingness to expand quickly out of Key West and the Pensacola area then left the rich recruiting ground of Middle Florida, where most slaves had labored and most freedmen lived in the post–Civil War era, largely untouched by Zion missionaries until long after AME and Baptist preachers had won the region for their denominations. Even when tentative steps were taken to extend the church's reach, the efforts provoked little resonance among rural dwellers beyond low-key viability on a short-term basis.

As proved eventually to be the case generally, the tentative early steps seldom involved planning or commanded prolonged preparation. Instead, Zionites reacted more to AME drives to build churches in locales claimed by Zion than they opted to proceed in any proactive manner. Early AME expansion had given that denomination a commanding position within the state, a fact that meant for some time that AMEZ opposition could amount to little more than frustration coupled with symbolic defiance. The AMEZ Church did earn a reputation for being more progressive than the AME in certain respects such as in the involvement of women in church affairs and the recruitment of women for the ministry. But, even with women added to the AMEZ rolls as leaders in Florida, Zionites still fell short of the level of human resources necessary to contest effectively the supremacy of the AME Church (much less the Baptists) in the state.

The dilemma of rural outreach and AME predominance eased somewhat as Florida began to emerge as more of an urban state as the nineteenth century neared its conclusion. Yet denominational policies and beliefs forestalled permanent expansion on the scale desired. Here, the Florida AMEZ Church's reluctance to address political matters during times of critical concerns for the state's African American community made a real—and negative—difference. As the Republican Party's power waned and its ability to protect black residents evaporated, Floridians desperately sought leadership within some sort of institutional framework. An episcopal organization such as that utilized by Zion offered the potential for statewide leadership of the type earlier furnished by Bethel. Institutional resistance to such involvements, even though based not in formal policy but in history and unofficial preference, kept AMEZ bishops and ministers from some important forms of meaningful interaction with the larger community.

Had the mother church desired to provide the leadership required within the state, it would not have been able to meet the challenge, because it had additional internal problems. Its financial situation, for one thing, precluded any larger commitment as the examples of failed missionary efforts proved on any number of occasions. Zion's banner had arrived in Florida without any preparatory planning, and the church's growth thereafter had been haphazard and sporadic. The two main centers of church activity lay hundreds of miles apart at a time when communications were difficult at best and travel posed serious and sometimes dangerous challenges. Only two congregations matured sufficiently under the circumstances to support themselves over time, with the remainder of the church's functions taxing the national organization.

The never-ending funding problems also restricted AMEZ ability to recruit and maintain a pool of trained clergy. Fortuitous circumstances and skillful leadership at times opened windows of opportunity for church growth, but the paucity of personnel and an inability to offer reward for good service blunted many initiatives. Even so basic a matter as a high school for the training of AMEZ laymen and ministers remained out of reach during the time period under consideration. By itself, the problem loomed bad enough. It grew larger by comparison, though, with the colleges opened during the same period by the AME Church and black Baptists.

Meanwhile, the AMEZ General Conference evidenced its resentments at the demands of the Florida mission field. It repeatedly declined to allocate from its already scarce resources a level of funding sufficient to meet continuing needs much less the costs of outreach and greater involvement. The conference and the church's bishops illustrated, in yet another manner, resentment of Florida's chronic problems during the church's formative years. Specifically, they assigned the Florida Conference during the 1870s and early 1880s to bishops who either cared little about the panhandle and peninsular churches or else were unable for a variety of reasons to do much for them. This circumstance brought forth remarkable leadership from men such as Thomas H. Darley, Joseph Sexton, and Warren C. Vesta, but their best efforts could not make up for the loss of steady and farsighted leadership from the top.

That stated, the AMEZ Church nonetheless played a vital role in meeting the religious needs of many black Floridians. Faced with challenge after challenge and what at times amounted to insurmountable odds, Zion preachers offered much to their members and the state during trying times. Their duties differed from church to church and from place to place, but Zion ministers typically preached, administered rites and ceremonies of the church, and assisted their members and others in need during times of natural disasters and other crises. This, for the most part, the church did well. Importantly, AMEZ ministers helped, as well, to set a fitting moral tone during a time of widespread racism, discrimination, segregation, and lynching in the state. Their resources often may have been found wanting, but their group dedication to Florida never wavered. The clergy would serve as an example of strong institutional commitment and untiring dedication to the black community even though not all AMEZ policies, programs, and beliefs met with general satisfaction.

Measured by its function as a denomination established for the religious uplift of African Americans, the AMEZ Church has played a critically important role in the lives of many black Floridians. It has given and continues to offer helpful leadership, service, and comfort to black Floridians. Indeed, if this study tells one significant story, it is the marvelous and even heroic saga of how this church accomplished, with so little, so much of an enduring quality. A Mt. Sinai layman offered a fitting summation from Tampa in 1923. "Zion is still showing her colors in the state," he wrote. "Pray for us that we might go on and make Zion what she ought to be in the State of Florida."[5]

APPENDIX 1.

AMEZ FLORIDA CHRONOLOGY, 1864–1905

1864 AMEZ and AME churches tentatively agree to merge, subject to ratification in 1868. First Florida AMEZ Church established at Key West (Cornish Chapel) by Wilbur G. Strong with authority from Bishop Joseph J. Clinton.

1865 Civil War ends. Bishop Joseph J. Clinton brings AMEZ Church to Pensacola vicinity, establishing congregation at Warrington (Navy Yard). Joseph Sexton plants Zion banner at Tampa (Mt. Sinai).

1866 Pensacola church established (eventually Talbot Chapel).

1867 Ultimately unsuccessful attempt made to carry church from Tampa to Hernando County.

1868 Bishop Joseph J. Clinton organizes Florida District of Alabama Conference. By year's end, Zion churches in Santa Rosa and Polk counties. Congressional or "Radical" Reconstruction begins. Republicans draft new constitution for the state and take charge of government. AMEZ General Conference declines union with AME Church and votes to refer to superintendents thereafter as bishops.

1869 Bishop Joseph J. Clinton organizes Florida Conference.

1871 Expansion attempted into Levy County at Cedar Keys. Yellow fever at Tampa.

1872 Bishop Samson D. Talbot begins four-year term as bishop for Florida.

1873 National economic depression known as the Panic of 1873 commences, with effects lasting for years.

1875 Yellow fever at Key West; hurricane at Tampa.

1876 General Conference names Joseph P. Thompson as bishop for Florida and revises church discipline to eliminate term "male." Congregations established at Nassau, Bahama Islands (St. Joseph's Chapel) and at Jacksonville, Duval County (St. Lukes).

1877 Congressional Reconstruction ends; Democrats "redeem" Florida. Yellow fever at Jacksonville.

1878 Bahamas Conference organized by Bishop Joseph P. Thompson with assistance from Wilbur G. Strong. Hurricanes at Key West and Tampa; yellow fever along Gulf coast.

1880 General Conference begins electing bishops for life and returns Joseph P. Thompson as bishop for Florida. Yellow fever at Nassau and Key West.

1881 Efforts undertaken to expand church missions up the railroad northeasterly from Cedar Key into Alachua County. Federal court lifts order prohibiting state support of railroad construction after state sells four million acres of land to Philadelphia developer Hamilton Disston for twenty-five cents per acre. Railroad construction eastward from Pensacola and southward from northeast Florida commences or accelerates.

1882 Railroad construction spurs creation and growth of towns in panhandle and peninsula. Yellow fever at Pensacola and Key West; smallpox at Jacksonville.

1883 Railroads link Jacksonville with Pensacola. Smallpox at Jacksonville.

1884 General Conference names Singleton T. W. Jones as bishop for Florida. South Florida Railroad reaches Tampa, providing link to Jacksonville and points north. State elects former Confederate general Edward A. Perry as governor.

1885 Church expands into Osceola County. Democrats rewrite state constitution to dilute the power of state government and to require racial segregation in public education.

1886 Church expands into Sumter County. Many black Republicans begin to cooperate with the Knights of Labor to contest municipal elections. Railroad reaches Charlotte Harbor in Manatee (now Charlotte) County.

1887 Florida Conference officially adopts position of presiding elder. Thomas H. Darley named to the position. Church expands into Manatee (now Charlotte) and Jackson counties. Yellow fever at Key West, Pensacola, and Tampa. Labor violence at Pensacola. Tide of racial violence rising.

1888 General Conference names Thomas H. Lomax as bishop for Florida. Church expands into Walton and Lee counties and returns to Polk.

1889 If not earlier, Florida Conference officially divided into two districts, one centered at Pensacola and the other covering South Florida including the former Bahamas Conference. S. L. McDonald and Warren C. Vesta named as presiding elders, with Thomas H. Darley acting as conference steward. Church expands into Lake County. Florida legislature adopts poll tax, a measure that dramatically undercuts black political strength. Phosphate mining craze rocks peninsula.

1890 Florida Conference votes to divide into Florida (West Florida) and South Florida conferences. Church expands into Washington, Okaloosa, Marion, and Seminole counties, returns to Alachua County, and opens numerous additional congregations in counties previously served. Henry Flagler's railroad has linked Daytona with Jacksonville.

1891 Florida (West Florida) and South Florida conferences established. Efforts mapped to expand church into Leon, Jefferson, Suwannee, and Columbia counties. Ministerial recruitment problems proliferate. The Florida conferences agree to build a denominational high school at Bartow, Polk County, and commence fund-raising efforts.

1892 General Conference returns Thomas H. Lomax as bishop for Florida conferences. Church expansion abruptly halts, although growth temporarily sustained. Mary V. Anderson named Florida Conference missionary. Controversy flares over nepotism allegations after Bishop Lomax receives AME minister Joseph N. Clinton, son of Bishop Joseph J. Clinton, into the AMEZ clergy and names him presiding elder of the Florida Conference's Pensacola District. Henry Flagler orders railroad construction south from Daytona.

1893 Mary Frances Green named Florida Conference missionary. National economic depression known as the Panic of 1893 begins, and Democrat Grover Cleveland takes oath of office as president of the United States. Yellow fever at Pensacola. Flagler railroad reaches Palm Beach.

1894 Renewed church expansion, with Putnam, Madison, Orange, Hamilton, Volusia, and St. Johns counties now served. Julia Foote ordained first female deacon in AMEZ Church.

1895 The "great freeze" seriously damages peninsular agriculture. Many congregations quickly lapse with "devastation at most every hand." Membership totals plummet. One-time Zion clergyman and long-time Florida political figure Robert Meacham shot by Tampa policeman.

1896 General Conference returns Thomas H. Lomax as bishop for Florida Conference, names conservative clergyman Cicero R. Harris as bishop for South Florida Conference, and creates Varick Christian Endeavor Society to focus on needs of young people and to offer women enlarged role in church work. Rebuilding process begins. Flagler railroad reaches Miami.

1897 Bishop Harris reorganizes South Florida Conference, but growth frustrated through his four-year term. Problems of clergy recruitment and training reemerge. Republican president William McKinley takes office.

1898 Cornerstone laid for new Talbot Chapel (Pensacola), Florida's first brick AMEZ church. Florida Conference inaugurates new mission events in panhandle heartland. Mary J. Small ordained first woman elder in AMEZ Church. Bishop Lomax possibly ordains Mary V. Anderson an elder or else does so within the next year. Spanish-American War brings racial violence to Tampa, Lakeland, and other Florida locales.

1899 Two church pioneers die: Thomas H. Darley at Tampa and Harrison Williams at Pensacola.

1900 General Conference returns Cicero R. Harris as bishop for South Florida Conference and names Isom C. Clinton as bishop for the West Florida Conference (officially renamed). Harris launches major expansion initiative aimed at new communities on lower Atlantic coast and older settlements in the Bahama Islands.

1901 Bishop Clinton reorganizes West Florida Conference and initiates a modest expansion program based upon ministerial recruitment and training effort. President William McKinley assassinated; Vice President Theodore Roosevelt becomes president.

1903 South Florida Conference expansion efforts fall victim to shortfalls in financial support and lack of a sufficiently large, trained, and energetic clergy. Intra-church feuding erupts. Conference appointments cut by half. A "grave condition of affairs" confronts black Floridians.

1904 General Conference renames Bishop Isom C. Clinton as bishop for West Florida Conference and designates Bishop Alexander Walters as bishop for South Florida Conference. Bishop Clinton passes away; Bishop John W. Alstork replaces him. West Florida Conference has enjoyed sustained, modest, growth.

1905 The AMEZ Church's pioneer era has passed. As new leadership takes the helm of the Florida conferences, Governor Napoleon Bonaparte Broward urges a mandatory white Democratic primary for all state elections and advocates forcible emigration of African Americans from the United States.

Appendix 2.

AMEZ Churches and Ministerial Assignments

Although surviving records do not permit identification of all Florida AMEZ churches, specify the time of creation and termination of every congregation, or detail complete listings of ministers assigned to specific societies, at least some pertinent information can be gleaned for most of the state's churches. The following material was gathered from the church's *Star of Zion* newspaper, WPA Florida Writers' Project historical records survey questionnaires, and other sources listed in the bibliography of this book.

Alachua (Alachua County)
  1902–1903—W. B. Gibbs (Wade, High Springs, and Alachua)
  1904–1905—J. W. Warren (Alachua and Cadillac)
Alafia (Little Zion) (Polk County)
  1868—Joseph Sexton
  1887–1888—James R. Harris (Missionary)
  1889–1890—W. A. Bain (Bartow)
  1890—R. R. Frederick (Bartow)
  1890–1891—R. W. Ballard (Bartow)
  1891–1892—R. R. Frederick (Bartow)
  1892–1893—Warren C. Vesta (Bartow)
  1893–1894—S. L. McDonald (Bartow)
  1894–1897—Warren C. Vesta (Bartow)
  1897–1898—Wiley Walker (Alafia and Homeland)
  1898–1900—A. H. Evans (Bartow Circuit)
  1900—W. J. Sanders (Bartow Circuit)
  1900–1902—J. H. Sliger (Bartow Circuit)
  1902—L. A. Patrick (Bartow Circuit)
  1902–1904—Joseph Sexton (Bartow Circuit)
  1904–1905—J. H. Sliger

Albion (Levy County?)
    1900–1901—Joseph Robinson (Albion and circuit)
    1902–1903—W. C. Adams (Albion and Bronson)
    1903–1904—A. Barber? (Cedar Key Circuit)
    1904–1905—J. M. Jenkins (Cedar Key and Albion)
Altamonte Springs (Seminole)
    1904–1905—G. W. Cook (Altamonte, Sanford, and Oveido)
Anthony (Marion)
    1895–1896—H. Black (Anthony Mission)
Apopka (Orange County)
    1901–1902—H. Redding (Apopka and Higley)
Arcadia (De Soto County)
    1902–1903—J. W. White (Tiger Bay, Arcadia, and Fort Meade)
Archer (Alachua County)
    1901—P. C. Jordan (Archer, Otter Creek, and Newberry)
    1902–1903—T. M. Martin (Newberry and Archer)
    1903–1904—B. J. Martin (Archer Circuit)
Argyle (Walton County)
    1903–1904—R. Farrell (Argyle and Choctawhatchee)
Ashville (Pleasant Grove) (Jefferson County)
    1898–1899—Lee Cobb (Ashville)
    1899–1900—Robert Williams (Ashville Circuit)
    1900–1901—B. J. Jelks (Asheville)
Aucilla (Jefferson County)
    1898–1899—R. H. Hurst (Monticello, Ocilla, and Pin Hook Missions)
    1902–1903—J. W. Anderson (Aucilla)
Bagdad or Blackwater (Santa Rosa County)
    1878–1879—Alexander Robinson (Santa Rosa)
    1880–1882—George W. Maize (Santa Rosa)
    1892–1893—B. F. Stevens (Milton Station and Blackwater)
    1897—B. F. Stevens (Bagdad and Galt City Circuit)
Bartow (Star of Zion) (Polk County)
    1889–1890—W. A. Bain (Bartow)
    1890—R. R. Frederick (Bartow)
    1890–1891—R. W. Ballard (Bartow)
    1891–1892—R. R. Frederick (Bartow)
    1892–1893—W. C. Vesta (Bartow)
    1893–1894—S. L. McDonald (Bartow)
    1894–1897—W. C. Vesta (Bartow)
    1897–1898—L. G. Brookins (Bartow and E. Bartow Mission)
    1898–1900—A. H. Evans (Bartow Circuit)

1900—W. J. Sanders (Bartow Circuit)

1900–1901—R. W. Ballard (East Bartow and Circuit)

1900–1902—J. H. Sliger (Bartow Circuit)

1902—L. A. Patrick (Bartow Circuit)

1902–1904—Joseph Sexton (Bartow Circuit)

1904–1905—W. A. Bain (Bartow Circuit)

Bell (Gilchrist County)

1902–1903—J.E.S. Brown (Dutton, Bell, and Williston)

Bellamy (Alachua County?)

1902–1903—J. R. Montgomery (Sampson City, Bellamy, and Ft. White)

1903–1904—J. D. Lundy (Bellamy)

Bishopville (Jacksonville District)

1899–1900—Silas L. Adger (Bishopville)

Boardman (Marion County)

1902–1903—S. E. Kinsler (Fairfield and Boardman)

Bowling Green (then De Soto County, now Hardee County)

1901–1902—J. W. White (Fort Meade and Bowling Green Mission)

Bradenton (Manatee County)

1904–1905—F. R. Smith (Plant City and Manatee)

Bronson (Levy County)

1902–1903—W. C. Adams (Albion and Bronson)

Brooksville (Hernando County)

1867–1868—James H. Roberts

Bryant (Milton District)

1903–1905—M. Godfrey (Bryant Mission)

Cadillac (Alachua County)

1904–1905—J. W. Warren (Alachua and Cadillac)

Campbell (Osceola County)

1901–1902—Wiley Walker? (Kissimmee Circuit)

1902–1903—A. A. Marshall (Kissimmee and Campbell Mission)

1903–1904—F. R. McIntyre (Campbell Mission)

Carrabelle (Franklin County)

1898—M. Mohorne (Hilliardville and Carrabelle)

Carter's Mill (Polk County)

1902–1903—A. L. Wilkerson (Lakeland and Carter's Mill)

Caryville (New Hope) (Washington County)

1891–1892—Louis Johnson (Caryville, Mossy Head, and Lake De Funiak)

1892–1893—Simon Brown (Caryville Circuit)

1897–1898—T. D. Upshaw (Caryville, New Hope Chapel)

1898–1900—T. D. Upshaw (Caryville Station)

1900–1901—C. W. Thomas (Caryville)

1901–1902—J. W. Booker (Caryville Station)

1902–1903—R. P. Perry (Caryville)

1903–1904—W. K. Killingsworth (New Hope Chapel)

1904–1905—S. Williams (New Hope #1)

—W. K. Killingsworth (New Hope #2)

Cedar Key(s) (Levy County)

1871–1878—John G. Williams

1878–1879—Israel Furby

1883–1884—John A. Bain

1900–1901—P. C. Jordan (Albion and Otter Creek)

1901–1902—P. C. Jordan (Archer, Otter Creek, and Newberry)

1902–1903—B. J. Martin (Cedar Key and Rosewood)

1903–1904—A. Barber (Cedar Key Circuit)

1904–1905—J. M. Jenkins (Cedar Key and Albion)

Center Hill (Zion) (Sumter County)

1886–1887—J. M. Sims

1890–1891—W. J. Sanders

1891–1892—J. M. Sims

1892–1893—J. R. Harris (Leesburg and Center Hill)

1894–1895—J. H. Jordan (Center Hill)

1896–1897—A. Jackson

1898–1899—G. B. Wilson (Leesburg and Center Hill)

1901–1902—J. M. Jenkins (Center Hill Circuit)

1903–1904—M. Edward Church (Center Hill Circuit)

Century (Escambia County)

1902–1903—R. Ford (Century)

1903–1904—R. W. Houser (Century Mission and Warrington)

1904–1905—H. J. Davis (Quintette and Century)

Choctawhatchee (Walton County)

1903–1904—R. Farrell (Argyle and Choctawhatchee)

Clearwater (Pinellas County)

1901–1902—J.A.W. Robinson (St. Petersburg and Clearwater)

Cocoa (Brevard)

1902–1903—J. J. Smith (Cocoa Mission)

Cottondale (St. Paul) (Jackson County)

1887–1888—W. A. Bain (Cottondale)

1888–1889—W. A. Bain (Cottondale Circuit)

1889–1890—Vincent F. White (Cottondale Circuit)

1890–1891—Israel Furby (Cottondale Circuit)

1891–1892—Louis Johnson (Marianna, Cottondale, and Cypress)

1892–1893—G.W.T. Wynns and J. M. Sims (Marianna Circuit)
1897–1898—C. S. Scarborough
1898–1899—G. W. Wallace (Cottondale Circuit)
1900–1901—R. Kemp (Cottondale Circuit)
1901—G. W. Wallace (Cottondale and St. Paul)
1901–1902—C. B. Buie (local preacher)
1902—S. Williams
1902—Joseph Lennox
1902–1903—E. C. Leonardy (St. Paul and Wynn's Chapel)
1903–1904—R. Martin
1904–1905—J. H. Wheeler
Crescent City (Putnam County)
1901–1902—J. H. Hamilton (Crescent City and Ina Missions)
Cypress (Jackson County)
1891–1892—Louis Johnson (Marianna, Cottondale, and Cypress)
Daytona (Volusia County)
1901–1902—("to be supplied")* (Daytona Mission)
1902–1903—James DeVaughn (Daytona and Ormond)
—S. E. Kinsler (Seville, DeLand, and Daytona)
Deerfield (then Dade, now Broward)
1903–1904—William M. Johnson (Deerfield Mission)
De Funiak Springs (Friendship) (Walton County)
1888–1890—Henry Taylor
1891–1892—Louis Johnson (Caryville, Mossy Head, and Lake De
    Funiak)
1892–1893—W. A. Neal
1896–1897—J. L. Cook
1897–1899—H. Taylor (Lake De Funiak Circuit, Wilson Station,
    and Flow River Mission, including Laurel Hill)
1899–1900—B. F. Stevens
1901–1904—H. Taylor (De Funiak Springs)
1904–1905—H. Taylor (De Funiak Circuit)
DeLand (Volusia County)
1895–1896—A. A. Marshall (DeLand)
1902–1903—Oscar V. Jackson (Seville, DeLand, and Daytona)
Drifton (Jefferson County)
1896–1897—R. H. Hurst (Monticello and Drifton)
1897–1898—R. H. Hurst (Drifton)
1898–1899—R. H. Hurst (Monticello, Ocilla, and Pin Hook Mission)
1900–1901—Ephraim Jordan (Drifton)

*The phrase "to be supplied" in church records meant that no minister was ap-
pointed for that year.

1901–1902—J. Finley (Drifton Mission)

1902–1903—E. Jordan (Drifton)

1903–1904—S. L. Adger (Drifton)

1904–1905—J. W. Anderson (Drifton)

Dunnellon (Marion County)

1901–1902—Ed Stevens (Romeo and Dunnellon)

1902–1903—W. H. Frazier (Dunnellon, Romeo, and Morrison)

Dutton's (Alachua County)

1901–1902—J. R. Montgomery (Dutton's and Circuit)

1902–1903—J.E.S. Brown (Dutton's, Bell, and Williston)

Ellaville (Zion Grove) (Suwannee)

1898–1899—G. W. Jordan (Ellaville)

1901–1902—G. W. Jordan (Ellaville Circuit)

1902–1903—R. P. Perry (Ellaville)

Emporia (Volusia County)

1897–1898—A. A. Marshall

Escambia (Escambia County)

1889–1891—Joshua Edwards (East Pensacola Mission)

1891–1892—Henry Taylor (Escambia and Edwards Chapels)

1892–1893—Henry Taylor (Escambia Circuit)

1894–1895—H. McKinney (Escambia Circuit)

1896–1898—J. H. Simons (Escambia Station)

1898–1899—B. J. Arnold (Escambia and Gabroon)

1900–1901—B. F. Stevens (Escambia)

1901–1902—R. W. Houser (Escambia Station)

1902—J. M. Simons (Escambia)

1902–1903—E. J. McKenzie (St. Mark Station)

—L. W. Williams (Escambia)

1903—E. J. McKenzie (St. Mark Station) (resigns)

1903–1904—E. Johnson (St. Mark Station)

—A. Shinn (Escambia Circuit)

—G. W. Jones (Escambia Mission)

1904–1905—A. Shinn (St. Mark)

—E. C. Seward (Escambia)

Eucheeanna (Walton County)

1899–1900—R. H. Hurst (Eucheeanna)

Evinston (Jones Chapel) (Marion County at Alachua County line)

1891–1892—R. W. Ballard

1892–1893—W. J. Sanders

1894–1895—H. E. Jones

1895–1896—J. H. Green

1898–1899—W. C. Cato (Evinston and Micanopy)

1901–1902—B. J. Jelks

1902–1903—Wiley Walker (Evinston and Clinton Chapel)

1904–1905—M. E. Church (Evinston and Romeo)

Fairfield (Marion County)

1902–1903—S. E. Kinsler (Fairfield and Boardman)

Fernandina (Nassau County)

1899–1901—S. R. Rembert (Fernandina Mission)

W. H. Frazier (Fernandina Mission)

1901–1902—James DeVaughn (local preacher)

1902–1903—H. M. Moore (Fernandina Mission)

1903–1905—E. Stevens (Fernandina Mission)

Fligdon (Hamilton County?)

1899–1900—G. W. Jordan (Side Camp Circuit)

1900–1901—G. W. Jordan (Side Camp and Circuit)

1901–1902—G. W. Jordan (Ellaville Circuit, including Side Camp,
Fligdon, and Jennings)

Fort Meade (Polk County)

1901–1902—J. W. White (Fort Meade and Bowling Green Mission)

1902–1903—J. W. White (Tiger Bay, Arcadia, and Fort Meade)

Fort Myers (Lee County)

1888–1890—Robert Meacham (Fort Myers)

1889–1890—M.T.B. Thomas?

1897–1898—A. Jackson (Fort Myers)

1902–1903—("to be supplied") (Fort Myers and Punta Gorda)

Fort White (Columbia County)

1901–1902—J. R. Robinson (Fort White)

1902–1903—J. R. Montgomery (Sampson City, Bellamy, and Fort
White)

Gainesville (Harris Chapel) (Alachua)

1890–1891—B. F. Stevens

1891–1892—D. A. Forbes

1892–1893—R. W. Ballard

1893–1894—Wiley Walker

1894–1895—James R. Harris (Gainesville)

—D. J. Young (Gainesville Mission)

1895–1896—J. M. Jenkins (Gainesville Mission)

1895–1898—I. J. Cousins (local preacher?) (Gainesville)

1898–1899—S. E. Kinsler

1898–1900—E. S. Burney (Gainesville Circuit)

1900–1901—L. A. Patrick (Gainesville and Circuit)

1901–1902—M. Edward Church (Gainesville Station)

1902–1903—William Jacobs (Gainesville Circuit)

1903–1904—F. R. Smith (Gainesville Circuit)

1904–1905—Lewis E. Carr

Galt City (Santa Rosa)

1897—B. F. Stevens (Bagdad and Galt City Circuit)

Georgetown (Putnam)

1894–1895—J. H. Green (Georgetown)

Golden Mission (Pensacola District)

1901–1902—Wesley Killingsworth (Golden Mission)

Grandin (Putnam County)

1894–1895—A. A. Marshall (Grandin)

1898–1900—B. J. Jelks (Grandin Mission)

Grand Ridge (Jackson)

1897–1898—J. L. Cook (Grand Ridge)

1901–1902—F. Ward (Grand Ridge)

Green Cove Springs (Clay County)

1898–1899—S. Gilyard (Green Cove Mission)

Greenville (Shiloh) (Madison County)

1894–1895—A. A. Ponder (Greenville)

1895–1896—A. Jackson (Greenville)

—G. H. May (Jefferson County Mission)

1898–1901—S. L. Adger (Greenville)

1901–1902—E. D. Wood (Greenville Station)

—W. M. Jacobs (Greenville Mission)

1901–1902—R. Ford (Greenville Circuit)

1902–1903—R. P. Perry (Shiloh, Greenville)

—J. W. Anderson (Greenville Chapel)

1903–1904—J. W. Anderson (Greenville)

—G. H. May (Shiloh Mission)

1904–1905—G. H. May (Shiloh Circuit)

Grove Park (Alachua County)

1900–1901—John Warren (Grove Park Mission)

1902–1903—J. W. Warren (Grove Park and Rochelle)

Hawthorne (Alachua County)

1894–1895—G. H. May (Hawthorne)

1898–1899—S. E. Kinsler (Hawthorne, including Gainesville Station)

Higdon (Union AMEZ) (Jacksonville District)

1898–1900—S. W. Haynes (Hayes?)

High Springs (Alachua County)

    1899–1900—J. H. Jordan (High Springs Circuit—Waldo, New Bethel, and High Springs)

    1900–1902—B. J. Grant (replaced by W. B. Gibbs of Rome, Ga.) (High Springs Circuit)

    1902–1903—W. B. Gibbs (Wade, High Springs, and Alachua)

    1903–1904—J. M. Jenkins (High Springs Circuit)

    1904–1905—A. A. Marshall (Clinton Chapel and West High Springs)

Higley (Orange County?)

    1901–1902—H. Redding (Apopka and Higley)

Hilliardville (Wakulla)

    1898—M. Mohorne (Hilliardville and Carrabelle)

Holmes Valley (Holmes County)

    1890–1891—("to be supplied") (Holmes Valley)

    1897—R. P. Perry (Holmes Valley)

    1897–1898—E. M. Sheffield (Holmes Valley)

    1898–1899—E. M. Sheffield (Holmes Valley and Spring Hill Mission)

    1902–1903—E. M. Sheffield (Holmes Valley)

Homeland (Mt. Olive) (Polk County)

    1887–1888—James R. Harris (Missionary)

    1889–1890—W. A. Bain (Bartow)

    1890—R. R. Frederick (Bartow)

    1890–1891—R. W. Ballard (Bartow)

    1891–1892—H. E. Jones (Homeland)

    1892–1893—Warren C. Vesta (Bartow)

    1893–1894—S. L. McDonald (Bartow)

    1894–1897—Warren C. Vesta (Bartow)

    1897–1898—Wiley Walker (Alafia and Homeland)

    1898–1899—A. Jackson (Homeland Circuit)

    1899–1900—M. Edward Church (Homeland Mission)

    1900—W. J. Sanders (Bartow Circuit)

    1900–1902—J. H. Sliger (Bartow Circuit)

    1902—L. A. Patrick (Bartow Circuit)

    1902–1903—Joseph Sexton (Bartow Circuit)

    1903—W. J. Sanders (Homeland and Gardiner)

    1904–1905—W. A. Bain (Bartow Circuit?)

Ina (Putnam County?)

    1901–1902—J. H. Hamilton (Crescent City and Ina Missions)

Jacksonville (St. Lukes) (Duval)

    1876–1877—Israel Furby

    1877–1882—Vincent F. White

1882–1884—Joseph Sexton
1884–1886—R. N. Andrews
1886–1887—George R. Morris
1887–1888—James R. Harris
1888–1889—S. L. McDonald
1889–1890—J. M. Sims
1890–1891—B. F. Stevens
1891–1892—Alex Robinson
1892–1894—S. L. McDonald
1894—Benjamin Roberts
1894–1895—A. Jackson
1895–1896—J. W. Wright
1896–1897—A. H. Evans
1897—J. W. Wright?
1898—R. R. Frederick
1898–1899—E. S. Burney
1899–1901—A. Jackson
1901–1902—W. J. Sanders
1902–1903—J. H. Sliger
1903–1904—E. Stevens
1904–1905—A. Jackson

Jacksonville (Jacksonville Mission or Welcome) (Duval)
1892–1893—Mary Anderson
1893–1897—J. W. Wright
1898–1899—Lewis E. Carr (West Jacksonville)
1901–1902—A. L. Wilkerson (East Jacksonville Mission)
—Ed Stevens (North City Mission)
1902–1903—W. J. Sanders
1903–1904—W. C. Cato (Jacksonville Circuit)

Jennings (Hamilton County)
1899–1900—G. W. Jordan (Side Camp Circuit)
1900–1901—G. W. Jordan (Side Camp and Circuit Mission)
1901–1902—G. W. Jordan (Ellaville Circuit, including Side Camp, Fligdon, and Jennings)

Jupiter (Palm Beach County)
1901–1902—("to be supplied") (New Smyrna, Titusville, and Jupiter)

Key West (Cornish Chapel) (Monroe County)
1864–1869—Sandy Cornish
1870–1882—Thomas H. Darley
1882–1886—Edward Hunter

1886–1887—Robert Meacham
1887–1892—W. C. Vesta
1892—Joseph Sexton
1892–1894—W. G. Strong
1894–1898—G. W. Maize
1898–1901—T.F.H. Blackman
1901–1903—G. W. Johnson (G. W. Hawkins, asst. pastor)
1903–1905—S. M. Gaines

Key West (Key West Mission) (Monroe County)
1889–1890—B. B. Bonner (Key West Mission)
1891–1892—A. L. Higgs (Key West "Ebenezer" Mission)
1901–1902—C. A. Mayo, P. E., Cuban Mission District
1901–1902—("to be supplied") (Cuban Mission)

Kissimmee (St. James) (Osceola County)
1886–1887—J. R. Harris
1887–1890—A. H. Erwin?
1890–1894—W. A. Bain
1894–1895—Joseph Sexton
1895–1896—A. H. Erwin and S. W. Cunningham
1896–1897—W. A. Bain
1897–1898—R. R. Frederick
1898–1900—R. W. Ballard
1900–1902—Wiley Walker
1902–1903—A. A. Marshall
1903–1904—W. A. Bain (Kissimmee Circuit)
1904–1905—Joseph Sexton

Knight's Station (Hillsborough County)
1900–1901—J. G. Gooden (Knight's Station Mission)

Lake City (Columbia County)
1891–1892—("to be supplied") (Lake City)
1894–1895—John Warren (Lake City and White Springs Mission)
1901–1902—J. R. Harris (Lake City)

Lakeland (Polk County)
1897–1898—S. W. Cunningham (Simmons Hammock and Plant
    City Circuit)
1898–1900—Wiley Walker (Lakeland Circuit)
1900–1901—A. L. Higgs (Lakeland Circuit)
1902–1903—A. L. Wilkerson (Lakeland and Carter's Mill)
1903–1904—W. A. Bain
1904–1905—Wiley Walker

Leesburg (Lake County)

  1890–1891—(lot purchased June 9)

  1891–1892—J. H. Jordan and J. M. Sims

  1892–1893—J. R. Harris (Leesburg and Center Hill)

  1895–1896—W. A. Bain

  1898–1900—G. B. Wilson (Leesburg and Center Hill)

  1900–1901—J. M. Jenkins (Leesburg and Circuit)

  1901–1902—Lewis E. Carr (Leesburg Circuit)

  1902–1903—George W. Maize (Leesburg Circuit)

  1903–1904—J. H. Sliger (Leesburg Circuit)

  1904–1905—Oscar V. Jackson (Leesburg Circuit)

Live Oak (Suwannee County)

  1891–1892—Wilson Perry (Live Oak Mission)

  1894–1895—S. L. Adger (Live Oak Mission)

  1898–1899—J. W. Jones (Live Oak Mission)

  1901–1902—James G. Gooden (Live Oak)

Marianna (Jackson County)

  1891–1892—Louis Johnson (Marianna, Cottondale, and Cypress)

  1892–1893—("to be supplied") (Marianna Circuit)

Miami (Harris Chapel) (Dade County)

  1899–1900—("to be supplied") (Miami)

  1900–1901—William Johnson (Miami)

  1901–1902—Joseph Sexton (Miami)

  —William Johnson (Coconut Grove)

  1902–1903—Joseph Sexton

  1903–1904—W. Pericles Pickens (Miami Circuit)

  —L. J. Hobbs (Coconut Grove Mission)

  1904–1905—F. A. Hamilton (Miami Station)

Micanopy (Alachua County)

  1894–1895—S. E. Kinsler (Micanopy)

  1895–1896—S. E. Kinsler (Micanopy Mission)

  1898–1999—W. C. Cato (Evinston and Micanopy)

  1899–1902—S. E. Kinsler (Micanopy and Circuit)

  1902–1903—William Jacobs? (Gainesville Circuit)

  1903–1904—S. E. Kinsler (Micanopy Mission)

Millers Ferry (Walton County)

  1902–1903—E. M. Sheffield (Holmes Valley)

  1903–1904—E. M. Sheffield (Elizabeth and Little Zion Circuit)

  1904–1905—E. M. Sheffield (Elizabeth Circuit)

Milligan (then Walton County, now Okaloosa County)
    1891–1892—G. G. Hornsby (Milligan's Mill)
    1892–1893—J. D. Peterson (Milligan Mission)
    1893–1894—A. L. Green (Milligan)
    1894–1895—H. Taylor (Milligan)
    1897–1898—Lum Williams (Milligan Station)
    1898–1899—J. M. Simons (Milligan Station)
    1902–1903—F. R. Smith (Milligan)
    1903–1904—G. W. Hogan (Milligan Circuit, including Lalhill and
      Florilla Missions)
Millview (Brown's Chapel) (Escambia County)
    1889–1890—Israel Furby (Millview)
    1890–1891—Henry Taylor (Millview)
    1891–1892—M. S. Arnold (Millview and Pine Orchard)
    1892–1893—Alex Robinson (Millview Circuit)
    1893–1895—B. F. Stevens (Millview)
    1897–1898—M. Mohorne (Muscogee and Millview)
    1898–1900—J. W. Murray (Millview and Muscogee Circuits)
    1900—W. C. Vesta (Millview)
    1900–1902—J. W. Murray (Millview Circuit)
    1902–1903—T. M. Moore (Millview and Muscogee)
    1903–1904—A. Gregory (Millview and Muscogee)
    1904–1905—H. Graves (Millview and Muscogee)
Milton (Isaiah Chapel) (Santa Rosa County)
    186?-1870—Gabriel Sexton
    1872–1876—Joseph Sexton
    1876–1877—Vincent F. White
    1877–1879—Oscar V. Jackson
    1879–1881—Joseph Sexton
    1881–1884—Robert N. Andrews
    1884–1889—George W. Maize
    1889–1890—J. R. Harris
    1890–1891—W. H. Smith
    1891–1893—B. F. Stevens
    1893–1894—E. J. Carter
    1894—B. F. Stevens
    1894–1895—A. L. Green
    1895–1896—Henry Taylor
    1896–1897—J. M. Sims

1897–1898—Solomon Derry
1898–1900—M. Mohorne
1900–1902—T. M. Moore
1902–1903—J. R. Sheppard
1903–1904—H. Graves
1904–1905—Simon Brown
1905–1906—Mary V. Anderson
Milton Ferry (Tallahassee District)
1901–1902—S. Williams (Milton Ferry)
Monticello (Jefferson County)
1891–1892—("to be supplied") (Monticello)
1895–1896—G. W. May (Jefferson County)
1897–1898—R. H. Hurst (Monticello and Drifton)
1898–1899—R. H. Hurst (Monticello, Ocilla, and Pin Hook Missions)
1902–1903—("to be supplied") (Monticello)
Morriston (Levy County)
1901–1902—James Dudley (Morrison Mission)
1902–1903—W. H. Frazier (Dunnellon, Romeo, and Morrison)
1903–1904—J. G. Gooden (West Tampa and Morrison Mission)
1904–1905—James Dudley (Morrison Mission)
Muscogee (St. Paul Chapel) (Escambia County)
1890–1892—Simon Brown (Powelton and Muscogee)
1892–1893—J. L. Cook (Powelton and Muscogee Circuit)
1893–1895—B. F. Stevens (Millview)
1897–1898—M. Mohorne (Muscogee and Millview)
1898–1900—J. W. Murray (Millview and Muscogee Circuits)
1900—Warren C. Vesta (Millview)
1901–1902—Israel Furby (Muscogee)
1902–1903—T. M. Moore (Millview and Muscogee)
1903–1904—A. Gregory (Millview and Muscogee)
1904–1905—H. Graves (Millview and Muscogee)
Narcoosee (Osceola County)
1899–1900—F. McIntyre (Narcoosee Circuit)
Nassau, Bahamas (St. Joseph's Chapel)
1876–1878—Joseph Sexton (Nassau)
1878–1881—Robert N. Andrews (Nassau)
1881–1882—Joseph Sexton (Nassau)
1884–1889—Joseph Sexton (Nassau)
1885–1890—David Thomas (Nassau District)
—Thomas Lynn (Bahamas)

1889–1890—David Thomas (Nassau District)
1891–1892—Oscar V. Jackson
1892–1898—A. L. Higgs
1898–1899—W. A. Bain (Nassau)
1899–1900—L. A. Patrick (Nassau)
—Ed Dean (Fox Hill)
1900–1901—Edward Dean (Nassau Station)
—Henry J. Johnston (Fox Hill)
1901–1902—H.W.J. Johnston (Nassau Station)
—Edward Dean (Fox Hill and Baintown)
—F. Douglass (New Road Mission)
—Charles Maesa (Harbour Island and East Nassau)
—J. Adderly (Andros Island)
1902–1903—A. Jackson (Nassau Station)
—Ed Dean (Fox Hill)
—H.W.J. Johnston (Abaco)
—("to be supplied") (New Road, Tarpon Bay, and Governor's Harbour)
1903–1904—A. Jackson (Nassau Station)
—W. Harrison Lane (Nassau Mission)
—Ed Dean (Fox Hill Mission)
—H.W.J. Johnston (Abaco Mission)
—J. A. Bain (Baintown Mission)
—("to be supplied") (Eleuthera Mission)
1904–1905—R. P. Perry (Nassau Station)
—Ed Dean (Nassau Mission)
Newberry (Alachua County)
   1900–1901—J. R. Montgomery
   1901—P. C. Jordan (Archer, Otter Creek, and Newberry)
   1902–1903—T. M. Martin (Newberry and Archer)
New Smyrna (Volusia)
   1901–1902—("to be supplied") (New Smyrna, Titusville, and Jupiter)
Ocala (Marion County)
   1899–1900—W. C. Cato (Ocala Circuit)
Ola (then De Soto County, now Hardee County)
   1902–1903—("to be supplied") (Ola Mission)
Olive (Escambia County)
   1898–1899—H. J. Davis (Olive and Cantonment Mission)
   1901–1903—Wilson Perry (Spring Hill and Olive Missions)
   1903–1904—A. Gregory (St. Luke and Olive Missions)
   1904–1905—S. Allen (Pine Barren and Olive)

Orange Bend (Sanders Chapel) (Lake County)
   1889–1890—W. J. Sanders (local preacher)
   1893–1896—W. J. Sanders (Orange Bend and Lake Eustis)
   1898–1899—J. E. Rivers
   1900–1901—J. M. Jenkins (Leesburg Circuit)
   1901–1902—Lewis E. Carr (Leesburg Circuit)
Orange Heights (Alachua County)
   1894–1895—E. D. Wood (Orange Heights)
   1895–1896—C. S. Thompson (Orange Heights)
   1898–1900—James R. Montgomery (Orange Heights)
   1900–1901—E. M. Freeman (Orange Heights and Circuit)
   1901–1902—W. C. Cato
   1902–1903—B. J. Jelks (Orange Heights and Waldo)
Orlando (Orange County)
   1894–1895—F. R. McIntyre
   1902–1903—("to be supplied") (Orlando)
Ormond (Volusia County)
   1902–1903—James DeVaughn (Daytona and Ormond)
Otter Creek (Levy County)
   1901—P. C. Jordan (Archer, Otter Creek, and Newberry)
Oveido (then Orange, now Seminole)
   1904–1905—G. W. Cook (Altamonte, Sanford, and Oveido)
Palatka (Putnam County)
   1895–1896—W. M. Reid (Palatka Mission)
   1899–1900—S. L. Burkett (Palatka Mission)
   1900–1901—W. T. Walker (Putnam Hall and Circuit)
   1901–1902—A. A. Marshall (Palatka and Seville)
   1902–1903—Lewis E. Carr (Palatka and Putnam Hall)
   1903–1904—L. W. Garnett (West Palatka)
   1904–1905—E. D. Wood (Palatka and Putnam Hall)
Palmetto (Manatee County)
   1904–1905—E. S. Burney (Plant City and Palmetto)
Pensacola (Clinton's Chapel) (Escambia County)
   1904–1905—W. M. Witherspoon (Clinton and Edwards Chapels)
   1905–1906—H. B. Wells (Clinton's Chapel)
Pensacola (Edwards Chapel) (Escambia County)
   1879–1880—Joshua Edwards (local preacher?)
   1882–1884—Alexander Robinson (Edwards Chapel, Zion Church)
   1888–1889—Israel Furby (Edwards Chapel)
   1889–1890—M. S. Arnold (Edward's Chapel)
   1890–1891—Joshua Edwards (East Pensacola Mission)

1891–1892—Henry Taylor (Escambia and Edwards Chapels)
1892–1893—Henry Taylor (Escambia Circuit)
1898—G. W. Powell (Edwards Chapel Circuit; Edwards Chapel #1
    and #2)
1898–1899—Squire Allen (Edwards Chapel)
—William M. Moseley (Edwards Chapel #2)
1901–1902—R. M. Simmons (Edwards Chapel)
1902–1903—A. Gregory (Edwards Chapel and Powelton)
1903–1904—J. R. Sheppard (Edwards Chapel)
1904–1905—W. M. Witherspoon (Clinton and Edwards Chapels)
1905–1906—Israel Furby
Pensacola (Mt. Moriah, Tan Yard Church, or Little Zion) (Escambia
County)
    1888–1889—Oscar V. Jackson (Tanyard Church)
    1889–1890—Alex Robinson (Tan Yard Church)
    1890–1891—Alex Robinson (Warrington Circuit)
    1891–1892—Israel Furby (Tanyard and Warrington)
    1892–1893—H. M. Martin (Mt. Moriah)
    1893–1894—Simon Brown (Tanyard Church)
    1894–1895—S. M. Brown (Warrington Circuit)
    1897–1898—Simon Brown (Mt. Moriah and St. Luke)
    1898–1900—T. L. Holt (Mt. Moriah)
    1900–1901—J. C. Lee (Mt. Moriah)
    1902–1904—Simon Brown (Mt. Moriah Station)
    1904–1905—J. R. Sheppard (Mt. Moriah)
    1905–1906—Simon Brown (Mt. Moriah)
Pensacola (St. Lukes) (Escambia County)
    1892–1893—J. D. Peterson (St. Lukes)
    1893–1895—J. D. Peterson (St. Luke's Chapel)
    1897–1898—Simon Brown (Mt. Moriah and St. Luke)
    1898–1899—J. C. Lee (St. Luke and Warrington Circuit)
    1901–1902—T. M. Moore (St. Lukes)
    1902–1903—F. A. Hogans (St. Luke)
    1903–1904—A. Gregory (St. Luke and Olive Mission)
    1904–1905—A. Shinn (St. Luke Circuit)
    1905–1906—R. P. Perry (St. Luke's)
Pensacola (Talbot Chapel) (Escambia County)
    1866–1869—E. S. Winn
    1869–1871—Alexander C. Fisher
    1871–1874—W. C. Vesta
    1874–1880—J. M. Butler

1880–1882—W. C. Vesta?

1882–1887—Thomas H. Darley

1887–1888—S. L. McDonald

1888—F. A. Clinton

1888–1891—Thomas H. Darley

1891–1894—W. H. Smith

1894–1895—E. J. Carter

1895–1898—J. H. Manley

1898–1902—G. W. Gaines

1902–1904—H. S. McMullen

1904–1906—William M. Massey

Pine Barren (Escambia County)

1891–1892—J. L. Cook (Pine Barren Mission)

1892–1893—Sam Allen (Pine Barren Mission)

1894–1895—Sam Allen (Chumuckla Circuit, including Pine Barren, Quintette, and Carpenter's Creek)

1897–1898—H. J. Davis (Chumuckla and Pine Barren Circuit)

1898–1899—J. D. Peterson (Molino and Pine Barren)

1901–1902—R. Ford (Pine Barren)

1902–1903—W. M. Moseley (Pine Barren Circuit)

1903–1904—A. J. Liggett (Pine Barren)

1904–1905—S. Allen (Pine Barren and Olive)

Pine Orchard (Escambia County)

1891–1892—M. S. Arnold (Millview and Pine Orchard)

1892–1894—Wilson Perry (Orchard Church)

1894–1895—S. M. Brown (Warrington Circuit)

Plant City (Little Zion) (Hillsborough County)

1892–1893—J. H. Jordan (Simmons Hammock)

1894–1897—R. R. Frederick

1897–1899—S. W. Cunningham (Simmons Hammock and Plant City Circuit)

1899–1900—W. A. Bain (Plant City Circuit)

1900–1904—E. S. Burney (Plant City Circuit)

1904–1905—F. R. Smith (Plant City and Manatee)

Point Washington (Thomas Chapel) (Walton County)

1890–1891—W. A. Neal (Point Washington)

1891–1892—W. A. Neal (Thompson Chapel and Point Washington)

1892–1893—J. M. Sims (Thompson Chapel Circuit)

1896–1897—J. L. Cook (Point Washington, Hogtown, Shipyard Point, Red-bay, and Burnout Churches)

1897–1898—J. C. Bellamy (Thomas' Chapel)

1898—J. L. Cook (Point Washington and Hogtown Circuit)
1898–1900—R. Ford
1901–1902—D. D. Peoples (Point Washington)
1902–1903—W. K. Killingsworth (Point Washington)
1904–1905—P. W. Wilkens (Point Washington Circuit)
Pomona (Putnam County)
1902–1903—L. W. Garnett (Welaka and Pomona)
Powelton (Escambia County)
1891–1892—Simon Brown (Powelton and Muscogee)
1892–1893—J. L. Cook (Powelton and Muscogee Circuit)
1894–1895—G. W. Powell (Powelton Circuit)
1897–1898—F. R. Smith (Powelton)
1898—Sam Allen (Powelton and Cedar Town)
1898–1899—F. R. Smith (Powelton and Cedar Town)
1901–1902—G. W. Powell (Powelton Station)
1902–1903—A. Gregory (Edwards Chapel and Powelton)
1903–1905—G. W. Powell (Powelton)
Punta Gorda (then De Soto County, now Charlotte County)
1887–1888—Robert Meacham (Punta Gorda)
1902–1903—("to be supplied") (Ft. Myers and Punta Gorda)
Putnam Hall (Putnam County)
1894–1895—J. H. Hamilton (Putnam Hall)
1899–1900—S. L. Burkett? (Palatka Mission)
1900–1901—W. T. Walker (Putnam Hall and Circuit)
1901–1902—A. Jackson (Putnam Hall)
1902–1903—Lewis E. Carr (Palatka and Putnam Hall)
1903–1904—L. W. Garnett? (West Palatka)
1904–1905—E. D. Wood (Palatka and Putnam Hall)
Quincy (Gadsden)
1896–1897—H. M. Martin (River Junction and Quincy)
Quintette (Ascend) (Escambia County)
1894–1895—S. Allen (Chumuckla Circuit)
1897–1898—H. Graves (Spring Hill and Quintette)
1898–1899—R. P. Perry (Quintette)
1903–1904—Wilson Perry (Quintette)
1904–1905—H. J. Davis (Quintette and Century)
Ridgewood (Polk County)
1898–1899—A. A. Marshall (Ridgewood)
Rochelle (Alachua County)
1901–1902—S. E. Kinsler (Rochelle Circuit)
1902–1903—J. W. Warren (Grove Park and Rochelle)

1903–1904—S. E. Kinsler? (Micanopy Mission)
1904–1905—S. E. Kinsler (Rochelle Mission)
Romeo (Mount Carmel) (Marion County)
    1898–1899—L. A. Patrick (Romeo)
    1900–1901—W. C. Cato (Romeo Mission)
    1901–1902—Ed Stevens (Romeo and Dunnellon)
    1902–1903—W. H. Frazier (Dunnellon, Romeo, and Morrison)
    1904–1905—M. Edward Church (Evinston and Romeo)
Rosewood (Levy County)
    1902–1903—B. J. Martin (Cedar Key and Rosewood)
St. Augustine (St. Johns County)
    1894–1895—William Reid (St. Augustine)
    —John Horton (St. Augustine Mission)
    1895–1896—J. W. Whitman (St. Augustine)
    1901–1902—L. A. Patrick (St. Augustine Mission)
St. Petersburg (Pinellas County)
    1901–1902—J.A.W. Robinson (St. Petersburg and Clearwater)
    1902–1903—M. Edward Church and M. C. Kelley
    1903–1904—M. C. Kelley (St. Petersburg Circuit)
Sampson City (Bradford County)
    1899–1900—Emory Freeman (Sampson City)
    1902–1903—J. R. Montgomery (Sampson City, Bellamy, and Ft. White)
Sanford (Seminole County)
    1891–1892—J. R. Harris
    1892–1893—R. R. Frederick and Benjamin Roberts
    1899–1900—A. A. Marshall (Sanford Mission)
    1901–1902—Oscar V. Jackson (Sanford Mission)
    1902–1903—("to be supplied") (Sanford Mission)
    1904–1905—G. W. Cook (Altamonte, Sanford, and Oveido)
Satsuma (Putnam County)
    1894–1895—R. H. Williams (Satsuma)
Seffner (Mt. Zion) (Hillsborough County)
    1868—Joseph Sexton
    1891–1892—R. R. Frederick (Simmons Hammock)
    1892–1893—J. H. Jordan (Simmons Hammock)
    1894–1896—R. R. Frederick (Plant City)
    1897–1899—S. W. Cunningham (Simmons Hammock and Plant City
        Circuit)
    1899–1900—W. A. Bain (Plant City Circuit)
    1900–1901—W. A. Bain (Seffner)

1901–1902—J. H. Hale (Seffner Circuit)
1902–1903—F. A. Hamilton (Seffner and Ybor City)
1903–1904—F. A. Hamilton (Seffner)
1904–1905—E. S. Burney (Seffner and Palmetto)
Seminole (then Walton, now Okaloosa County)
    1903–1904—A. Fry (Seminole)
Seville (Philips Chapel) (Volusia County)
    1895–1896—J. W. Horton (Seville and Georgetown)
    1896–1897—S. Moses Houston
    1897–1900—S. M. Houston (Seville Circuit)
    1900–1901—A. A. Marshall (Seville and Circuit)
    1901–1902—A. A. Marshall (Palatka and Seville)
    1902–1903—Oscar V. Jackson (Seville, DeLand, and Daytona)
    1903–1904—H. M. Moore (Seville Circuit)
    1904–1905—L. W. Garnett (Seville Mission)
Side Camp (Suwannee County)
    1899–1900—G. W. Jordan (Side Camp Circuit)
    1900–1901—G. W. Jordan (Side Camp and Circuit Mission)
    1901–1902—G. W. Jordan (Ellaville Circuit; Side Camp, Fligdon, and
      Jennings)
    1902–1905—G. W. Jordan (Side Camp)
Spring Hill (Escambia County)
    1894–1895—Wilson Perry (Spring Hill)
    1897–1898—H. Graves (Spring Hill and Quintette)
    1898–1899—Wilson Perry (Spring Hill Circuit)
    1901–1902—Wilson Perry (Spring Hill and Olive Missions)
    1902–1903—Wilson Perry (Spring Hill)
    1903–1904—H. J. Davis (Spring Hill)
    1904–1905—E. J. George (Spring Hill Circuit)
Spring Hill (Holmes County?)
    1898–1899—E. M. Sheffield (Holmes Valley and Spring Hill Mission)
Starke (Bradford County)
    1902–1903—B. J. Jelks (Orange Heights, Waldo, and Starke)
Sugarloaf Key (Monroe County)
    1902–1903—James Dudley (Sugarloaf Key and surroundings)
Summerville (Cottondale District)
    1897–1898—W. D. Lennox (Summerville)
    1898–1899—S. Williams (Summerville and Valley Mission)
Syril (Alachua County?)
    1903–1904—J. R. Montgomery

Tallahassee (Leon County)
    1891–1892—("to be supplied") (Tallahassee)
    1896–1898—J. C. Lee (Tallahassee)
    1897–1898—A. H. Evans (Tallahassee)
    1898–1899—F. R. Smith (Pleasant Valley)
    —J. N. Raspberry (Tallahassee Station)
    1899–1900—J. D. Peterson (Tallahassee) (Mt. Pleasant)
    1900–1901—Fillmore R. Smith (Tallahassee Station)
    —C. J. Powell (Lomax Chapel)
    1901–1902—Fillmore R. Smith (Tallahassee Station)
    —C. W. Thomas (Lomax Chapel)
    1902–1903—R. W. Simmons (Tallahassee) (Pleasant Valley)
    1903–1904—J. D. Peterson (Tallahassee) (Mt. Pleasant)
    1904–1905—H. P. Norris (Tallahassee Circuit)
Tampa (Mt. Sinai) (Hillsborough County)
    1865–1868—Joseph Sexton
    1868–1869—James H. Roberts
    1869–1872—Joseph Sexton
    1874–1875—Joseph Healey?
    1875–1876—Israel Furby
    1877–1878—R. N. Andrews
    1878–1879—Joseph Sexton
    1879–1882—Oscar V. Jackson
    1885–1886—J. W. Bowen
    1886–1887—Edward Hunter
    1887–1889—Alex Robinson
    1889–1894—G. W. Maize
    1894–1895—W. G. Strong
    1895–1896—F. R. Smith
    1896–1897—Thomas H. Darley
    1897–1898—W. J. Sanders
    1898–1899—G. L. White
    1899–1900—J. W. Randolph
    1900–1903—A. H. Evans
    1903—James C. Thompson
    1903–1905—W. J. Sanders
Tampa (Port Tampa City) (Hillsborough County)
    1899–1900—A. L. Higgs
    1904–1905—Mack Kelley (St. Petersburg and Port Tampa Missions)

Tampa (West Tampa) (Hillsborough County)

    1901–1902—A. L. Higgs

    1902–1903—G. W. Luckey

    1903–1904—J. G. Gooden (West Tampa and Morrison Mission)

Tampa (Ybor City) (Hillsborough County)

    1891–1892—W. J. Sanders

    1892–1893—James Dudley (Ybor City)

    1899–1900—J. M. Jenkins (Ybor City)

    —James Dudley (East Ybor City)

    1900–1901—James Dudley (Ybor City Mission)

    1902–1903—F. A. Hamilton (Seffner and Ybor City)

Thomas City (Jefferson County)

    1904–1905—C. J. Powell (Thomas City)

Tiger Bay (Polk County)

    1902–1903—J. W. White (Tiger Bay, Arcadia, and Ft. Meade)

Titusville (Brevard County)

    1895–1896—M.T.B. Thomas

    1901–1902—("to be supplied") (New Smyrna, Titusville, and Jupiter)

Valdosta (Lowndes County, Ga.)

    1901–1902—E. C. Leonardy (Valdosta Mission)

Wade (New Bethel) (Alachua County)

    1897–1898—G. B. Wilson (Wade)

    1898–1899—J. M. Jenkins (Wade)

    1899–1900—J. H. Jordan (High Springs Circuit; Waldo, New Bethel, and High Springs)

    1900–1901—J. H. Jordan (Wade Circuit)

    1901–1902—W. T. Walker (Wade Circuit)

    1902–1903—W. B. Gibbs (Wade, High Springs, and Alachua)

    1903–1904—Lewis E. Carr (Wade Circuit)

    1904–1905—J. R. Montgomery (Syril and Wade)

Waldo (Alachua County)

    1899–1900—J. H. Jordan (High Springs Circuit; Waldo, New Bethel, and High Springs)

    1900–1902—B. J. Grant (High Springs Circuit)

    1902–1903—B. J. Jelks (Orange Heights and Waldo)

    1903–1904—J. H. Hamilton (Waldo Mission)

Warrington (Good Hope or Navy Yard) (Escambia County)

    1865—Harrison Williams (church originally organized at Turpentine Orchard)

1870—Harrison Williams (church reorganized at New
Warrington)
1889–1891—Alex Robinson (Warrington Circuit)
1891–1892—Israel L. Furby (Tan Yard and Warrington)
1892–1894—Israel L. Furby (Warrington)
1894–1895—S. M. Brown (Warrington Circuit)
1897–1898—R. P. Perry (Warrington and St. Marks)
1898–1899—J. C. Lee (St. Luke and Warrington Circuit)
1901–1902—J. M. Simons (Warrington Station)
1902–1903—Mary V. Anderson (Navy Yard)
Welaka (Putnam County)
1900–1901—M. Edward Church (Welaka Mission)
1901–1902—L. W. Garnett (Welaka Mission)
1902–1903—L. W. Garnett (Welaka and Pomona)
1904–1905—J. H. Hamilton (Welaka Mission)
West Palm Beach (Palm Beach County)
1898–1899—J. M. Jenkins (Palm Beach) (at Wade by Aug.)
1901–1902—W. Pericles Pickens (West Palm Beach Circuit)
1902–1903—("to be supplied") (West Palm Beach)
1903–1904—W. Pericles Pickens? (Miami Circuit)
1904–1905—W. Pericles Pickens (West Palm Beach)
White Springs (Hamilton County)
1894–1895—John Warren (Lake City and White Springs Mission)
Wildwood (Sumter County)
1899–1900—("to be supplied") (Wildwood)
Williston (Levy County)
1902–1903—J.E.S. Brown (Dutton, Bell, and Williston)
Wynn Chapel (Jackson County?)
1897–1898—("to be supplied") (Wynn's Chapel)
1898–1899—F. A. Hogans (Cottondale Circuit, St. Paul, and Wynn
Chapel)
1899—G. W. Wallace (Cottondale Circuit, including Wynn
Chapel)
1900–1901—R. Kemp (Cottondale Circuit)
1901–1902—J. E. Battles (St. Paul Circuit)
1902–1903—E. C. Leonardy (St. Paul and Wins Chapel)

ABBREVIATIONS

AME African Methodist Episcopal
AMEZ African Methodist Episcopal Zion
Census Manuscript returns, U.S. Decennial Census or Florida State Census, as appropriate
CH-RECS Church Records. Questionnaires of the Historical Records Survey of the Florida Writers' Program, WPA
CSZ *Charlotte Star of Zion*
FSA Florida State Archives, Tallahassee
JDFU *Jacksonville Daily Florida Union*
JET *Jacksonville Evening Telegram*
JFT-U *Jacksonville Florida Times-Union*
JFU *Jacksonville Florida Union*
MSCA *Macon Southern Christian Advocate*
NA National Archives, Washington, D.C.
NYA *New York Age*
NYF *New York Freeman*
NYG *New York Globe*
PCR *Philadelphia Christian Recorder*
PDN *Pensacola Daily News*
PKY P. K. Yonge Library of Florida History, University of Florida, Gainesville
PSZ *Petersburg Star of Zion*
RG Record Group
SMN *Savannah Morning News*
SSZ *Salisbury Star of Zion*
TFP *Tampa Florida Peninsular*
TG *Tampa Guardian*
TMT *Tampa Morning Tribune*
TS Tallahassee Sentinel
TST *Tampa Sunland Tribune*
TWF *Tallahassee Weekly Floridian*
WPA Work Projects Administration

NOTES

INTRODUCTION

1. Minutes, AMEZ General Conference, 1884, 93; Walls, *African Methodist Episcopal Zion Church*, 192–93.

2. Bradley, *History of the A.M.E. Zion Church*, vol. 1, 42–45; PDN, May 29, 1892. For more on Peter Williams, see Swift, *Black Prophets of Justice*, 6, 27, 41, 60–69, 73–74, 117, 166.

3. Bradley, *History of the A.M.E. Zion Church*, vol. 1, 47–57.

4. Rivers and Brown, *Laborers in the Vineyard of the Lord*, 19–21; Hood, *One Hundred Years*, 56–129.

5. Walls, *African Methodist Episcopal Zion Church*, 43–83.

6. Bradley, *History of the A.M.E. Zion Church*, vol. 1, 80–82, 150–51, 155; Walls, *African Methodist Episcopal Zion Church*, 71–83.

7. Walls, *African Methodist Episcopal Zion Church*, 97, 102.

8. Ibid., 105–6; Martin, *For God and Race*, 178–79; Gravely, *Gilbert Haven*, 191–92.

9. Bradley, *History of the A.M.E. Zion Church*, vol. 1, 158–60.

10. Walls, *African Methodist Episcopal Zion Church*, 172–83; Bradley, *History of the A.M.E. Zion Church*, vol. 1, 131–44.

11. Bradley, *History of the A.M.E. Zion Church*, vol. 1, 107–8; Martin, *For God and Race*, 13–14. See also Swift, *Black Prophets of Justice*.

12. Angell, *Bishop Henry McNeal Turner*, 64–67; Hood, *One Hundred Years*, 130–53; Rivers and Brown, *Laborers in the Vineyard of the Lord*, 1–22.

13. Stuckey, *Slave Culture*, 37–64; Raboteau, *Slave Religion*; Blassingame, *Slave Community*, 130–48; Boles, *Masters and Slaves*; Hall, "Do Lord, Remember Me"; Genovese, *Roll, Jordan, Roll*; Heyrman, *Southern Cross*; Mathews, *Religion in the Old South*; Fitts, *History of Black Baptists*; Lincoln and Mamiya, *Black Church*; Higginbotham, *Righteous Discontent*; McKinney and McKinney, *History of the Black Baptists of Florida*; Jordan, *Negro Baptist History*; Joyner, *Down by the Riverside*.

14. Rawick, *American Slave*, vol. 14, 32–38, 93–99, 109–10, 347–54.

15. Ibid., 32–37; Burton, *In My Father's House*.

16. Bradley, *History of the A.M.E. Zion Church*, vol. 1, 16–19; Angell, *Bishop*

Henry McNeal Turner, 46–53; Rivers and Brown, *Laborers in the Vineyard of the Lord*, 4–8.

17. Rivers, *Slavery in Florida*, 106–24; *MSCA*, March 4, 1874; Temple, *Florida Flame*, 32–33, 40–41, 52; Brooks, *From Saddlebags to Satellites*, 23–24; Martin, *Florida during the Territorial Days*, 36, 108–12; Smith, *Slavery and Plantation Growth*, 9–12; Groene, *Ante-Bellum Tallahassee*, 3–22.

18. See McKinney and McKinney, *History of the Black Baptists of Florida*, 9–27; Rivers, *Slavery in Florida*, 114–24; Rivers, "Baptist Minister James Page"; Rivers and Brown, *Laborers in the Vineyard of the Lord*, 9–10, 16–19; Long, *History of the A.M.E. Church in Florida*, 55–57; Rawick, *American Slave*, vol. 14, 166–67, 242–47; Raboteau, *Slave Religion*, 212–88.

19. *Tallahassee Daily Democrat*, April 16, 1928. See also, for example, Burton, *In My Father's House*, 242–59; Rivers and Brown, *Laborers in the Vineyard of the Lord*; Lincoln and Mamiya, *Black Church*; Fitts, *History of Black Baptists*; Higginbotham, *Righteous Discontent*; McKinney and McKinney, *History of the Black Baptists of Florida*; Angell, *Bishop Henry McNeal Turner*; Walker, *Rock in a Weary Land*; Bradley, *History of the A.M.E. Zion Church*; Walls, *African Methodist Episcopal Zion Church*; Martin, *For God and Race*; Johnson and Jersild, *"Ain't Gonna Lay My 'Ligion Down"*; Montgomery, *Under Their Own Vine and Fig Tree*; Rivers, *Slavery in Florida*, 120–24.

20. Woodward, *Strange Career of Jim Crow*, 1–109; Brown, *Florida's Black Public Officials*, 59–69; *JFT-U*, November 18, 1905; Colburn and Scher, *Florida's Gubernatorial Politics*, 220–21; Proctor, *Napoleon Bonaparte Broward*, 252.

21. Tebeau, *History of Florida*, 278–308, 327–43.

1. CORNISH CHAPEL, 1864–1865

1. Walls, *African Methodist Episcopal Zion Church*, 402, 571–72; Hood, *One Hundred Years*, 172; *SSZ*, October 5, 1893.

2. Hood, *One Hundred Years*, 172–73; Bradley, *History of the A.M.E. Zion Church*, vol. 1, 127, 154, 157; Walls, *African Methodist Episcopal Zion Church*, 185–86, 570–71.

3. Walls, *African Methodist Episcopal Zion Church*, 186; Hood, *One Hundred Years*, 172–73.

4. Minutes, AMEZ General Conference, 1896, 110; Martin, *For God and Race*, 157, 209; Angell, *Bishop Henry McNeal Turner*, 64–65.

5. Bradley, *History of the A.M.E. Zion Church*, vol. 1, 158–59.

6. Martin, *For God and Race*, 34–35, 51–56; Bradley, *History of the A.M.E. Zion Church*, vol. 1, 160–61.

7. Walls, *African Methodist Episcopal Zion Church*, 188–93; Bradley, *History of the A.M.E. Zion Church*, vol. 1, 152–53; Hood, *One Hundred Years*, 87.

8. Minutes, AMEZ General Conference, 1884, 93; Walls, *African Methodist Episcopal Zion Church*, 191–92.

9. Browne, *Key West*, 174; Brown, *Ossian Bingley Hart*, 68–72; Mayo, *Sixth Census of the State of Florida*, 90.

10. Browne, *Key West*, 171–73; Rivers, *Slavery in Florida*, 79–81; Brown, *Ossian Bingley Hart*, 69–70; *Savannah Daily Georgian*, May 14, 1853.

11. Rivers, *Slavery in Florida*, 79–80; Browne, *Key West*, 171; *Boston Daily Journal*, September 12, 1862.

12. The 1870 Monroe County census; Browne, *Key West*, 171–72; *CSZ*, November 30, 1899; Thomas H. Darley to Ossian B. Hart, July 5, 1867, Correspondence of Ossian B. Hart, Superintendent of Registration, RG 156, series 626, FSA; 1866 Monroe County tax roll.

13. *NYG*, August 18, 1883; *JFT-U*, July 14, 1883; Brown, *Florida's Black Public Officials*, 125; Manley, Brown, and Rise, *Supreme Court of Florida*, 128–31; Brown, *Tampa before the Civil War*, 129–30, 145–46; 1866 Monroe County tax roll.

14. Schmidt, "From Slavery to Freedom and Success," 12–13. On Samuel Cornish see, for example, Swift, *Black Prophets of Justice*.

15. John A. Wilder to "My Dear Mother," March 5, 1864, Loomis-Wilder Family Papers, Yale University Library.

16. Hay, *Letters of John Hay and Extracts from Diary*, vol. 1, 176–77; Reid, *After the War*, 182–85.

17. Brown and Brown, *Family Records*, 86–88; *JFT-U*, July 27, 29, 1883; Rivers, *Slavery in Florida*, 13, 185, 219, 246.

18. Hawes, "Tampa-born Sheriff"; Hillsborough County Day Book (March 18, 1837–March 2, 1846), 326; 1873 Monroe County tax roll; Brown, "As Far as Our Eyes Will Let Us See," 48; Brown and Brown, *Family Records*, 35–37.

19. *TST*, March 16, 1878; Brown and Brown, *Family Records*, 220–21; Brown, "Bartow Is the Place for Our People to Go," 2; Brown, *Florida's Peace River Frontier*, 165–69; Brown, *Fort Meade*, 16, 19–20, 23–24, 42–48.

20. Coles, "They Fought Like Devils," 40; Coles, "Far from Fields of Glory," 265–71; James A. Roberts military pension record 681174, Veterans Administration, RG 15, NA; Brown, *Florida's Black Public Officials*, 120.

21. Newman, "History of Cornish," 1; Rivers and Brown, *Workers in the Vineyard of the Lord*, 16–17; Lewis, "Bartow, West Bartow, and the Andy Moore Family," 52–53; Tarbox, *Memoirs of James H. Schneider*, 172.

22. Newman, "History of Cornish," 1; Tarbox, *Memoirs of James H. Schneider*, 161–62.

23. Newman, "History of Cornish," 1; Tarbox, *Memoirs of James H. Schneider*, 166.

24. Tarbox, *Memoirs of James H. Schneider*, 177–78.

25. Ibid., 181.

26. Nuwer, "1878 Yellow Fever Epidemic," 51–58; Rivers, "They . . . Exalt Humbug at the Expense of Science and Truth," 9–10; *New York Herald*, July 1, August 14, 1864.

27. *New York Herald*, May 5, August 31, 1864; *New York Freedmen's Advocate*, June 1864.

28. *New York Freedmen's Advocate*, June 1864; Minutes, AMEZ General Conference, 1884, 93.

29. Minutes, AMEZ General Conference, 1884, 93; Walls, *African Methodist Episcopal Zion Church*, 192–93.

30. Minutes, AMEZ General Conference, 1884, 93.

31. *CSZ*, July 18, 1901; Minutes, AMEZ General Conference, 1884, 93.

32. Hood, *One Hundred Years*, 367.

33. Cornish Chapel AMEZ Church, Monroe County, in CH-RECS; Newman, "History of Cornish," 1; Maloney, *Key West*, 35–36; Browne, *Key West*, 172; Reid, *After the War*, 189; *Miami Herald*, June 7, 1964.

34. Bradley, *History of the A.M.E. Zion Church*, vol. 1, 161–62; Hood, *One Hundred Years*, 87, 312; *SSZ*, September 24, 1891; *MSCA*, April 26, 1871.

35. Hood, *One Hundred Years*, 312; Minutes, AMEZ General Conference, 1884, 93; Walls, *African Methodist Episcopal Zion Church*, 192–93.

36. *Key West Daily Equator-Democrat* (Trade Edition), March 1889; Newman, "History of Cornish," 1; *TS*, April 30, 1867.

2. OUTREACH, 1865–1868

1. Hood, *One Hundred Years*, 297, 367.

2. Walls, *African Methodist Episcopal Zion Church*, 103.

3. Ibid., 103–4.

4. *Key West Daily Equator-Democrat* (Trade Edition), March 1889; Newman, "History of Cornish," 1; Maloney, *Key West*, 36; *CSZ*, November 30, 1899; *TST*, March 16, 1878; Brown and Brown, *Family Records*, 220–21.

5. Wynn, "History of Mt. Sinai A.M.E. Zion Church"; Mt. Sinai AMEZ Church, Hillsborough County, in CH-RECS; Brown, *Tampa in Civil War and Reconstruction*, 55, 61, 101–2.

6. Wynn, "History of Mt. Sinai A.M.E. Zion Church"; Polk County Marriage Records, A ("Marriage License Records for Colored Persons"), 6.

7. Martin, *For God and Race*, 93; Shofner, *Nor Is It Over Yet*, 53.

8. Monroe County Deed Records, F, 949, 952; "Tampa Church" in Federal Writers' Project, *Negro in Florida's Cities*, unpaginated; *Key West Equator-Democrat* (Trade Edition), March 1889.

9. Hood, *One Hundred Years*, 312, 365, 370–72; Walls, *African Methodist Episcopal Zion Church*, 193, 197; *Mobile Nationalist*, May 10, 1866. On Mobile and its political and religious significance, see Fitzgerald, *Urban Emancipation*.

10. Hood, *One Hundred Years*, 312, 365, 370–72; Walls, *African Methodist Episcopal Zion Church*, 193, 197.

11. *CSZ*, February 20, 1902; *MSCA*, December 21, 1866; 1870, 1885 Escambia County censuses.

12. Wilson, "Pensacola and Its Colored People," 328; Richardson, "Negro History in Pensacola," 8–10, in Federal Writers' Project, *Negro History in Florida.*

13. Durkin, *Confederate Navy Chief,* 391; William Fiske to George Whipple, April 25, 1866 (two letters), American Missionary Association Archives; Hoskins, *History of Methodism in Pensacola,* 75.

14. *New York World,* November 2, 1865; E. B. Cole to Mrs. Millikin, March 23, 1866, and Fiske to Whipple, April 25, 1866, American Missionary Association Archives.

15. *Mobile Nationalist,* May 10, 17, 1866.

16. *CSZ,* February 20, 1902; Escambia County Marriage Records, E, 124½, 147½, 161½; *Guide to Supplementary Vital Statistics from Church Records in Florida,* vol. 1, 297.

17. *CSZ,* February 20, 1902; 1870 Escambia County census.

18. *Guide to Supplementary Vital Statistics from Church Records in Florida,* vol. 1, 297; *Milton Santa Rosa Press-Gazette,* June 29, 1967; *MSCA,* November 5, 1869; Hoskins, *History of Methodism in Pensacola,* 75.

19. Martin, *For God and Race,* 64; Temple, *Florida Flame,* 140.

20. Temple, *Florida Flame,* 140–41, 146; Thrift, *Trail of the Florida Circuit Rider,* 107.

21. *MSCA,* November 5, 1869; *Savannah Daily Republican,* March 18, 1867; Temple, *Florida Flame,* 149; Mitchell, *African American Religious History in Tampa Bay,* 6.

22. *JFU,* August 6, 1868.

23. Rivers, *Slavery in Florida,* 16–84; Shofner, *Nor Is It Over Yet,* 123–34.

24. Rivers and Brown, *Workers in the Vineyard of the Lord,* 23–50; *PCR,* July 13, 1867.

25. Monroe County Deed Records, F, 949, 952; Stanaback, *History of Hernando County,* 11–27; Landers, "Freedmen's Bureau Becomes a Force in Hernando"; *JFU,* August 6, 1868.

26. *Florida Voter Registration Lists, 1867–68,* 6; Richard Comba to Allen H. Jackson, February 29, March 31, May 31, June 17, 1868, Records of the Assistant Commissioner and Subordinate Field Offices for the State of Florida, Bureau of Refugees, Freedmen, and Abandoned Lands, 1865–1872, M-1869, roll 8, NA. On missionary efforts in the South generally during this period, see Montgomery, *Under Their Own Vine and Fig Tree,* 38–96.

27. Hood, *One Hundred Years,* 365; Walls, *African Methodist Episcopal Zion Church,* 197; *CSZ,* July 18, 1901.

28. Landers, "Freedmen's Bureau Becomes a Force in Hernando"; Bentley, *History of the First South Florida Missionary Baptist Association,* 28–29; Brown and Brown, *Family Records,* 165–71, 248–50; Brown, *Florida's Black Public Officials,* 95, 128; Brown, *African Americans on the Tampa Bay Frontier,* 55, 57–60.

29. Foner, *Reconstruction,* 176–227; Shofner, *Nor Is It Over Yet,* 31–58; Brown, *Ossian Bingley Hart,* 150–62, 171–73.

30. Foner, *Reconstruction*, 228–80; Brown, *Florida's Black Public Officials*, 6–13.

31. *Pensacola West Florida Commercial*, February 4, 1868; petition to Major Richard Comba, August 30, 1867, Letters Received, Dept. and Dist. of Florida, 1865–1869, RG 393, box 5, NA; *TFP*, August 22, October 3, 24, 1868; *Tampa True Southerner*, October 29, December 3, 1868.

32. Brown, *Florida's Black Public Officials*, 97; Martin, *For God and Race*, 69–71, 78, 114.

33. Rivers and Brown, *Laborers in the Vineyard of the Lord*, 43–58, 74–75; Brown, *Florida's Black Public Officials*, 1–22; *PCR*, July 29, 1871.

34. Rivers, "Baptist Minister James Page," 47–53; McKinney and McKinney, *History of the Black Baptists of Florida*, 21–27, 33–35; Brown, *Florida's Black Public Officials*, 114, 125, 128.

35. Walls, *African Methodist Episcopal Zion Church*, 192.

36. Richard Comba to Allen H. Jackson, March 31, 1868, roll 8, and E. B. Duncan, Report of Inspection Tour of Schools from Pensacola to Key West, May 17, 1867, roll 9, M-1869, NA; Hillsborough County Deed Records, C, 633; *Pensacola West Florida Commercial*, October 15, 1868.

37. Fahey, *Black Lodge in White America*, 5–9; Greenbaum, "Comparison of African American and Euro-American Mutual Aid Societies," 95–102; *Pensacola Commercial*, March 4, 16, 1869.

38. *Savannah Daily News and Herald*, June 28, 1866; Davis, *Civil War and Reconstruction in Florida*, 431; Brown, *Tampa in Civil War and Reconstruction*, 104–6.

39. T. Seymour to Allen H. Jackson, October 5, 1867, M-1869, roll 9, NA; *Pensacola Commercial*, January 19, 1869; *New York Herald*, November 10, 1865; Brown, *Tampa in Civil War and Reconstruction*, 122–24; *TFP*, February 16, 1868.

40. *New York Herald*, November 10, 1865; Seymour to Jackson, October 5, 1867; *TFP*, August 17, 1867, July 28, 1869; Shofner, *Nor Is It Over Yet*, 208; *St. Augustine Examiner*, September 21, 1867; Brown, *Tampa in Civil War and Reconstruction*, 120–24.

3. THE FLORIDA CONFERENCE, 1868–1875

1. *CSZ*, June 27, 1901.

2. Walls, *African Methodist Episcopal Zion Church*, 197.

3. Rivers and Brown, *Laborers in the Vineyard of the Lord*, 45–48, 52.

4. Bradley, *History of the A.M.E. Zion Church*, vol. 1, 154, 157; Angell, *Bishop Henry McNeal Turner*, 100.

5. Hood, *One Hundred Years*, 380; Walls, *African Methodist Episcopal Zion Church*, 202.

6. Hood, *One Hundred Years*, 380; Walls, *African Methodist Episcopal Zion Church*, 202; Bradley, *History of the A.M.E. Zion Church*, vol. 1, 163; *CSZ*, November 19, 1903; *Tampa Journal*, December 8, 1888; 1870 Hillsborough County census.

7. Escambia County Marriage Records, F, 86, 88, 93, G, 94; *Pensacola West Florida Commercial,* February 4, 1868; *Tallahassee Sentinel,* January 22, 1870; Santa Rosa County Marriage Records, Marriage License Record 1869–1877, 24; Hillsborough County Marriage Records, B-2, 18–20; Hillsborough County Deed Records, C, 633; Monroe County Deed Records, G, 618–19, 628, 629; 1870 Escambia, Hillsborough, and Polk County censuses; Schmidt, "From Slavery to Freedom and Success," 14.

8. Walker, *Ninth Census—Volume I,* 19, 98; Brown, *Tampa in Civil War and Reconstruction,* 120–37.

9. John G. Williams to B. H. Bristow, September 26, 1874, Department of the Treasury, Customs Service Appointment Records, Cedar Key, RG 56, entry 246, box 63, NA; Brown, *Florida's Black Public Officials,* 140.

10. James A. Roberts military pension record, Records of U.S. Department of Veterans Affairs, RG 15, NA; Roberts to John F. Horr, August 22, 1890, Department of the Treasury, Customs Service Appointment Records, Key West, RG 56, entry 246, box 69, NA; *JDFU,* February 28, 1876; Brown, *Florida's Black Public Officials,* 120.

11. Brown and Brown, *Family Records,* 10–16, 86–88; *CSZ,* December 20, 1900.

12. Brown and Brown, *Family Records,* 35–40; Brown, *Florida's Black Public Officials,* 78.

13. Foner, *Reconstruction,* 245–46; Rivers and Brown, "Rejoicing in Their Freedom," 6–11; Brown, *Tampa in Civil War and Reconstruction,* 119, 167–68; Brown, *In the Midst of All That Makes Life Worth Living,* 116; Brown, *Florida's Peace River Frontier,* 205–7; *TG,* April 21, 1886.

14. Rivers, *Slavery in Florida,* 77–78; Stephen Harvell slave interview, Florida Negro Papers, box 7, USF Special Collections; *CSZ,* October 4, 1900; Brown and Brown, *Family Records,* 106–9.

15. Stone, "Profile of Lloyd Davis," 25–26; Brown, *Florida's Peace River Frontier,* 195–200; Brown, *"Bartow Is the Place for Our People to Go,"* 4–5; *Fort Meade Leader,* April 19, 1928; Polk County Marriage Records, B, 25, vol. 1, 114, 149.

16. Pettengill, *Story of the Florida Railroads,* 114–15; *Pensacola Tri-Weekly Observer,* October 19, 1868.

17. Drobney, *Lumbermen and Log Sawyers,* 26–27; Pettengill, *Story of the Florida Railroads,* 39; Mayo, *Sixth Census,* 90; *Pensacola Semi-Weekly Commercial,* November 5, 1869.

18. Browne, *Key West,* 125–26; Mayo, *Sixth Census,* 90; *New York Daily Tribune,* October 16, 1872; *MSCA,* May 5, 1874.

19. Roberts to Horr, August 22, 1890; *Cornish/Matthews Family Reunion,* 25; Saunders, *Bridging the Gap,* 29; Robert W. Saunders Sr., interviews, January 30, 1997, December 4, 1998.

20. Shofner, "Militant Negro Laborers," 407; Shofner, *Nor Is It Over Yet,* 236; *Cornish/Matthews Family Reunion,* 25.

21. Brown, *Tampa in Civil War and Reconstruction,* 142–45, 175–76.

22. *TFP,* December 15, 1869; Mitchell, *African American Religious History in*

Tampa Bay, 6; Mt. Sinai AMEZ Church, Hillsborough County, in CH-RECS; Santa Rosa County Deed Records, A, 355–57; *Milton Santa Rosa Press-Gazette*, June 29, 1967; Nathan Woolsey to Canter Brown Jr., June 22, 1998, collection of Canter Brown Jr.

23. *Pensacola Semi-Weekly Commercial*, July 16, November 19, 1869; *Guide to Supplementary Vital Statistics from Church Records in Florida*, vol. 1, 280.

24. *PDN*, February 1890 (West Florida Trade and Industrial Number); *Guide to Supplementary Vital Statistics from Church Records in Florida*, vol. 1, 296.

25. Escambia County Deed Records, S, 555; *Guide to Supplementary Vital Statistics from Church Records in Florida*, vol. 1, 297; *PDN*, February 1890 (West Florida Trade and Industrial Number), April 28, 1893.

26. *Pensacola Semi-Weekly Commercial*, August 6, 1869; *SMN*, November 19, 1872; Escambia County Deed Records, X, 41.

27. On Cedar Keys, see Fishburne, *The Cedar Keys in the Nineteenth Century*, and Dees and Dees, *"Off the Beaten Path."*

28. Brown, *Tampa in Civil War and Reconstruction*, 144–45; Elliott, *Best of Its Kind*, 145; *Diary of Eliza Horn*, 10.

29. Brown, *Tampa in Civil War and Reconstruction*, 149–50; *FP*, September 30, 1871; *Diary of Eliza Horn*, 10.

30. *TFP*, September 23, November 18, 1871.

31. *Diary of Eliza Horn*, 10; *TS*, December 2, 1871; Brown, *Florida's Black Public Officials*, 140; Levy County Marriage Records, A, 75–76, Marriage License Record 1874–1879, 9, 20, 25–26; John G. Williams to B. H. Bristow, September 26, 1874, and John V. Cornell to Bristow, October 30, 1874, Department of the Treasury, Customs Service Appointment Records, Cedar Keys, RG 56, entry 246, box 63, NA.

32. *TS*, January 20, 1872; Hillsborough County Marriage Records, B, 131, C, 62, 67; Santa Rosa County Marriage Records, Marriage Record Book 1869–1877, 69–70, 75–76.

33. The 1870 Escambia County census; *Florida Voter Registration Lists, 1867–68*, 223; Escambia County Marriage Records, H, 19, I, 92, 108; Santa Rosa County Marriage Records, Marriage Record Book 1869–1877, 24; Duval County Marriage Records, Book 4, 227, 235, 530, 640, 654.

34. *PCR*, June 17, 1875; *SSZ*, September 24, 1891; Walls, *African Methodist Episcopal Zion Church*, 202, 575.

35. *PCR*, December 28, 1872.

36. Rivers and Brown, *Workers in the Vineyard of the Lord*, 69–72; *PCR*, January 22, 1870.

37. Rivers and Brown, *Workers in the Vineyard of the Lord*, 69, 97–98; *PCR*, August 20, 1874.

38. *PCR*, June 10, 1871, June 17, 1875.

39. Ibid., August 19, 1880.

40. Montgomery, *Under Their Own Vine and Fig Tree*, 121; Brown, *Florida's*

Black Public Officials, 105–6, 142; Brown, *Ossian Bingley Hart*, 251–68; Brown and Brown, *Family Records*, 129–30; Brady, *Things Remembered*, 179.

41. Brown, *Florida's Black Public Officials*, 140; Fishburne, *Cedar Keys*, 87; Commissions of Office, vol. 30, unpaginated, RG 156, series 259, and Resignations from Office, vol. 1, 345, RG 156, series 260, FSA; Escambia County Marriage Records, I, 18, 21, 90, 103, 110; Hood, *One Hundred Years*, 367.

42. *Savannah Daily Republican*, January 12, 1872; *Savannah Daily Advertiser*, March 8, 1872; *Jacksonville Tri-Weekly Florida Union*, January 16, 1873; *TWF*, September 30, December 16, 1873, September 22, October 6, 1874; *Diary of Eliza Horn*, 13; Barnes, *Florida's Hurricane History*, 68; *Savannah Advertiser-Republican*, September 4, 1873; Foner, *Reconstruction*, 512–17; Shofner, *Nor Is It Over Yet*, 273; Bailey, *Narrative Reports of County Superintendents*, 55; *MSCA*, July 21, 1875.

43. *PCR*, June 17, 1875.

4. CONSEQUENCES OF NEGLECT, 1875–1884

1. *PCR*, June 17, 1875; Walls, *African Methodist Episcopal Zion Church*, 575; Martin, *For God and Race*, 92–93.

2. *TST*, March 16, 1878; *PCR*, October 10, 1878; Escambia County Marriage Records, J, 64, 96.

3. *PCR*, July 8, 1875; Rivers and Brown, *Laborers in the Vineyard of the Lord*, 89, 110; *TST*, March 16, 1878; Santa Rosa County Marriage Records, Marriage Record Book 1869–1877, 137, 164.

4. Martin, *City Makers*, 108–17; Rivers and Brown, *Laborers in the Vineyard of the Lord*, 18, 28, 100–101, 112–16, 119; Duval County Marriage Records, Book 4, 244, 320.

5. Walls, *African Methodist Episcopal Zion Church*, 226.

6. Minutes, AMEZ General Conference, 1880, 16–17; *SSZ*, January 3, 1895.

7. Foner, *Reconstruction*, 564–601; Shofner, *Nor Is It Over Yet*, 300–341.

8. *JDFU*, August 14, 1876; Duval County Marriage Records, Book 4, 320, 348; *TST*, March 16, 1878; *JFT-U*, February 7, 1908; *Guide to Supplementary Vital Statistics from Church Records in Florida*, vol. 1, 246.

9. Rivers and Brown, *Laborers in the Vineyard of the Lord*, 89–91, 102–3, 120, 124, 135–36, 145–47, 162; *PCR*, June 4, 1885.

10. Martin, *For God and Race*, 79, 121–23.

11. Fahey, *Temperance and Racism*, 106, 121–22; Rivers and Brown, *Workers in the Vineyard of the Lord*, 103–6; *TS*, October 28, 1876.

12. *Birmingham (Eng.) Good Templars' Watchword*, December 27, 1876, March 12, 1879; *TS*, October 28, 1876; *PCR*, October 10, 1878; *Jacksonville Florida Daily Times*, February 2, 1883; "Senior Grand Lodge of Florida," 300–301.

13. *SSZ*, April 14, 1892, March 9, 1893, August 23, 1894.

14. Montgomery, *Under Their Own Vine and Fig Tree*, 188.

15. *Bartow Courier-Informant*, July 26, 1893; *TWF*, June 19, July 10, 1877; *Jacksonville Daily Sun and Press*, July 8, 1877; Warner, *Free Men in an Age of Servitude*, 122.

16. *TWF*, June 19, July 10, 1877; *Jacksonville Daily Sun and Press*, July 8, 1877; Warner, *Free Men in an Age of Servitude*, 122.

17. *TST*, March 31, 1877; *TWF*, March 20, 1877; Menard, *Lays in Summer Lands*, 103–16, 125, 131; Brown, *Ossian Bingley Hart*, 262.

18. Montgomery, *Under Their Own Vine and Fig Tree*, 95, 114, 139.

19. Schmidt, "From Slavery to Freedom and Success," 13–14; Brown and Brown, *Family Records*, 35; *CSZ*, February 20, 1902.

20. Haywood, *Prophesying Daughters*, xiii, 6–13, 121; Bradley, *History of the A.M.E. Zion Church*, vol. 1, 122–23. Additional recent and worthy works have touched on the story of early African American women preachers. They include, among others, Collier-Thomas, *Daughters of Thunder*; Dodson, "Nineteenth-Century A.M.E. Preaching Women"; and Higginbotham, *Righteous Discontent*.

21. Walls, *African Methodist Episcopal Zion Church*, 111–12; Minutes, AMEZ General Conference, 1884, 135.

22. *SSZ*, February 11, 1892; *CSZ*, July 1, 1897.

23. *Key West Key of the Gulf*, May 7, 1881.

24. *Pensacola Commercial*, March 20, 1869; *TWF*, March 23, 1880; *TST*, July 29, 1880.

25. Montgomery, *Under Their Own Vine and Fig Tree*, 280–81; *Pensacola Semi-Weekly Commercial*, October 15, 1869.

26. Montgomery, *Under Their Own Vine and Fig Tree*, 281–82; *PSZ*, November 7, 1884.

27. Santa Rosa County Marriage Records, Marriage Record Book 1869–1877, 164, Marriage Record Book 1877–1887, 3, 13; 1880 Hillsborough and Monroe County censuses; Duval County Marriage Records, Book 4, 235, 244, 530, 640, 654; Levy County Marriage Records, A, 17; Hillsborough County Marriage Records, C, 110; Escambia County Marriage Records, I, 332, 372, 378, 384–85, 399, 402–3, 441.

28. Walls, *African Methodist Episcopal Zion Church*, 248.

29. Hood, *One Hundred Years*, 399–400; Walls, *African Methodist Episcopal Zion Church*, 248–49.

30. Monroe County Marriage Records, Book 1, 17; *SSZ*, September 24, 1891; *TST*, March 16, July 6, September 28, 1878; Rivers and Brown, "Rejoicing in Their Freedom," 11–12; Brown, *Tampa in Civil War and Reconstruction*, 163–70.

31. Santa Rosa County Marriage Records, Marriage Record Book 1877–1887, 25–42; 1885 Santa Rosa County census; *CSZ*, October 25, 1923.

32. Escambia County Marriage Records, I, 507, 519, 531, J, 7–8, 53; Escambia County Deed Records, X, 41; *JDFU*, October 16, 1876; Levy County Marriage Records, Marriage License Record 1874–1879, 20, 26; Levy County Deed Records, C, 445; 1880 Chatham County, Georgia, census.

33. *SSZ*, December 6, 1888; Levy County Marriage Records, Marriage License Record 1874–1879, 28, 32–33; *Bronson Levy County Enterprise*, February 23, 1883; Escambia County Marriage Records, J, 220, 223, 296; Santa Rosa County Marriage Records, Marriage Record Book 1877–1887, 69; *TST*, March 5, 1881; Duval County Marriage Records, Book 5, 729, 789; *CSZ*, November 28, 1901; Monroe County Marriage Records, Book 1, 307–8; Hillsborough County Marriage Records, D, 48, 51–52, 83; Polk County Marriage Records, B, 25.

34. *Pensacola Pensacolian*, January 22, 1887; *CSZ*, November 28, 1901; Hood, *One Hundred Years*, 380; *JDFU*, February 10, 1882.

35. *Guide to Supplementary Vital Statistics from Church Records in Florida*, vol. 1, 295; *SSZ*, April 27, 1893; Escambia County Deed Records, Book 5, 84–85, Book 7, 353, Book 10, 196.

36. *PCR*, August 11, 1881; "Rev. John A. Mulligan," 150–53.

37. Minutes, AMEZ General Conference, 1884, 8.

5. THE REKINDLING OF SPIRIT, 1884–1888

1. For additional information concerning these events and circumstances, see chapter 4.

2. Mayo, *Seventh Census*, 10–11.

3. Ibid., 9.

4. Ibid., 10.

5. Walker, *Ninth Census—Volume I*, 97–99; Mayo, *Sixth Census*, 90.

6. Shofner, *Nor Is It Over Yet*, 115–16, 122, 251, 256, 274, 344; Brown, *Ossian Bingley Hart*, 245–48, 259, 277, 279, 286, 291, 299–300; Williamson, *Florida Politics in the Gilded Age*, 8, 32–33; Knetsch, "Hamilton Disston," 9–13.

7. Pettengill, *Story of the Florida Railroads*, 115–22; Shofner, *Jackson County*, 345.

8. Pettengill, *Story of the Florida Railroads*, 41–43, 69–73; Brown, *Henry Bradley Plant*, 8–15; Peeples, "Charlotte Harbor Division," 291–97.

9. Drobney, *Lumbermen and Log Sawyers*, 35; *Fernandina Florida Mirror*, February 25, 1882; *Pensacola Pensacolian*, February 16–17, 1884.

10. *PCR*, January 10, 1884; *NYG*, April 26, 1884; *NYF*, February 28, 1885.

11. *NYG*, April 26, 1884; Payne, *Recollections*, 316; Jackson, "Booker T. Washington's Tour," 268; *TFP*, June 16, 1869; Tingley, "Dr. Alexander H. Darnes"; Charles Tingley, telephone interview, April 29, 2003; Hutchins, "William John Gunn."

12. *Fernandina Florida Mirror*, February 4, 1882; *JFT-U*, September 5, 1885; *NYA*, December 1, 1888.

13. *JFT-U*, October 7, 1885; Grismer, *Tampa*, 181–84; Mormino and Pozzetta, *Immigrant World of Ybor City*, 43, 63–66; *Tampa Journal*, June 23, 1887; Rivers and Brown, "Rejoicing in Their Freedom," 11–15; Brown and Rivers, "The Negroes Are There to Stay," 58–62.

14. Williamson, *Florida Politics in the Gilded Age*, 1–143; Brown, *Florida's Black Public Officials*, 43–60.

15. Williamson, *Florida Politics in the Gilded Age*, 59–143; Rivers and Brown, *Laborers in the Vineyard of the Lord*, 120–21; Brown, *Florida's Black Public Officials*, 55–58; Brown, "Where Are Now the Hopes I Cherished?" 32–33.

16. Brown, *Florida's Black Public Officials*, 43–54, 62–63, 84, 86; Brown, "Prelude to the Poll Tax," 73–79; Hawes, "Tampa-born Sheriff."

17. *Pensacola Semi-Weekly Commercial*, December 22, 29, 1882; Manley, Brown, and Rise, *Supreme Court of Florida*, 273–74, 304–6; Brown, *Florida's Black Public Officials*, 58.

18. Williamson, *Florida Politics in the Gilded Age*, 61, 65, 67, 85, 89, 91, 132; Rivers and Brown, *Laborers in the Vineyard of the Lord*, 145; Brown, "George Washington Witherspoon," 68–70.

19. *JFT-U*, December 17, 24, 30, 1884; Rivers and Brown, *Laborers in the Vineyard of the Lord*, 145; Brown, *Florida's Black Public Officials*, 58, 86; *NYA*, June 30, 1888; Brown, "George Washington Witherspoon," 71.

20. Raper, *Tragedy of Lynching*, 28.

21. *PCR*, October 27, 1887.

22. *NYF*, July 16, 1887.

23. Rivers and Brown, *Laborers in the Vineyard of the Lord*, 142–56.

24. *PCR*, July 24, 1884, April 29, 1886; *CSZ*, September 26, November 14, 1901; Welch, "Black Churches in Tampa," unpaginated; *SSZ*, June 30, 1886, April 2, 1889; Brown, *Florida's Black Public Officials*, 87.

25. *NYF*, February 19, 1887; *JFT-U*, March 6, 1886.

26. Minutes, AMEZ General Conference, 1884, 8, 1888, 37.

27. *SSZ*, May 14, 1891; Hood, *One Hundred Years*, 178–80; Walls, *African Methodist Episcopal Zion Church*, 577–78.

28. St. James AMEZ Church, Seminole County, in CH-RECS; "St. James A.M.E. Zion Church"; Orange County Marriage Records, Book 3, 262; *CSZ*, July 5, August 2, 1900.

29. *PSZ*, January 23, 1885; *SSZ*, April 16, 1886; *TG*, June 30, 1886; Duval County Marriage Records, Book 6, 728, 736, 943; *PCR*, April 29, 1886.

30. *PSZ*, January 23, May 22, 1885.

31. *TG*, February 10, 17, 1886; *SSZ*, April 16, 1886.

32. *PCR*, April 29, 1886; *JFT-U*, March 12, 1886; Zion AMEZ Church, Sumter County, in CH-RECS.

33. *SSZ*, April 16, November 5, 1886; *JFT-U*, September 17, 1886.

34. *TG*, June 30, 1886.

35. *JFT-U*, January 22, 1887; *NYF*, February 12, 1887; *SSZ*, October 8, 1886; *Philadelphia Journal of United Labor*, September 17, 1887.

36. *Pensacola Pensacolian*, January 22, 1887; *SSZ*, February 24, 1887.

37. *SSZ*, September 8, 29, 1887, September 4, 1890; *Fort Myers Weekly Press*, November 8, 1888; *NYF*, April 16, 1887.

38. *SSZ*, September 8, 15, October 13, 1887; *PCR*, March 1, 1888; Rivers and Brown, *Laborers in the Vineyard of the Lord*, 149–52, 168–69.

39. *SSZ*, February 24, 1887; *JFT-U*, July 21, 1887; Welch, "Black Churches in Tampa," 1; *Tampa Tribune*, August 4, 1887.

40. Barker, "Sneaky, Cowardly Enemy," 6–15; *JFT-U*, October 14, 1887; *SSZ*, November 17, 1887.

41. *SSZ*, March 15, 1888, September 4, 1890; Barker, "Sneaky, Cowardly Enemy," 16; *NYA*, January 14, 1888.

42. *NYA*, February 18, 1888; *Pensacola Daily Commercial*, February 18, 1888; *SSZ*, March 21, 1889; September 4, 1890, September 3, 1891; *Fort Myers Weekly Press*, November 8, 1888.

43. *NYA*, May 5, June 2, 1888; *SSZ*, November 8, 1888, April 14, 1892; Hood, *One Hundred Years*, 425; Walls, *African Methodist Episcopal Zion Church*, 216.

44. Minutes, AMEZ General Conference, 1888, 37.

45. Rivers and Brown, *Laborers in the Vineyard of the Lord*, 163–64; *NYA*, June 2, 1888.

46. *NYA*, June 16, 23, 1888; *PCR*, September 20, 1888; *Pensacola Daily Commercial*, August 25, 1888; *JFT-U*, April 22, 1889.

6. BISHOP LOMAX AND THE GOSPEL HORSE, 1888–1893

1. Hood, *One Hundred Years*, 191–92; Walls, *African Methodist Episcopal Zion Church*, 580; *CSZ*, March 1, 1900.

2. Hood, *One Hundred Years*, 192–95; Martin, *For God and Race*, 92–95; *CSZ*, March 1, 1900.

3. *SSZ*, March 9, 1893.

4. Ibid.

5. Rivers and Brown, *Laborers in the Vineyard of the Lord*, 149; *SSZ*, February 27, 1890.

6. Barker, "Sneaky, Cowardly Enemy," 18; *NYA*, September 1, October 2, 1888; Walls, *African Methodist Episcopal Zion Church*, 216; Davis, *History of Jacksonville*, 180–86; *SSZ*, November 8, 1888, April 14, 1892.

7. Drobney, *Lumbermen and Log Sawyers*, 35–43; Tebeau, *History of Florida*, 278–86; Blakey, *Florida Phosphate Industry*, 15–17; *JFT-U*, January 3, 1890; Brown, *Florida's Peace River Frontier*, 312–21.

8. Brown, *In the Midst of All That Makes Life Worth Living*, 161–70, 179–83; *SSZ*, March 21, 1889.

9. *SSZ*, September 4, 1890.

10. Ibid., March 21, September 26, December 5, 1889, February 27, 1890.

11. Ibid., September 26, 1889, May 11, 1893, June 28, 1894.

12. Ibid., March 21, 1889; Brown, *Florida's Black Public Officials*, 47, 71, 84, 86; *NYA*, December 1, 1888.

13. *SSZ*, March 21, 1889.

14. Ibid.

15. *PCR*, January 12, 1890.

16. *PDN*, February 13, 14, 1890; *SSZ*, March 27, 1890.

17. *SSZ*, February 27, March 27, 1890.

18. U.S. Department of the Interior, Census Office, *Report on Statistics of Churches in the United States at the Eleventh Census: 1890*, 566; *SSZ*, July 31, 1890, February 5, 1891.

19. *SSZ*, September 4, November 27, 1890, April 2, 1891; Lake County Deed Records, Book 23, 127; *Tampa Journal*, May 1, 1890; U.S. Department of the Interior, Census Office, *Report on Statistics of Churches in the United States at the Eleventh Census: 1890*, 565.

20. *SSZ*, April 2, 1891, May 19, 1892; Hood, *One Hundred Years*, 439–40.

21. *JFT-U*, February 20, 1891; *SSZ*, February 5, 1891.

22. *JFT-U*, February 20, 1891.

23. *SSZ*, July 2, September 3, 1891; *JFT-U*, February 12, March 10, 1892.

24. *PDN*, July 3, 1892; *SSZ*, April 23, 1891.

25. *PDN*, July 28, 1892.

26. Escambia County Deed Records, Book 13, 263; *SSZ*, February 5, 1891, March 16, 1893.

27. Martin, *For God and Race*, 164–65; 1900 Escambia County census; *JFT-U*, February 12, 1892. On Julia Foote, see also Douglass-Chin, *Preacher Woman Sings the Blues*.

28. 1885 Escambia County census; *SSZ*, April 27, 1893.

29. *SSZ*, June 21, August 30, 1894; Minutes, AMEZ General Conferences, 1896, 9, 1900, 92.

30. *SSZ*, February 11, May 19, 1892, March 16, April 27, 1893, May 31, 1894, July 18, 1901; *PDN*, December 14, 24, 1893.

31. *SSZ*, December 10, 1891, May 19, 1892, June 7, 1894; *JFT- U*, February 22, 1892; *JET*, February 23, March 3, 1892.

32. Brown and Brown, *Family Records*, 58–60; Richardson, *National Cyclopedia*, 380–81; Hawes, "One Official's Untold Story"; *JFT-U*, February 23, 1891.

33. *JET*, March 1, 1892; *SSZ*, March 10, April 14, 1892.

34. *SSZ*, September 3, 1891.

35. McKinney and McKinney, *History of the Black Baptists of Florida*, 54–55; McKinney, "American Baptists and Black Education in Florida"; Rivers and Brown, *Laborers in the Vineyard of the Lord*, 136–38, 140, 174, 182; Foster and Foster, *Beechers, Stowes, and Yankee Strangers*, 80–81, 114, 126–27; Neyland and Riley, *History of Florida Agricultural and Mechanical University*, 1–32.

36. *SSZ*, July 2, 1891.

37. *JET*, August 12, 1891; *SSZ*, July 31, 1890, September 3, 1891; Polk County Deed Records, Book 34, 330.

38. Rivers and Brown, *Laborers in the Vineyard of the Lord*, 182–84, 186–87; *SSZ*, March 10, April 2, May 19, 1892; *JET*, January 13, March 1, 1892; *JFT-U*, February 11, 12, 1892; Minutes, AMEZ General Conference, 1892, 32.

39. *SSZ*, March 2, 16, 1893.

40. Ibid., March 2, 1893.

7. AFFLICTIONS OF MAN AND GOD, 1893–1900

1. Ayers, *Promise of the New South*, 249–77; Williamson, *Florida Politics in the Gilded Age*, 179–89; *JET*, December 10, 31, 1892.

2. Woodward, *Origins of the New South*, 264–65; Ayers, *Promise of the New South*, 283–84.

3. *SSZ*, September 14, 1893.

4. Ibid., September 28, 1893.

5. Ibid., August 3, September 28, 1893, May 31, 1894.

6. Ibid., November 8, December 13, 1894.

7. *PDN*, January 14, 1894; *SSZ*, May 31, 1894.

8. *SSZ*, June 7, August 23, December 13, 1894, May 16, 1895.

9. *PDN*, January 14, 1894; *SSZ*, July 5, 1894.

10. *SSZ*, May 31, July 5, 26, August 23, 30, 1894.

11. Ibid., June 7, August 23, 1894, August 29, 1895.

12. *PDN*, March 24, 1894; *SSZ*, June 21, August 30, September 20, October 25, December 13, 1894.

13. *SSZ*, August 30, 1894.

14. Walls, *African Methodist Episcopal Zion Church*, 289–90; *CSZ*, July 1, August 12, 1897.

15. Brown, *Florida's Peace River Frontier*, 321–22; Brown, *In the Midst of All That Makes Life Worth Living*, 183, 185–88, 190–91; *Bartow Courier-Informant*, February 13, 1895; Polk County Deed Records, Book 48, 156; *SSZ*, February 28, May 16, 1895.

16. Minutes, AMEZ General Conference, 1896, 178–79.

17. *SSZ*, August 29, 1895; *CSZ*, February 18, 1897.

18. *SSZ*, February 28, May 16, 1895; *CSZ*, November 19, 1896; *Tampa Tribune*, May 9, 1895.

19. *CSZ*, February 18, July 1, 1897; *TMT*, February 14, 1896.

20. *SSZ*, February 28, 1895, April 1, 1897, August 17, 1899, July 18, August 15, 1901.

21. Martin, *For God and Race*, 126–27; Hall, *Magic Mirror*, 146–47.

22. Rogers and Denham, *Florida Sheriffs*, 160–73; Hawes, "Tampa-born Sheriff"; *JFT-U*, June 16, 1891.

23. Brown, "Where Are Now the Hopes I Cherished?" 33–35; Hawes, "Robert Meacham Left a Florida Legacy"; *JFT-U*, January 30, 1894.

24. Minutes, AMEZ General Conferences, 1896, 9, 1900, 129, 135; *CSZ*, April 1, 1897.

25. Hood, *One Hundred Years*, 202–7; Walls, *African Methodist Episcopal Zion Church*, 581–82; *SSZ*, April 6, 1904.

26. Walls, *African Methodist Episcopal Zion Church*, 582.

27. Hood, *One Hundred Years*, 206.

28. Martin, *For God and Race*, 124.

29. *CSZ*, April 3, 1902, April 30, 1903.

30. Ibid., January 21, July 1, 1897.

31. *Kissimmee Valley Gazette*, February 17, 1897; *CSZ*, March 11, July 1, 1897.

32. Minutes, AMEZ General Conference, 1900, 139.

33. Brown, *Florida's Peace River Frontier*, 321–25; Gatewood, "Black Troops in Florida," 17–28; Hubener, "Army Life in Lakeland," 33–34.

34. *CSZ*, February 18, July 1, 1897, March 17, September 29, 1898, April 6, 1899, March 22, 1900.

35. Brown and Brown, *Family Records*, 59; *JFT-U*, March 31, 1899; Minutes, AMEZ General Conference, 1900, 139, 240; *CSZ*, March 11, 1897, November 30, 1899; *TMT*, November 28, 1899.

36. *CSZ*, March 22, 1900, August 1, 1901.

37. Minutes, AMEZ General Conference, 1900, 129; *CSZ*, July 28, August 18, 1898.

38. Walls, *African Methodist Episcopal Zion Church*, 587; *CSZ*, September 8, 15, 22, 1898.

39. *CSZ*, February 18, April 1, 1897, February 3, March 10, 1898, March 2, 1899, April 12, September 27, 1900.

40. Drobney, *Lumbermen and Log Sawyers*, 130; *CSZ*, February 3, March 10, May 19, 1898, February 1, March 2, 1899, March 1, September 27, 1900.

41. Minutes, AMEZ General Conference, 1900, 241; *CSZ*, February 18, April 1, 1897.

42. *CSZ*, July 28, 1898.

43. Ibid., July 28, 1898, February 26, 1903; Martin, *For God and Race*, 163–75.

44. *CSZ*, March 10, August 18, 1898, March 21, 28, 1901, April 17, 1902, March 10, 1904; Santa Rosa County Marriage Records, Marriage License Book 1898–1906, 450.

8. CLIMBING TO THE MOUNTAINTOP, 1900–1905

1. Nolan, *Fifty Feet in Paradise*, 80–83, 95–119; Graham, *Awakening of St. Augustine*, 166–218; Brown, *Henry Bradley Plant*, 13–19; Brown, "A Late Victorian Romp," 2–18.

2. Akin, *Flagler*, 123–63.

3. McRae, *Fourth Census*, 15–17; Mayo, *Sixth Census*, 90–91.

4. Crawford, *Third Census*, 29–30, 44–47; McRae, *Fourth Census*, 15.

5. Brown, *Florida's Black Public Officials*, 63–69; Lempel, "Mayor's 'Henchmen and Henchwomen,'" 271–73; Iorio, "Colorless Primaries," 297–303; Kerstein, *Politics and Growth in Twentieth-Century Tampa*, 42–51.

6. Woodward, *Strange Career of Jim Crow*, 6–7, 69–70; *Orlando Sentinel-Reporter*, quoted in *Tallahassee Weekly Tallahassean*, January 17, 1901.

7. *JFT-U*, October 18, November 9, 18, 24, 25, 1905; *Pensacola Journal*, October 28, 1905; Moore, "Life and Career of Judson Douglas Wetmore"; Brown, *Florida's Black Public Officials*, 134–35.

8. *CSZ*, July 5, 1900; March 14, 30, 1901; Minutes, AMEZ General Conference, 1900, 139–40.

9. *CSZ*, March 14, 30, June 27, 1901.

10. Ibid., August 7, 1902.

11. Ibid., February 14, 1901, February 27, May 8, 1902, February 12, 1903, February 4, 1904.

12. Walls, *African Methodist Episcopal Zion Church*, 249; *CSZ*, February 26, June 18, 1903.

13. *CSZ*, August 6, 1903.

14. *TMT*, March 24, 25, 27, 1904; *CSZ*, May 15, 1902, April 21, 1904.

15. *CSZ*, February 18, 1904.

16. Ibid., January 7, 1904.

17. Lewis, *W.E.B. Du Bois*, 277.

18. *CSZ*, March 26, 1903.

19. Ibid.

20. *TMT*, March 25, 27, April 4, 1904; *CSZ*, April 30, 1903, April 21, 1904.

21. *TMT*, March 25, 1904.

22. *CSZ*, October 1, November 12, 1903.

23. Hood, *One Hundred Years*, 207–9; Walls, *African Methodist Episcopal Zion Church*, 582–83; *CSZ*, March 21, 1901.

24. Walls, *African Methodist Episcopal Zion Church*, 582; *CSZ*, March 21, 1901.

25. *CSZ*, October 24, 1901.

26. Ibid., March 28, 1901, April 17, August 7, 1902, May 21, 1903, March 10, 1904.

27. Walls, *African Methodist Episcopal Zion Church*, 208–9; *CSZ*, August 5, 1901, April 10, 17, 1902.

28. *CSZ*, August 7, 1902.

29. Ibid., March 19, October 29, 1903.

30. Ibid., March 10, 1904.

31. Minutes, AMEZ General Conference, 1900, 129; *CSZ*, March 10, 1904, December 17, 1908; Bureau of the Census, *Religious Bodies: 1906*, vol. 2, 460.

32. *CSZ*, October 29, 1903.

33. Ibid., June 20, 1901, October 8, 1903.

34. Ibid., October 8, 1903; Colburn and Scher, *Florida's Gubernatorial Politics*, 221; Proctor, *Napoleon Bonaparte Broward*, 173–74, 252, 296; Walls, *African Methodist Episcopal Zion Church*, 583, 587; *JFT-U*, February 7, 1908; *Pensacola Journal*, October 29, 1908.

35. *CSZ*, February 4, 1904.

36. Ibid.

AFTERWORD

1. U.S. Department of Commerce, Bureau of the Census, *Religious Bodies: 1916*, vol. 1, 162; *CSZ*, December 14, 1922.

2. *CSZ*, December 13, 1923.

3. Ibid., January 18, December 13, 1923.

4. Ibid., October 7, 1920, October 11, 1923.

5. Ibid., April 19, 1923.

BIBLIOGRAPHY

MANUSCRIPTS, COLLECTIONS, AND CHURCH MINUTES

American Missionary Association. Archives. Amistad Research Center, New Orleans.

Church Records. Questionnaires of the Historical Records Survey of the Florida Writers' Project, WPA. Florida Collection, State Library of Florida.

Florida Negro Papers. University of South Florida Special Collections, Tampa.

Loomis-Wilder Family. Papers. Yale University Library, New Haven, Conn.

Minutes, General Conference of the AMEZ Church, 1880, 1884, 1888, 1892, 1896, 1900, 1904. Heritage Hall Archives and Research Center, Livingstone College, Salisbury, N.C.

PUBLIC DOCUMENTS AND PUBLIC RECORDS

Alachua County. Marriage Records. Available on microfilm at FSA.

Bailey, Thomas D., comp. *Narrative Reports of County Superintendents, 1869–70 to 1879–80*. Tallahassee: State Superintendent of Public Instruction, 1962.

Brevard County. Marriage Records. Available on microfilm at FSA.

Bureau of Refugees, Freedmen, and Abandoned Lands. Records of the Assistant Commissioner and Subordinate Field Offices for the State of Florida, 1865–1872. RG 105, NA. Microcopy No. M-1869. Available on microfilm at PKY.

Crawford, H. Clay, comp. *The Third Census of the State of Florida Taken in the Year 1905*. Tallahassee: Capital, 1906.

Duval County. Marriage Records. Available on microfilm at FSA.

Escambia County. Deed Records. Available on microfilm at FSA.

———. Marriage Records. Available on microfilm at FSA.

Florida State Archives. Elections, Division of. Commissions of Office, 1827–1978. RG 156, series 259 and 259A.

———. Correspondence of Ossian B. Hart, Superintendent of Registration, 1867. RG 156, series 626.

———. Resignations from Office, 1868–1975. RG 156, series 260.

Florida State Census, 1885. Available on microfilm at FSA.

Guide to Supplementary Vital Statistics from Church Records in Florida. 3 vols. Jacksonville: Florida Historical Records Survey, 1942.

Hillsborough County. Day Book (March 18, 1837–March 2, 1846). Hillsborough County Courthouse, Tampa.

———. Deed Records. Available on microfilm at FSA.

———. Marriage Records. Available on microfilm at FSA.

Lake County. Deed Records. Available on microfilm at FSA.

———. Marriage Records. Available on microfilm at FSA.

Lee County. Marriage Records. Available on microfilm at FSA.

Levy County. Deed Records. Available on microfilm at FSA.

———. Marriage Records. Available on microfilm at FSA.

———. Tax Lists, 1866–1879. Available on microfilm at FSA.

Mayo, Nathan, comp. *The Sixth Census of the State of Florida, 1935.* Tallahassee: Florida Department of Agriculture, 1935.

———. *The Seventh Census of the State of Florida, 1945.* Tallahassee: Florida Department of Agriculture, 1945.

McRae, W. A., comp. *The Fourth Census of the State of Florida Taken in the Year 1915.* Tallahassee: T. J. Appleyard, 1915.

Monroe County. Deed Records. Available on microfilm at FSA.

———. Marriage Records. Available on microfilm at FSA.

———. Tax Lists, 1866–1879. Available on microfilm at FSA.

Polk County. Marriage Records. Available on microfilm at FSA.

Santa Rosa County. Deed Records. Available on microfilm at FSA.

———. Marriage Records. Available on microfilm at FSA.

Sumter County. Marriage Records. Available on microfilm at FSA.

U.S. Decennial Censuses, 1860, 1870, 1880, 1900. Manuscript returns. Available on microfilm at FSA.

U.S. Department of Commerce, Bureau of the Census. *Religious Bodies: 1916.* 2 vols. Washington, D.C.: Government Printing Office, 1919.

U.S. Department of Commerce and Labor, Bureau of the Census. *Religious Bodies: 1906.* 2 vols. Washington, D.C.: Government Printing Office, 1910.

U.S. Department of the Interior, Census Office. *Report on Statistics of Churches in the United States at the Eleventh Census: 1890.* Washington, D.C.: Government Printing Office, 1894.

U.S. Department of the Treasury. Customs Service appointment records. RG 56, NA.

U.S. Department of War. Department and District of Florida. Letters Received, 1865–1869. RG 393, NA.

U.S. Veterans Administration. Military pension records. RG 15, NA.

Walker, Francis A., comp. *Ninth Census—Volume I. The Statistics of the Population of the United States . . . Compiled from the Original Returns of the Ninth Census (June 1, 1870).* Washington, D.C.: Government Printing Office, 1872.

NEWSPAPERS AND PERIODICALS

Bartow Courier-Informant, 1893, 1895
Birmingham (Eng.) Good Templars Watchword, 1876–1879
Boston Daily Journal, 1862
Bronson Levy County Enterprise, 1883
Brooksville Hernando Today, 1999
Charlotte (N.C.) Star of Zion, 1896–1928
Fernandina Florida Mirror, 1882
Fort Meade Leader, 1928
Fort Myers Weekly Press, 1888
Jacksonville Daily Florida Union, 1876
Jacksonville Daily Sun and Press, 1877
Jacksonville Evening Telegram, 1891–1894
Jacksonville Florida Times-Union, 1883–1908
Jacksonville Florida Union, 1868
Jacksonville Tri-Weekly Florida Union, 1873
Key West Daily Equator-Democrat, 1889
Key West Key of the Gulf, 1881
Kissimmee Valley Gazette, 1897
Macon (Ga.) Southern Christian Advocate, 1866–1878
Miami Herald, 1964
Milton Santa Rosa Press-Gazette, 1967
Mobile Nationalist, 1866
New York Age, 1888
New York Freedmen's Advocate, 1864
New York Freeman, 1885–1887
New York Globe, 1883–1884
New York Herald, 1864–1865
New York World, 1865
Pensacola Commercial, 1868–1869
Pensacola Daily Commercial, 1888
Pensacola Daily News, 1890–1894
Pensacola Journal, 1905, 1908
Pensacola Pensacolian, 1884, 1887
Pensacola Semi-Weekly Commercial, 1869, 1882
Pensacola Tri-Weekly Observer, 1868
Pensacola West Florida Commercial, 1868
Petersburg (Va.) Star of Zion, 1884–1885
Philadelphia Christian Recorder, 1867–1905
Philadelphia Journal of United Labor, 1886–1890
St. Augustine Examiner, 1867

Salisbury (N.C.) Star of Zion, 1886–1895
Savannah Advertiser-Republican, 1873
Savannah Daily Advertiser, 1872
Savannah Daily Georgian, 1853
Savannah Daily News and Herald, 1866
Savannah Daily Republican, 1867, 1872
Savannah Morning News, 1872
Tallahassee Daily Democrat, 1928
Tallahassee Sentinel, 1867–1872, 1876
Tallahassee Weekly Floridian, 1873–1880
Tallahassee Weekly Tallahassean, 1901
Tampa Florida Peninsular, 1868–1871
Tampa Guardian, 1880, 1886
Tampa Journal, 1887–1890
Tampa Morning Tribune, 1896
Tampa Sunday Tribune, 1995
Tampa Sunland Tribune, 1877–1880
Tampa Tribune, 1887, 1892–1895
Tampa True Southerner, 1868

SECONDARY SOURCES

Akin, Edward N. *Flagler: Rockefeller Partner and Florida Baron*. Kent, Ohio: Kent State University Press, 1988.
Angell, Stephen Ward. *Bishop Henry McNeal Turner and African- American Religion in the South*. Knoxville: University of Tennessee Press, 1992.
Ayers, Edward L. *The Promise of the New South: Life After Reconstruction*. New York: Oxford University Press, 1992.
Barker, Eirlys. "'A Sneaky, Cowardly Enemy': Tampa's Yellow Fever Epidemic of 1887–88." *Tampa Bay History* 8 (Fall–Winter 1986): 4–22.
Barnes, Jay. *Florida's Hurricane History*. Chapel Hill: University of North Carolina Press, 1998.
Bentley, Altermese Smith. *History of the First South Florida Missionary Baptist Association (1888–1988)*. Chuluota, Fla.: Mickler House, 1988.
Blakey, Arch Fredric. *The Florida Phosphate Industry: A History of the Development and Use of a Vital Mineral*. Cambridge, Mass.: Wertheim Committee, Harvard University, 1973.
Blassingame, John W. *The Slave Community: Plantation Life in the Antebellum South*. 2nd ed. New York: Oxford University Press, 1979.
Boles, John B., ed. *Masters and Slaves in the House of the Lord: Race and Religion in the American South, 1740–1870*. Lexington: University Press of Kentucky, 1988.
Bradley, David Henry, Sr. *A History of the A.M.E. Zion Church*. 2 vols. Nashville, Tenn.: Parthenon Press, 1956–70.

Brady, Rowena Ferrell. *Things Remembered: An Album of African Americans in Tampa*. Tampa: University of Tampa Press, 1997.

Brooks, William E., ed. *From Saddlebags to Satellites: A History of Florida Methodism*. Nashville: Parthenon, 1969.

Brown, Canter, Jr. *African Americans on the Tampa Bay Frontier*. Tampa: Tampa Bay History Center, 1997.

———. *"Bartow Is the Place for Our People to Go": Race and the Course of Life in Southern Polk County, 1865–1905*. Bartow, Fla.: Polk County Historical Association, 2000.

———. "Bishop Payne and Resistance to Jim Crow in Florida during the 1880s." *Northeast Florida History* 2 (1994): 23–40.

———. *Florida's Black Public Officials, 1867–1924*. Tuscaloosa: University of Alabama Press, 1998.

———. *Florida's Peace River Frontier*. Orlando: University of Central Florida Press, 1991.

———. *Fort Meade, 1849–1900*. Tuscaloosa: University of Alabama Press, 1995.

———. "George Washington Witherspoon: Florida's Second Generation of Black Political Leadership." *A.M.E. Church Review* 119 (January–March 2003): 66–74.

———. *Henry Bradley Plant, the Nineteenth-Century "King of Florida."* Tampa: Henry B. Plant Museum, 1999.

———. *In the Midst of All That Makes Life Worth Living: Polk County, Florida, to 1940*. Tallahassee: Sentry Press, 2001.

———. *Jewish Pioneers of the Tampa Bay Frontier*. Tampa: Tampa Bay History Center, 1999.

———. *"A Late Victorian Romp"; or, The World As Seen from the Tampa Bay Hotel's Veranda, 1891–1901*. Tampa: Henry B. Plant Museum, 1999.

———. *Ossian Bingley Hart, Florida's Loyalist Reconstruction Governor*. Baton Rouge: Louisiana State University Press, 1997.

———. "Prelude to the Poll Tax: Black Republicans and the Knights of Labor in 1880s Florida." In *Florida's Heritage of Diversity: Essays in Honor of Samuel Proctor*, edited by Mark I. Greenberg, William Warren Rogers, and Canter Brown Jr. Tallahassee: Sentry Press, 1997.

———. "Race Relations in Territorial Florida, 1821–1845." *Florida Historical Quarterly* 73 (January 1995): 287–307.

———. *Tampa before the Civil War*. Tampa: University of Tampa Press, 1999.

———. *Tampa in Civil War and Reconstruction*. Tampa: University of Tampa Press, 2000.

———. "'Where Are Now the Hopes I Cherished?': The Life and Times of Robert Meacham." *Florida Historical Quarterly* 69 (July 1990): 1–36.

Brown, Canter, Jr., ed. "'As Far as Our Eyes Will Let Us See': The 'Peas Creek Expedition' of 1860." *Tampa Bay History* 12 (Spring–Summer 1990): 43–79.

Brown, Canter, Jr., and Barbara Gray Brown. *Family Records of the African Ameri-*

can Pioneers of Tampa and Hillsborough County. Tampa: University of Tampa Press, 2003.

Brown, Canter, Jr., and Larry Eugene Rivers. "'The Negroes Are There to Stay': The Development of Tampa's African American Community, 1891–1916." *Sunland Tribune* 29 (2003): 57–76.

Browne, Jefferson B. *Key West: The Old and the New*. St. Augustine: Record Company, 1912. Reprint, Gainesville: University of Florida Press, 1973.

Burton, Orville Vernon. *In My Father's House Are Many Mansions: Family and Community in Edgefield, South Carolina*. Chapel Hill: University of North Carolina Press, 1985.

Call, C. F. *History of Allen Chapel A.M.E. Church, Pensacola, Florida*. Pensacola: Allen Chapel AME Church, 1939.

Colburn, David R., and Richard K. Scher. *Florida's Gubernatorial Politics in the Twentieth Century*. Tallahassee: Florida State University Press, 1980.

Coles, David James. "Far from Fields of Glory: Military Operations in Florida during the Civil War." Ph.D. diss., Florida State University, 1996.

———. "'They Fought Like Devils': Black Troops in Florida during the Civil War." In *Florida's Heritage of Diversity: Essays in Honor of Samuel Proctor*, edited by Mark I. Greenberg, William Warren Rogers, and Canter Brown Jr. Tallahassee: Sentry Press, 1997.

———. "Unpretending Service: The *James L. Davis*, the *Tahoma*, and the East Gulf Blockading Squadron." *Florida Historical Quarterly* 71 (July 1992): 41–62.

Collier-Thomas, Bettye. *Daughters of Thunder: Black Women Preachers and Their Sermons, 1850–1879*. San Francisco: Jossey-Bass, 1998.

The Cornish/Matthews Family Reunion, July 13, 14, 15, 16, 1989. Tampa: Cornish/Matthews Family Reunion Committee, 1989.

Davis, T. Frederick. *History of Jacksonville, Florida, and Vicinity, 1513 to 1924*. Jacksonville: Florida Historical Society, 1925. Reprint, Jacksonville: San Marco Bookstore, 1990.

Davis, William Watson. *The Civil War and Reconstruction in Florida*. New York: Columbia University Press, 1913. Reprint, Gainesville: University Press of Florida, 1964.

Dees, Jesse Walter, Jr., and Vivian Flannery Dees. *"Off the Beaten Path": The History of Cedar Key, Florida, 1843–1990*. Chiefland, Fla.: Rife Publishing, 1990.

Diary of Eliza Horn, Way Key, East Florida, 1867–1869. Jacksonville: Works Progress Administration Historical Records Survey, 1937.

Dodson, Jualyne. "Nineteenth-Century A.M.E. Preaching Women: Cutting Edge of Women's Inclusion in Church Polity." In *Women in New Worlds: Historical Perspectives on the Wesleyan Tradition*, edited by Hilah F. Thomas, Rosemary Skinner Keller, and Louise L. Queen. Nashville: Abingdon Press, 1981.

Douglass-Chin, Richard J. *Preacher Woman Sings the Blues: The Autobiographies of Nineteenth-Century African American Evangelists*. Columbia: University of Missouri Press, 2001.

Drobney, Jeffrey A. *Lumbermen and Log Sawyers: Life, Labor, and Culture in the North Florida Timber Industry, 1830–1930*. Macon, Ga.: Mercer University Press, 1997.

Durkin, Joseph T. *Confederate Navy Chief: Stephen R. Mallory*. Chapel Hill: University of North Carolina Press, 1954. Reprint, Columbia: University of South Carolina Press, 1987.

Elliott, Brenda J. *The Best of Its Kind: The Incredible American Heritage of the Dixon Ticonderoga Company since 1795*. Kissimmee, Fla.: Dixon Ticonderoga Company, 1996.

Ellis, Mary Louise. "North Florida and the Great Storm of 1873." *Florida Historical Quarterly* 62 (April 1984): 485–96.

Fahey, David M. *The Black Lodge in White America: "True Reformer" Browne and His Economic Strategy*. Dayton, Ohio: Wright State University Press, 1994.

———. *Temperance and Racism: John Bull, Johnny Reb, and the Good Templars*. Lexington: University of Kentucky Press, 1996.

Federal Writers' Project. *Negro History in Florida*. Jacksonville: Federal Writers' Project, 1936.

———. *The Negro in Florida's Cities*. Jacksonville: Federal Writers' Project, 1936.

Fishburne, Charles Carroll. *The Cedar Keys in the Nineteenth Century*. Quincy, Fla.: Sea Hawk Publications, 1993.

Fitts, Larry. *A History of Black Baptists*. Nashville: Broadman Press, 1999.

Fitzgerald, Michael W. *Urban Emancipation: Popular Politics in Reconstruction Mobile, 1860–1890*. Tuscaloosa: Louisiana State University Press, 2002.

Florida Voter Registration Lists, 1867–68. Tallahassee: Florida Genealogical Society, 1992.

Foner, Eric. *Reconstruction: America's Unfinished Business, 1863–1877*. New York: Harper and Row, 1988.

Foster, John T., Jr., and Sarah Whitmer Foster. *Beechers, Stowes, and Yankee Strangers: The Transformation of Florida*. Gainesville: University Press of Florida, 1999.

Futch, Ovid. "Salmon P. Chase and Civil War Politics in Florida." *Florida Historical Quarterly* 32 (April 1954): 163–88.

Gannon, Michael, ed. *The New History of Florida*. Gainesville: University Press of Florida, 1996.

Gatewood, Willard B., Jr. "Black Troops in Florida during the Spanish-American War." *Tampa Bay History* 20 (Spring–Summer 1998): 17–31.

Genovese, Eugene D. *Roll, Jordan, Roll: The World the Slaves Made*. New York: Pantheon Books, 1974.

George, Paul S. "Colored Town: Miami's Black Community, 1896–1930." *Florida Historical Quarterly* 56 (April 1978): 432–47.

Gordon, Julius J. *Afro-Americans of Hillsborough County, Florida, 1870–1890*. Tampa: Privately published, 1993.

Graham, Thomas. *The Awakening of St. Augustine: The Anderson Family and the Oldest City, 1821–1924*. St. Augustine: St. Augustine Historical Society, 1978.

Gravely, William. *Gilbert Haven, Methodist Abolitionist: A Study in Race, Religion, and Reform, 1850–1880.* New York: Abingdon Press, 1973.

Greenbaum, Susan D. "A Comparison of African American and Euro-American Mutual Aid Societies in Nineteenth-Century America." *Journal of Ethnic Studies* 19 (1991): 95–119.

Greenberg, Mark I., William Warren Rogers, and Canter Brown Jr. *Florida's Heritage of Diversity: Essays in Honor of Samuel Proctor.* Tallahassee: Sentry Press, 1997.

Grismer, Karl H. *Tampa: A History of the City of Tampa and the Tampa Bay Region of Florida.* St. Petersburg: St. Petersburg Printing Co., 1950.

Groene, Bertram. *Ante-Bellum Tallahassee.* Tallahassee: Florida Heritage Foundation, 1971.

Hall, Kermit L. *The Magic Mirror: Law in American History.* New York: Oxford University Press, 1989.

Hall, Robert L. "'Do Lord, Remember Me': Religion and Cultural Change among Blacks in Florida, 1565–1906." Ph.D. diss., Florida State University, 1984.

Harvey, Paul. *Redeeming the South: Religious Cultures and Racial Identities among Southern Baptists, 1865–1925.* Chapel Hill: University of North Carolina Press, 1997.

Hawes, Leland. "One Official's Untold Story." *Tampa Sunday Tribune,* February 13, 1994.

———. "Robert Meacham Left a Florida Legacy." *Tampa Sunday Tribune,* August 5, 1990.

———. "Tampa-born Sheriff." *Tampa Sunday Tribune,* July 23, 1995.

Hay, John. *Letters of John Hay and Extracts from Diary.* 3 vols. New York: Gordian Press, 1969.

Haywood, Chanta M. *Prophesying Daughters: Black Women Preachers and the Word, 1823–1913.* Columbia: University of Missouri Press, 2003.

Heyrman, Christine Leigh. *Southern Cross: The Beginnings of the Bible Belt.* New York: Alfred A. Knopf, 1997.

Higginbotham, Evelyn Brooks. *Righteous Discontent: The Women's Movement in the Black Baptist Church, 1880–1920.* Cambridge: Harvard University Press, 1993.

Hoggard, James Clinton. *The African Methodist Episcopal Zion Church, 1972–1996: A Bicentennial Commemorative History.* Charlotte, N.C.: A.M.E. Zion Publishing House, 1998.

Hood, James W. *One Hundred Years of the African Methodist Episcopal Zion Church; or, The Centennial of African Methodism.* New York: A.M.E.Z. Book Concern, 1895.

———. *Sketch of the Early History of the African Methodist Episcopal Zion Church.* N.p., 1914.

Hoskins, Frank W. *The History of Methodism in Pensacola, Florida.* Nashville: M. E. Church, South, Publishing House, 1928.

Hubener, Hal. "Army Life in Lakeland, Florida, during the Spanish-American War." *Tampa Bay History* 20 (Spring–Summer 1998): 32–47.

Hutchins, Jonathan. "William John Gunn: Florida's First Black Surgeon and Physician." Unpublished paper delivered at Third Annual Conference on the African American Heritage of Peninsular Florida, Bartow, January 31, 2003.

Iorio, Pam. "Colorless Primaries: Tampa's White Municipal Party." *Florida Historical Quarterly* 79 (Winter 2001): 297–318.

Jackson, David H., Jr. "Booker T. Washington's Tour of the Sunshine State, March 1912." *Florida Historical Quarterly* 81 (Winter 2003): 254–78.

Johnson, Alonzo, and Paul Jersild, eds. *"Ain't Gonna Lay My 'Ligion Down": African American Religion in the South.* Columbia: University of South Carolina Press, 1996.

Jordan, Lewis G. *Negro Baptist History: USA—1750–1930.* Nashville: Townsend Press, 1995.

Joyner, Charles. *Down by the Riverside: A South Carolina Slave Community.* Urbana: University of Illinois Press, 1984.

Jupiter, Del E. "Augustina and the Kelkers: A Spanish West Florida Line." *National Genealogical Society Quarterly* 80 (December 1992): 265–79.

———. "New Providence Missionary Baptist Church, Bagdad, Florida." *The Florida Genealogist* 14 (Fall 1991): 180.

Kerstein, Robert. *Politics and Growth in Twentieth-Century Tampa.* Gainesville: University Press of Florida, 2001.

Knetsch, Joe. "Hamilton Disston and the Development of Florida." *Sunland Tribune* 24 (1998): 5–19.

Landers, Roger. "Freedmen's Bureau Becomes a Force in Hernando." *Brooksville Hernando Today*, August 4, 1999.

Lempel, Leonard R. "The Mayor's 'Henchmen and Henchwomen, Both White and Colored': Edward H. Armstrong and the Politics of Race in Daytona Beach, 1900–1940." *Florida Historical Quarterly* 79 (Winter 2001): 267–96.

Lewis, Clifton P. "Bartow, West Bartow, and the Andy Moore Family: The Joy and Importance of Discovering African-American History." *Sunland Tribune* 24 (1998): 49–59.

Lewis, David Levering. *W.E.B. Du Bois: Biography of a Race, 1868–1919.* New York: Henry Holt, 1993.

Lincoln, Eric C., and Lawrence H. Mamiya. *The Black Church in the African American Experience.* Durham: Duke University Press, 1990.

Long, Charles Sumner. *History of the A.M.E. Church in Florida.* Philadelphia: AME Book Concern, 1939.

Maloney, Walter C. *A Sketch of the History of Key West, Florida.* Newark, N.J.: Advertiser Printing House, 1876. Reprint, Gainesville: University of Florida Press, 1968.

Manley, Walter W., Canter Brown Jr., and Eric W. Rise. *The Supreme Court of Florida and Its Predecessor Courts, 1821–1917.* Gainesville: University Press of Florida, 1997.

Martin, Richard A. *The City Makers.* Jacksonville: Convention Press, 1972.

Martin, Sandy Dwayne. *For God and Race: The Religious and Political Leadership of AMEZ Bishop James Walker Hood*. Columbia: University of South Carolina Press, 1999.

Martin, Sidney Walker. *Florida during the Territorial Days*. Athens: University of Georgia Press, 1944.

Mathews, Donald G. *Religion in the Old South*. Chicago: University of Chicago Press, 1977.

Matthews, Janet Snyder. "The African American Experience in Southwest Florida and the Origins of Dunbar High School in Fort Myers, 1841 to 1927." Ph.D. diss., Florida State University, 1999.

McDonogh, Gary W., ed. *The Florida Negro: A Federal Writers' Project Legacy*. Jackson: University Press of Mississippi, 1993.

McKinney, George Patterson, Sr., and Richard I. McKinney. *History of the Black Baptists of Florida, 1850–1985*. Miami: Florida Memorial College Press, 1987.

McKinney, Richard I. "American Baptists and Black Education in Florida." *American Baptist Quarterly* 11 (December 1992): 309–26.

Menard, John Willis. *Lays in Summer Lands*. Edited by Larry Eugene Rivers, Richard Mathews, and Canter Brown Jr. Tampa: University of Tampa Press, 2002.

Mitchell, Mozella. *African American Religious History in Tampa Bay*. Tampa: National Conference of Christians and Jews, 1992.

Montgomery, William E. *Under Their Own Vine and Fig Tree: The African-American Church in the South, 1865–1900*. Baton Rouge: Louisiana State University, 1993.

Moore, Torrenzo H. "The Life and Career of Judson Douglas Wetmore: Attorney and City Councilman of Duval County, 1899–1906." Master's seminar paper, Florida A&M University, 2003.

Mormino, Gary R., and George E. Pozzetta. *The Immigrant World of Ybor City: Italians and Their Latin Neighbors in Tampa, 1885–1985*. Urbana: University of Illinois Press, 1987. Reprint, Gainesville: University Press of Florida, 1998.

Mt. Sinai African Methodist Episcopal Zion Church, One Hundred and Twenty-fifth Anniversary, Sunday, February 28, 1988. Tampa: Mt. Sinai AMEZ Church, 1988.

Newman, Marion L. "History of Cornish." In *Cornish Chapel A.M.E. Zion Church Annual Women's Day Program—April 25, 1971*. Key West: Cornish Chapel AMEZ Church, 1971.

Neyland, Leedell W., and John W. Riley. *The History of Florida Agricultural and Mechanical University*. Gainesville: University of Florida Press, 1963.

Nolan, David. *Fifty Feet in Paradise: The Booming of Florida*. San Diego: Harcourt Brace Jovanovich, 1984.

Nuwer, Deanne Stephens. "The 1878 Yellow Fever Epidemic along the Mississippi Gulf Coast." *Gulf South Historical Review* 14 (Spring 1999): 51–73.

Parks, Virginia. *Pensacola: Spaniards to Space Age*. Pensacola: Pensacola Historical Society, 1986.

Payne, Daniel Alexander. *Recollections of Seventy Years*. New York: Arno Press and the *New York Times*, 1969.

Pearce, George F. *Pensacola during the Civil War: A Thorn in the Side of the Confederacy*. Gainesville: University Press of Florida, 2000.

Peeples, Vernon E. "Charlotte Harbor Division of the Florida Southern Railroad." *Florida Historical Quarterly* 58 (January 1980): 291–302.

Pettengill, George W., Jr. *The Story of the Florida Railroads*. Boston: Railway and Locomotive Historical Society, and Baker Library, Harvard Business School, 1952. Revised ed., Jacksonville: Southeast Chapter of the Railway and Locomotive Historical Society, 1998.

Proctor, Samuel. *Napoleon Bonaparte Broward, Florida's Fighting Democrat*. Gainesville: University of Florida Press, 1950.

Raboteau, Albert J. *Slave Religion: The "Invisible Institution" in the Antebellum South*. New York: Oxford University Press, 1978.

Raper, Arthur F. *The Tragedy of Lynching*. Chapel Hill: University of North Carolina Press, 1933.

Rawick, George P. *The American Slave: A Composite Autobiography*. 41 vols. Westport, Conn.: Greenwood Press, 1972.

Reid, Whitelaw. *After the War: A Tour of the Southern States, 1865–1866*. Edited by C. Vann Woodward. New York: Harper and Row, 1965.

"Rev. John A. Mulligan: Late Conference Steward of the Allegheny Conference." *A.M.E.Z. Church Quarterly* 1 (January 1891): 150, 153.

Richardson, Clement, ed. *National Cyclopedia of the Colored Race, Volume One*. Montgomery, Ala.: National Publishing, 1919.

Richardson, Joe M. *Christian Reconstruction: The American Missionary Society and Southern Blacks, 1861–1890*. Athens: University of Georgia Press, 1986.

Richardson, Martin. "Negro History in Pensacola." In *Negro History in Florida*, by Federal Writers' Project. Jacksonville: Federal Writers' Project, 1936.

Rivers, Larry Eugene. "Baptist Minister James Page: Alternatives for African American Leadership in Post–Civil War Florida." In *Florida's Heritage of Diversity: Essays in Honor of Samuel Proctor*, edited by Mark I. Greenberg, William Warren Rogers, and Canter Brown Jr. Tallahassee: Sentry Press, 1997.

———. "'He Treats His Fellow Man Properly': Building Community in Multi-Cultural Florida." In *Amid Political, Cultural, and Civic Diversity: Building a Sense of Statewide Community in Florida*. Dubuque, Iowa: Kendall/Hunt, 1998.

———. *Slavery in Florida: Territorial Days to Emancipation*. Gainesville: University Press of Florida, 2000.

———. "A Troublesome Property: Master-Slave Relations in Florida, 1821–1865." In *The African-American Heritage of Florida*, edited by David R. Colburn and Jane L. Landers. Gainesville: University Press of Florida, 1995.

Rivers, Larry Eugene, and Canter Brown Jr. "African Americans in South Florida: A Home and a Haven for Reconstruction-Era Leaders." *Tequesta* 56 (1996): 5–23.

———. *Laborers in the Vineyard of the Lord: The Beginnings of the AME Church in Florida, 1865–1895*. Gainesville: University Press of Florida, 2001.

———. "'Rejoicing in Their Freedom': The Development of Tampa's African-American Community in the Post–Civil War Generation." *Sunland Tribune* 27 (2001): 5–18.

Rivers, Larry Omar. "'They . . . Exalt Humbug at the Expense of Science and Truth': Dr. John P. Wall and the Fight against Yellow Fever in Late-Nineteenth Century Florida." *Sunland Tribune* 25 (1999): 9–18.

Rogers, William Warren, and James M. Denham. *Florida Sheriffs: A History, 1821–1945*. Tallahassee: Sentry Press, 2001.

"St. James A.M.E. Zion Church." In *Mt. Sinai African Methodist Episcopal Zion Church, One Hundred and Twenty-fifth Anniversary, Sunday, February 28, 1988*. Tampa: Mt. Sinai AMEZ Church, 1988.

Saunders, Robert W., Sr. *Bridging the Gap: Continuing the Florida NAACP Legacy of Harry T. Moore, 1952–1966*. Tampa: University of Tampa Press, 2000.

———. Personal interviews by Canter Brown Jr., January 30, 1997, December 4, 1998, notes in collection of Canter Brown Jr.

Schmidt, Lewis G. "From Slavery to Freedom and Success: Sandy Cornish (circa 1793–1869) and Lillah Cornish (circa 1813–1870s)." *Florida Keys Sea Heritage Journal* 4 (Spring 1994): 1, 12–15.

Scott, J. Irving E. *The Education of Black People in Florida*. Philadelphia: Dorrance, 1974.

"Senior Grand Lodge of Florida." *International Good Templar* 8 (May 1888): 300–301.

Shofner, Jerrell H. "The Chimerical Scheme of Ceding West Florida." *Alabama Historical Quarterly* 33 (Spring 1971): 5–36.

———. *Jackson County, Florida: A History*. Marianna: Jackson County Heritage Association, 1985.

———. "Militant Negro Laborers in Reconstruction Florida." *Journal of Southern History* 39 (August 1973): 397–408.

———. *Nor Is It Over Yet: Florida in the Era of Reconstruction, 1863–1877*. Gainesville: University Press of Florida, 1974.

Skinner, Emory Fiske. *Reminiscences*. Chicago: Vestal Printing, 1908.

Smith, Julia Floyd. *Slavery and Plantation Growth in Antebellum Florida*. Gainesville: University Press of Florida, 1973.

Souvenir Program of the Tenth Anniversary Celebration of the Reverend V. R. Hill, Pastor of Talbot Chapel, A.M.E. Zion Church, October 15 thru 19, 1958. Pensacola: Pastor's Aid Club, 1958.

Stanaback, Richard J. *A History of Hernando County, 1840–1976*. Brooksville, Fla.: Action '76 Steering Committee, 1976.

Stone, Spessard. "Profile of Lloyd Davis." *Sunland Tribune* 17 (November 1991): 25–26.

Swift, David E. *Black Prophets of Justice: Activist Clergy before the Civil War*. Baton Rouge: Louisiana State University Press, 1989.

Tarbox, Increase N. *Memoirs of James H. Schneider and Edward M. Schneider*. Boston: Massachusetts Sabbath School Society, 1867.

Tebeau, Charlton W. *A History of Florida*. Coral Gables: University of Miami Press, 1971.

Temple, Robert M., Jr. *Florida Flame: A History of the Florida Conference of the United Methodist Church*. Nashville: Parthenon Press, 1987.

Thomas, Hilah F., Rosemary Skinner Keller, and Louise L. Queen, eds. *Women in New Worlds: Historical Perspectives on the Wesleyan Tradition*. Nashville: Abingdon Press, 1981.

Thrift, Charles T., Jr. *The Trail of the Florida Circuit Rider*. Lakeland: Florida Southern College Press, 1944.

Tingley, Charles. "Dr. Alexander H. Darnes: Jacksonville's First Black Physician." Unpublished paper delivered at the Second Annual Conference on the African American Heritage of Peninsular Florida, Bartow, February 2, 2002.

———. Telephone interview, April 29, 2003. Notes in collections of the authors.

Walker, Clarence E. *A Rock in a Weary Land: The African Methodist Episcopal Church during the Civil War and Reconstruction*. Baton Rouge: Louisiana State University Press, 1982.

Walls, William J. *The African Methodist Episcopal Zion Church: Reality of the Black Church*. Charlotte: N.C.: A.M.E.Z. Publishing House, 1974.

Warner, Lee H. *Free Men in an Age of Servitude: Three Generations of a Black Family*. Lexington: University of Kentucky Press.

Welch, W. Curtis. "Black Churches in Tampa: 1886–1928." Typescript. Tampa: City of Tampa Archives, 1996.

Williamson, Edward C. *Florida Politics in the Gilded Age, 1877–1893*. Gainesville: University of Florida Press, 1976.

Wilson, William W. "Pensacola and Its Colored People." *Colored American Magazine* 8 (June 1905): 317–30.

Woodward, C. Vann. *Origins of the New South, 1877–1913*. Baton Rouge: Louisiana State University Press, 1951.

———. *The Strange Career of Jim Crow*. 3rd rev. ed. New York: Oxford University Press, 1974.

Wynn, Sarah. "History of Mt. Sinai A.M.E. Zion Church." In *Mt. Sinai African Methodist Episcopal Zion Church, One Hundred and Twenty-fifth Anniversary, Sunday, February 28, 1988*. Tampa: Mt. Sinai AMEZ Church, 1988.

INDEX

Larry Eugene Rivers is Distinguished University Professor of History and dean of the College of Arts and Sciences at Florida A&M University, Tallahassee, and the author of *Slavery in Florida: Territorial Days to Emancipation* (UPF, 2000). His work has been recognized with the Florida Historical Society's Arthur W. Thompson Prize, the Rembert W. Patrick Award, the Harry T. and Harriette V. Moore Book Award, and the Carolynn Washbon Award as well as the Association for the Study of African American Life and History's Carter G. Woodson Prize. He also received the Black Caucus of the American Library Association's Book Award and the American Association for State and Local History's Certificate of Commendation.

Canter Brown Jr. is the author of many works on Florida history, including *Florida's Peace River Frontier* (University of Central Florida Press, 1991); *Ossian Bingley Hart, Florida's Loyalist Reconstruction Governor*; and *Florida's Black Public Officials, 1867–1924*. He has received the Florida Historical Society's Rembert W. Patrick Award, the Harry T. and Harriette V. Moore Book Award, and the American Association for State and Local History's Certificate of Commendation. He is professor of history at Florida A&M University.

THE HISTORY OF AFRICAN-AMERICAN RELIGIONS
Edited by Stephen W. Angell and Anthony B. Pinn

This series will further historical investigations into African religions in the Americas, encourage the development of new paradigms and methodologies, and explore cultural influences upon African American religious institutions, including the roles of gender, race, leadership, regionalism, and folkways.

Laborers in the Vineyard of the Lord: The Beginnings of the AME Church in Florida, 1865–1895, by Larry Eugene Rivers and Canter Brown Jr. (2001)

Between Cross and Crescent: Christian and Muslim Perspectives on Malcolm and Martin, by Lewis V. Baldwin and Amiri YaSin Al-Hadid (2002)

The Quest for the Cuban Christ: A Historical Search, by Miguel A. De La Torre (2002)

For a Great and Grand Purpose: The Beginnings of the AMEZ Church in Florida, 1864–1905, by Canter Brown Jr. and Larry Eugene Rivers (2004)

Afro-Cuban Religiosity, Revolution, and National Identity, by Christine Ayorinde (2004)